Rethinking Therapeutic Reading

Rethinking Therapeutic Reading

Lessons from Seneca, Montaigne, Wordsworth and George Eliot

Kelda Green

With a foreword by Professor Michael Wood

ANTHEM PRESS

Anthem Press
An imprint of Wimbledon Publishing Company
www.anthempress.com

This edition first published in UK and USA 2022
by ANTHEM PRESS
75–76 Blackfriars Road, London SE1 8HA, UK
or PO Box 9779, London SW19 7ZG, UK
and
244 Madison Ave #116, New York, NY 10016, USA

First published in the UK and USA by Anthem Press in 2020

Copyright © Kelda Green 2022

The author asserts the moral right to be identified as the author of this work.

All rights reserved. Without limiting the rights under copyright reserved above,
no part of this publication may be reproduced, stored or introduced into
a retrieval system, or transmitted, in any form or by any means
(electronic, mechanical, photocopying, recording or otherwise),
without the prior written permission of both the copyright
owner and the above publisher of this book.

British Library Cataloguing-in-Publication Data
A catalogue record for this book is available from the British Library.

Library of Congress Control Number: 2020936291

ISBN-13: 978-1-83998-531-7 (Pbk)
ISBN-10: 1-83998-531-3 (Pbk)

This title is also available as an e-book.

Written with love for my parents
and with thanks to Professor Philip Davis

CONTENTS

List of Illustrations   ix

Foreword   xi

Introduction   1

Part I Four Models

1. Senecan Tragedy and Stoic Philosophy   9
2. Therapy and the Essay: Montaigne, after Seneca   27
3. Therapy and Poetry: Wordsworth, after Seneca   41
4. Therapy and the Novel: George Eliot, after Wordsworth   67

Part II Three Experiments

5. Experiment One: A First Reading   99
6. Experiment Two: Slowing Down and Tuning In   129
7. Experiment Three: Writing Back   163

Conclusion   181

Bibliography   187

Index   193

ILLUSTRATIONS

Figures

5.1	The three passages used in experiment one	104
5.2	Graph showing the most frequently quoted lines of poetry extract one	107
5.3	The most frequently quoted sections of poetry extract one	108
5.4	Graphs showing the order of direct quotations used in each participant response to poetry extract one	110
5.5	Graph showing the most frequently quoted lines of poetry extract two	112
5.6	The most frequently quoted sections of poetry extract two	113
5.7	Graphs showing the order of direct quotations used in each participant response to poetry extract two	114
5.8	Verbs used in the first person in response to the news article	121
5.9	Verbs used in the first person in response to the poetry extracts	121
7.1	The letters written by each participant in experiment three	169

Tables

5.1	Experiment one: Sample information	103
5.2	The order of direct quotations in participant A2's response to poetry extract one	108
6.1	Experiment two: Sample information	131
7.1	Experiment three: Sample information	165

FOREWORD

'All sorrows can be borne', the writer Karen Blixen once said, 'if you put them in a story, or tell a story about them', and this belief is often thought to lie behind much of the work of psychoanalysis: not just a talking cure but a telling cure. You won't be able to manage your need or distress or even think about them until you find a shape for them in a tale. There are problems with these claims of course. Nothing will take care of all sorrows, and we can't be cured from living. But stories do help in all kinds of ways, and it makes sense to speak of literature as a source of therapy, as this remarkable book does.

We just need to be careful about our stories. Or rather, we need to stay away from too careful stories, stories that are neat and settled, too eager to arrive at their plausible endings.

The philosopher Galen Strawson, cited at the end of this work, eloquently decries the fashionable belief that we all need stories (and/or stories are all we need). 'There is widespread agreement that human beings typically see or live or experience their lives as a narrative or story of some sort, or at least as a collection of stories.' But what exactly are the alternatives to story? We can all think of epiphanies, lyric moments, but what else is there? This book richly answers the question, and in this sense copes with one of its own most difficult paradoxes: how are we to be practical while remaining 'in the service of something deeper than empiricism'.

Kelda Green reaches her solution through a close consultation of the works of Seneca, Montaigne, Wordsworth and George Eliot, and especially through her subtle attention to the pressure each author puts upon his or her predecessor, so that the very idea of therapy becomes a story that doesn't end. Seneca's wonderful insight into the mind's remaking of the world – 'A man is as wretched as he has convinced himself that he is' – must be true in some sense if the notion of psychology (and indeed of much of philosophy) is to have any meaning, but the truth is not binary: wretchedness has many components apart from the wretch's conviction. And this is Dr Green's recurring theme. We need to look at what she calls fault lines, claims whose truth lies in their fragility, logical instances 'where the framework doesn't quite accommodate reality', and is faithful to reality for that reason.

Wordsworth offers the best examples here. Even the admirable Seneca and Montaigne lack his tolerance for disorder, although Montaigne's flexibility is, as Dr Green suggests, 'all the more constant for not being under fixed mental control'. Certainly Wordsworth goes further than anyone in his feeling that suffering and trauma cannot be 'mere waste'. It is Wordsworth too who intimately portrays the action of the unconscious well before it became a celebrity – in the work of Eduard von Hartman, for example.

> Strength came where weakness was not known to be,
> At least not felt; and restoration came
> Like an intruder knocking at the door
> Of unacknowledged weariness.[1]

We note that the unconscious here is offering 'implicit therapy', as Dr Green says, not clamouring for attention, as it so often does in Freud. 'For Wordsworth, help works best when it occurs on a subliminal level, almost by psychologically syntactic stealth.'

And again: 'Wordsworth's is a model of progress that exists [...] as an antidote to the overly linear, reductive pathways to recovery that are commonly prescribed by modern psychological therapies.'

George Eliot's special contribution to this practical but undogmatic version of literature as a form of care is made clear by a particularly insightful reading of her novelistic methods. Who listens when a narrator says what a character can't say (perhaps can't even think)? Who is helped when characters are revealed, again and again, to be beyond rescue? Well, there is a 'community of readers' – at least there is if we are willing to take on that responsibility. 'It is as if,' Dr Green says, 'unable to help her characters, George Eliot instead offers to her readers [...] that which might have prevented or mitigated the internal tragedies of the novels.' This is how we might imagine an alternative fate not for Dr Lydgate in *Middlemarch* but for some of the many (real and imaginary) persons enmeshed in marriages like his. 'George Eliot translates Lydgate's rough, deep approximations of feeling into language that can be seen and listened to, if not by Lydgate himself then instead by the reader who must then stand in for the character's absent "listening-experiencing self."'

The idea of literature as therapy seems attractive (or not) at first sight, and in any case appears to represent a large simplification of a complex set of possible relations between text and reader. This book makes an engaging case for the attraction of the idea, and firmly suggests that the second part of this impression is not the only available view. 'It is important to recognise,'

Dr Green writes, 'that much of what takes place, and much of what is of most value in the reading process is hidden, implicit, unquantifiable and entirely unsuitable for conventional formal study.' And having recognised that we may, if we are patient and inventive, go on to speak of what is hidden and implicit, to ignore quantities and to find new conventions. The practical experiments reported in the second part of this work do just this. We learn once again that literature does not force anything on its readers, it 'makes nothing happen', as W. H. Auden famously said of poetry. But it allows 'acts of returning and rethinking' that could not take place without it, and it addresses what may be the hardest therapeutical question of all: 'what to do with counsel that you know to be theoretically valuable but do not know how to make real?' There is no single answer, and sometimes there is no answer at all. But one of the things that literature does best is to help us to live with absences as well as conflicting forms of presence.

Michael Wood
Professor of English, Emeritus
Princeton University

Note

1 William Wordsworth, *The Prelude, The Four Texts (1798, 1799, 1805, 1850)*, ed. Jonathan Wordsworth (London: Penguin, 1995), Book IV, ll. 145–48.

INTRODUCTION

This book is an exploration of the therapeutic potential held within literature. It examines the ways in which literature has served – since ancient times – as a repository for collective human thinking and a source of what we would now call therapy. It argues for the ongoing need for literary thinking and literary models of care, repair and human connection in the world today. Through a combination of literary analysis and practical experimentation, I have sought to provide a contribution to the relation of the reading of literature to the practice of psychology, arguing throughout that literature has a vital role to play in the real world, while insisting that the methods of close literary analysis and literary thinking are preserved.

Chapter 1 considers Cognitive Behavioural Therapy in relation to the Stoic philosophy out of which, it has been argued, it derives its origins. Through an examination of the letters of Seneca and the tragic vision that precedes them in his plays, I have sought to reconstruct a context for Stoic therapy within a more profound world order than is understood within the modern psychological therapies that have partially evolved from it.

Chapter 2 explores the essays of the sixteenth-century philosopher Montaigne, as a reader of Seneca. It examines his adaptation of Stoicism into a personal form of thinking within praxis, adding a further dimension to Seneca's epistles. It is argued that through reading, writing and rewriting, Montaigne creates an individualistic model for, but also counterexample to, what we might today call self-examination and self-help. The essays are also linked forward to both the self-reflexive processes of psychoanalysis and to Freud's own work as an essayist and thinker preoccupied with the individual self, with relation (for example) to Adam Phillips's Freudian-based work on the linkage between psychoanalysis and the reading of serious literature.

Chapter 3 takes a second major creative reader of Seneca two hundred years after Montaigne. It examines William Wordsworth's poetic use of Stoicism and his move beyond Stoicism towards a philosophy of transmutation. More broadly, this chapter presents the case for the particular and distinctly therapeutic forms of literary thinking that are contained within Wordsworth's poetry, not least because, as representative of a reformed poetic to serve ordinary life, it was held by several readers and commentators to be vital to the recuperation of the Western psyche. The patterns of psychoanalysis, as outlined in Freud's essay 'Remembering, Repeating and Working Through', are an important point of comparison in Chapter 3, in relation to the restorative and revisionary patterns of Wordsworth's poetry.

Chapter 4 sets out the connections between George Eliot and Wordsworth. It examines George Eliot's contribution to the nineteenth-century development of psychology and argues that there is a specific and useful model of therapy contained with her realist novels, just as surely as within Wordsworth's poetry of common nature. It is argued that George Eliot is a 'proto-psychoanalyst' who in stern demand requires patients to stay *in* their difficulties, with relation to her own realist novelist's version of what Freud was to call 'the reality principle'.

Of course, these four central figures are my choices and could have been otherwise (St Augustine's reading of Seneca or Byron's reading of Montaigne are two specific examples). But the principle remains – that each author acts as a representative of a different literary form in relation to problems of human psychology: Seneca the philosopher-playwright, Montaigne the essayist, Wordsworth the poet and George Eliot the novelist. As such, this book demonstrates how different forms can create different – and yet analogous – spaces in which to do existential thinking.

The four authors were selected due to the strong links between them: Montaigne is a reader of Seneca, Wordsworth is a reader of Seneca and George Eliot is a reader of Wordsworth as well as the Senecan-influenced Spinoza. Furthermore, these four authors have had strong influence upon the future that came after them, with particular relation to what might now be called (albeit perhaps too reductively) mental health and well-being. There are well-established links between Seneca and modern psychological techniques for effecting calm (outlined in Chapter 1). Montaigne's *Essays* offer a vital model of personal and practical psychology, an individualistic experiment born out of his reading of Stoicism. Wordsworth became established for future generations as the archetypal 'healing poet', and the work of George Eliot, I will argue, had a significant role within the intellectual climate that helped found the discipline of psychology itself.

Chapters 5, 6 and 7 set out the results of three practical reading experiments. These studies were designed to test the theoretical and literary work that sits alongside them in ways that would not generally be accommodated by a traditional piece of literary scholarship. They are exploratory attempts at multidisciplinary thinking and try, in some way, to bridge the gap between the arts and sciences, between theory and practice, and between private concerns and public health. The experimental work of this book is indebted to research carried out by the Centre for Research into Reading, Literature and Society (CRILS) at the University of Liverpool. In particular, research into the impact of the Reader Organisation's shared reading model on mental health and well-being.

My methodology is rooted in the scholarly tradition of practical criticism. This is a form of literary study which is grounded in the attentive close analysis of primary texts, rather than a reliance on works of secondary criticism. It is a methodology which was first developed by I. A. Richards in his seminal work of 1929, *Practical Criticism*, in which he set out the results of a reading experiment which sought to demonstrate some of the limitations of methods of literary study which depend too heavily on the crutches of historical or theoretical context, at the expense of the actual words on the page. This approach is in line with what in the social sciences is now known as Grounded Theory, involving the bottom-up gathering and analysis of data, working inductively rather than being driven from above by the framework of a deductive hypothesis.[1]

I am concerned with the impact of literary texts on real lives and it was important therefore to select a methodology that would allow me to forge a direct connection to the literature being analysed and to get closer to the real, first-hand experience of serious reading. The chosen methodology also helped to establish a sense of continuity across the two distinct parts of this book – the theoretical and the practical – as it placed me, within my own terms, in the same testing position as the experimental participants of Chapters 5, 6 and 7: as a reader and struggling human, tasked with responding directly to a series of primary texts, without the assistance of external critical apparatus.

While certain critical approaches and theories have a tendency to make literature feel prohibitively distant and disconnected from the real and present struggles of individual modern life, the intention here has been to develop forms of interdisciplinary thinking and experimental design which firmly reconnect actual readers with texts and which demonstrate how literature might be of aid to human beings in those very struggles.

In her well-received monograph *The Limits of Critique*, Rita Felski offers a theoretical argument against the dominance of any one theoretical model of reading: in particular, critique based on the hermeneutics of suspicion. She makes the case for the encouragement of what she calls 'post-critical reading' in which 'the reader' is not an abstract concept as in reader-response theory, but a specific autonomous individual capable of a range of responses besides the trained default of intelligent suspicion:

> We need ways of thinking about individual readers that does not flatten and reduce them, that grasps their idiosyncrasy as well as their

importance. Texts cannot influence the world by themselves, but only via the intercession of those who read them, digest them, reflect on them, rail against them, use them as points of orientation, and pass them on.[2]

Such individual readers should not be restricted to those trained within the professionalised confines of a single approach, but should be allowed to offer from within themselves, Felski argues, riskily generous, personal and imaginative responses that arise prior to formalization:

> The import of a text is not exhausted by what it reveals or conceals about the social conditions that surround it. Rather, it is also a matter of what it sets alight in the reader – what kind of emotion it elicits, what changes of perception it prompts, what bonds and attachments it calls into being. One consequence of this line of thought is a perspective less dismissive of lay experiences of reading (which also precede and sustain professional criticism).[3]

It was with this aim of investigating lay reading that the memory of I. A. Richards is evoked in this book, and the techniques that he first introduced into English Literature scholarship are put to service.

If this book is to some degree an alternative to literary studies as conventionally carried out within the academy, it is also offered as a challenge by literature and literary study to certain therapeutic prescriptions adopted within the field of psychology. By separating itself off from the means through which humans have traditionally thought about and found ways of dealing with the psychological – whether that is art, literature, philosophy or religion – there is the risk that the discipline of psychology cannot help but become narrowed and diminished into popular instrumental programmes that offer up second-order solutions to problems that they cannot fully understand. As Philip Rieff writes in *The Triumph of the Therapeutic*, 'Scientific regression may occur in any discipline that does not insist upon mastery of its own historical development. A social science that refuses to remember its founders will not realise when it is being silly or repetitious.'[4]

Freud recognised the important role that literature played as a holding ground for the psychological, before psychology came into existence as a distinct concept or discipline: 'The poets and philosophers before me discovered the unconscious; what I discovered was the scientific method by which the unconscious can be studied.'[5] The psychoanalyst Adam Phillips claims in the introduction to his new edition of Freud's collected works that 'it would not be overstating the case to say that, for Freud, reading has been the modern equivalent of what, beginning in the eighteenth century, had been called the experience of the sublime. To write and to read was to be close to the source of something, close to the source of the most important something.'[6] Where in most contexts that 'something' may seem all too vague, in literature it becomes a powerful inner drive towards meaning in the secular age.

Notes

1 Barney G. Glaser, and Anselm L. Strauss, *The Discovery of Grounded Theory: Strategies for Qualitative Research* (New Brunswick, NJ: Aldine, 1967).
2 Rita Felski, *The Limits of Critique* (Chicago, IL: University of Chicago Press, 2015), pp. 171–72; hereafter cited as 'Felski'.
3 Ibid., p. 179.
4 Philip Rieff, *The Triumph of the Therapeutic* (Chicago, IL: The University of Chicago, 1966), p. 101.
5 Lionel Trilling, 'Freud and Literature', in *Freud: A Collection of Critical Essays*, ed. Perry Meisel (Upper Saddle River, NJ: Prentice Hall, 1971), p. 95.
6 Adam Phillips, Introduction to *The Penguin Freud Reader* (London: Penguin, 2006), p. xi.

Part I

Four Models

Chapter 1

SENECAN TRAGEDY AND STOIC PHILOSOPHY

In *Philosophy for Life and Other Dangerous Situations,* Jules Evans traces the origins of modern psychological therapies, including Cognitive Behavioural Therapy (CBT), back to their roots in the ancient philosophy of Stoicism, proposing that ancient philosophy lies at the heart of Western psychotherapy. As part of his research, Evans interviewed two of the founders of CBT, Albert Ellis and Aaron Beck; of Ellis he writes:

> Albert Ellis told me [...] that he had been particularly impressed by a saying of the Stoic philosopher Epictetus: 'Men are disturbed not by things, but by their opinions about them'. This sentence inspired Ellis's 'ABC' model of the emotions, which is at the heart of CBT: we experience an event (A), then interpret it (B), and then feel an emotional response in line with our interpretation (C). Ellis, following the Stoics, suggested that we change our emotions by changing our thoughts or opinions about events.[1]

The belief that 'we change our emotions by changing our thoughts or opinions about events' is fundamental to CBT and it is an idea of self-control that comes directly from Stoic philosophy. The most extensive surviving evidence that we have of ancient Stoic philosophy is provided by Lucius Annaeus Seneca, the Roman philosopher (4 BC–AD 65) described by Jules Evans as the author of 'one of the first works of anger management in Western culture'.[2] Within the 124 surviving philosophical letters in which many of the general principles of Stoicism are set out, Seneca outlines how by changing our thoughts or opinions about events, we can transform our emotions: 'It is according to opinion that we suffer. A man is as wretched as he has convinced himself that he is.'[3]

In the 40 years since CBT was first developed by Ellis and Beck, its popularity and prevalence has dramatically increased. Bestselling CBT self-help books such as *Mind over Mood* have translated Stoic philosophy into practical manuals for modern living, and today CBT is the most commonly prescribed evidence-based psychological therapy in the United Kingdom. Between 2016 and 2017, 31 per cent of the 567,000 programmes that were completed under the government's 'Increasing Access to Psychological Therapies Scheme' (IAPT) were in CBT, while a similar number of guided self-help programmes were completed – a low-intensity therapy which is based on the principles of CBT.[4]

A large number of studies have identified the benefits of CBT and shown it to be as effective – and in some cases more effective – than medication, particularly when used to treat depression and anxiety: 'Researchers have found that a 16 week course of CBT helps around 75 per cent of patients to recover from social anxiety, 65 per cent to recover from PTSD and as much as 80 per cent from panic disorders.'[5] Yet there are concerns – not least from among practising clinical psychologists – about the apparent dominance of CBT and its rigid, top-down and often overly manualised approach. A survey carried out in 2010 by the charity Mind found that only 8 per cent of patients deemed to require psychological therapy were offered any choice as to what that therapy might be: invariably patients were simply prescribed a course of CBT.[6] As the clinical psychologist Joanna Cates writes, 'There are a large number of people whose symptoms of anxiety and depression are caused by a myriad of other factors and for whom CBT is not necessarily the panacea it is sometimes promised to be. For this reason I question IAPT's overdependence on this model as a means of conceptualising and "treating" a person's emotional distress.'[7]

In response to some of the concerns surrounding CBT, a 'third-wave' of psychodynamic therapies have been developed, including Cognitive Analytic Therapy (CAT) and Acceptance and Commitment Therapy (ACT). These new therapies address some of the perceived limitations of CBT by incorporating elements of psychoanalysis, mindfulness and acceptance strategies.[8] However, while rooted in Greek and Roman philosophy, CBT and its new variants still offer, I will argue, only second-order versions of the original, ancient models of therapy of those philosophies. Evans himself acknowledges that they are fragmented over-simplifications of much more complicated thought-systems:

> It is inevitable that, in turning ancient philosophy into a sixteen-week course of CBT, cognitive therapists had to truncate it and narrow its scope, and the result is a rather atomised and instrumental form of self-help, which focuses narrowly on an individual's thinking style and ignores ethical, cultural and political factors [...] Self-help in the ancient

world was far more ambitious and expansive than modern self-help. It linked the psychological to the ethical, the political and the cosmic.[9]

By turning back to the classical antecedents of modern psychology, this chapter aims to rediscover the 'ambitious' and 'expansive' model of therapy that was originally developed by the Stoics. It will attempt to restore an understanding of Stoicism as a whole, rather than the 'truncated' version of it that has been co-opted by the discipline of psychology. In *After Virtue*, Alasdair MacIntyre writes of the broader threat of moral incoherence posed by the truncation or fragmentation of ideas into isolated disciples:

> What we possess, if this view is true, are the fragments of a conceptual scheme, parts which now lack those contexts from which their significance derived. We possess indeed simulacra of morality, we continue to use many of the key expressions. But we have – very largely, if not entirely – lost our comprehension, both theoretical and practical, of morality.[10]

By retaining only the vocabulary of self-mastery, regularity and moderation or only the surface appearance of Stoic strategies while rejecting the core of the 'conceptual scheme' that holds together and provides the motivation for those strategies, we are left with only a shadow of the original thought. Psychology is smaller than cosmology and secondary to cosmology and necessarily so because psychology seeks to fulfil the second-order need for a smaller, private, personal space in the midst of the great all or nothing extremes of the tragedies. But equally, I am arguing that a psychology that has stripped Stoicism of its cosmology is depleted and must seek to reformulate that core cosmology if it is to offer more expansive forms of therapy.

Seneca's surviving body of work consists of eight tragedies, a series of moral treatises, three consolations and one hundred and twenty-four letters to his friend Lucilius. The tragedies were written first and contain a degree of brutality and violence that does not sit comfortably alongside either the restraint of his later letters or our conventional understanding of Stoicism. In the centuries after Seneca's death the tragedies and letters were deemed to be so incompatible that the misconception developed that there must have been more than one Roman philosopher named Seneca. The fifth-century orator Sidonius Apollinaris and later Renaissance thinkers Erasmus and Diderot are among those who believed there were multiple Senecas.[11]

While the philosophical letters have been celebrated and absorbed by the discipline of psychology, Seneca's tragedies have been largely ignored in recent scholarship despite their noted influence on Shakespeare and other Renaissance dramatists.[12] Professor of Classical Philosophy Brad Inwood makes no mention of the tragedies in his collection of essays *Reading Seneca: Stoic Philosophy at Rome,* other than to explain his omission in the introduction:

> I have not said a word about Seneca's poetic works, his dramas [...] My decision rests partly on a sense of my own limitations and partly on the conviction that any philosophical influence probably runs from the prose works to the plays rather than the other way around [...] For the purpose of this collection, Seneca the philosopher writes in prose.[13]

Within the philosophical letters themselves, Seneca argues against the kind of scholarship which focuses on fragments of a body of work at the expense of the whole. He admonishes his friend Lucilius for attempting to subdivide the complex philosophical ideas that they are studying together: 'Look into their wisdom as a whole; study it as a whole. They are working out a plan and weaving together, line upon line, a masterpiece, from which nothing can be taken away without injury to the whole'.[14] By dividing Seneca's writing into two categories – namely the philosophical and literary texts – and examining each in isolation, scholars have marginalised Seneca's literary output and failed to acknowledge fully the unifying thought-system of Stoic cosmology which connects the two.

This chapter will begin by looking at Seneca's tragedies, arguing against Inwood's assertion that 'any philosophical influence probably runs from the prose works to the plays', not least because the tragedies were most likely to have been written first. More particularly, the tragedies are home to first things, primary emotions and forces that suggest to me that they should be read first. The chapter will then go on to look at Seneca's letters to Lucilius which contain his second-order attempts at setting out generalised guidance for living in adaptive accordance with the rules of Stoicism.

Contradictions and tensions are an important element of the Stoic cosmology and they exist within the tragedies and the prose as well as between them. In fact, internal contradiction is one thing which unifies these two seemingly disparate bodies of work. While on the surface, the tragedies are preoccupied with intense violence and unimaginable excess, they also contain places where small and very recognisably human pressure points are revealed. Similarly, within Seneca's letters there are places where the surface restraint of Stoic philosophy appears to crack and reveal underlying psychological fault lines.

The Tragedies

In Act Three of *Thyestes* – a tragedy about two vengeful royal brothers – the titular character is persuaded to leave behind the safety of a life of obscure poverty, tempted back to the royal palace by his brother Atreus's false promises of reconciliation. Some primitive part of himself – an almost archetypal version of anxiety – surfaces and attempts to halt the tragic momentum by which he is unknowingly being carried along:

> You ask me why, I cannot tell you why
> I am afraid; I see no cause for fear,
> And yet I am afraid. I would go on;
> But I am paralysed.[15]

A battle is taking place within these lines between surface logic and a lower, inner feeling of dread that can neither compromise nor explain itself in the language of reason. The instinctive, primal simplicity of 'I am afraid' comes from a different place within Thyestes to the second thought, the rational counterbalance of 'I see no cause for fear.' The two conflicting feelings exist simultaneously within him, each emerging from a different level or layer of his self. Reading vertically down the page, Thyestes's fear is as relentless as his opposing drive to keep moving, 'I am afraid / And yet I am afraid / But I am paralysed' is like the sound of ruminating cogs in his brain. Thyestes's logical half simultaneously struggles to understand how something can exist within him without evidence and without answers, 'I cannot tell you why'/ 'I see no cause for fear.' The result of this internal conflict is psychological paralysis. His fear is the last barrier holding back the destructive momentum of the tragedy. And yet in the face of what seems an external urge for life, Thyestes is persuaded in the next scene by the arguments of his son to return to the palace and 'I would go on; / But I am paralysed' quickly turns to 'Let us go on, then.'[16]

The impetus to keep driving onwards is the most powerful force within Seneca's tragedies. Even when some part of Thyestes is instinctively dragging him back and trying to halt, another part of his self is leading him onwards; it is hard to know which is the force for good. Thyestes overrides the survival mechanism that has been triggered within his body and now the only way he will finally come to a halt is at the end of the play when tragedy has piled on top of tragedy and everything has been destroyed. Seneca pushes his characters towards the extreme point of disintegration and that final point of impact is the only thing that can stop their momentum.

The tragic momentum is a damaging consequence of a Stoic cosmology in which everything belongs to one unified continuum which is held together by a system of tensions: '*Tonos* is the energy system that, for better or worse, welds the Stoic cosmos into a unity. The tensional relationship between the constituents of the cosmos, including the incorporation of man and his life in the larger world, Posidonius called *sumpatheia*.'[17] This is not sympathy in the modern sense, but rather a mutual interdependence or simultaneity of being at all levels in the cosmos. The concept of *krasis* – translated as 'blending' – was the epitome of *sumpatheia* for the Stoics. The 'tensional relationship' means that different elements within as well as between humans must be held together, and not necessarily in harmony:

> Another term by which Cicero chooses to render *sumpatheia* is *contagio*, which is contact, in the medical sense, hence, sadly, infection. Certainly medicine, though supportive of the notion of harmony and balance and healthy tension, is fully alive to the variety of causes that may trigger a breakdown of the harmony, and to the extreme narrow scope within which tension can be expected to operate successfully.[18]

Tragic relationships are characterised by the version of *sumpatheia* that is *contagion*, and revenge spreads like an infection between Seneca's characters. Generations of the same family are marked with violence as if their bloodline has been infected. The interconnected Stoic world view is dangerous because the set of conditions which are required to maintain healthy connections across the continuum are the same in nature as those that lead to sickness, but are much more difficult to sustain. The tragedies show what happens when the universe deviates from this 'extreme narrow scope' and is no longer operating successfully either on a macro, cosmic level or a micro, interpersonal level.

In Act Five of *Thyestes*, the tragic hero continues to struggle with a sense of dread and foreboding. Yet, at this point in fact, Thyestes has already unknowingly consumed the flesh of his own children, who have been murdered and fed to him by his brother Atreus:

> Why, fool, what griefs, what dangers
> Does your imagination see?
> Believe your brother with an open heart.
> Your fears, whatever they may be,
> Are either groundless, *or* too late.[19]

The formulation 'either groundless *or* too late' is disturbingly characteristic of the tragedies. In this instance, it is already 'too late', and the unarticulated fear that has hung over Thyestes since the beginning of the play has now overtaken him, coming to pass in a form beyond anything he could have imagined. The future has already happened and it is only by not yet knowing the truth that Thyestes is able partially, but only temporarily, to hold off its full realisation. In Act Five, Thyestes is the last to learn what it is that he has already done.

There is a strange relationship between time and fear and time and knowledge in the tragedies. Time can speed up or slow down, go forwards or turn back on itself, stretch out or stall in the presence or absence of knowledge or fear. In the moments after something bad is revealed to have happened, the time before a character found out the truth can feel to him retrospectively warped. The structure of this play reflects the real instability of time, a deep discrepancy between time as it is felt internally and how it exists externally. By refusing to follow a sequential timeline, Seneca creates a different kind of framework that feels more like how it is to be stuck inside the nightmare-like logic of a bad experience. We cannot return to the moments before we knew something bad had already happened. When a truth is discovered, the past is retrospectively reshaped by the present and what was small, insignificant and fleeting at the time becomes large. There is a sickening vertigo in this forwards-backwards motion which acts in defiance of simple cause and effect, for the effect almost creates its cause in retrospect. Boundaries that are crossed blindly in real time can only be seen afterwards and from a distance. The tragedies seem to be fixated with these boundary lines: Where does a tragedy start? Where does it finish? And where is 'too late' located if anywhere? Ignorance, like fear, is a mechanism for holding back or temporarily halting the flow of time, it creates a temporary safety. But fear, ignorance and paralysis are the unhealthy versions of stopping, just as revenge and greed, lies and secrets provide the fuel for a negative, unhealthy version of progress.

The tragedy of *Phaedra* is set in motion when Phaedra – the wife of Theseus – attempts to seduce her step-son Hippolytus, and when rejected, publicly accuses him of rape. As so often in Seneca's tragedies, the terrible consequences of the breakdown of natural relationships subsequently unfold like a distorted version of the genetic code.

When Theseus hears the allegations against his son, he calls on the Furies to exact a terrible punishment on Hippolytus. The innocent son is brutally killed and his body is torn into fragments. The image of the physically broken child lying in pieces before his guilty father powerfully recurs in *Thyestes*, *Phaedra* and *Hercules*. The fragmentation of human bodies – and more specifically of children's bodies – is another consequence of the forces at work within the tragedies that are breaking apart the connective bonds of the Stoic cosmos. There is a constant struggle and a constant failure within the tragedies to keep hold of the whole of something, whether that be the whole of a body, a family, or a much larger cosmic whole.

In Act Five of *Phaedra*, having discovered his wife's deception too late to save his son, Theseus weeps over his dismembered child and desperately attempts to rebuild Hippolytus's body out of the rubble of his limbs. As so often, it is only after time has run out and characters have reached rock bottom that a kind of space or stillness emerges that means that the tragedy has finally ground to a halt. I am interested in Seneca's work in these areas: what happens after the breaking point has been reached and what does a character do after it is already too late? Amid all the fury and chaos of the tragedies this is one of the moments of quiet where the resolve to repair and preserve something of what has been broken resurfaces:

> THESEUS: Trembling hands, be firm
> For this sad service; cheeks, dry up your tears!
> Here is a father building, limb by limb,
> A body for his son … Here is a piece,
> Misshapen, horrible, each side of it
> Injured and torn. What part of you it is
> I cannot tell, but it is part of you.
> So … put it there … not where it ought to be,
> But where there is a place for it.[20]

The father tries to reconstruct his offspring, but here in the chaotic world of the tragedies the starting point is utter fragmentation, and the process of rebuilding cannot hope to reconstruct the body as 'it ought to be'. In this world of physically and mentally broken people where minds and bodies have been mangled, there can only be this hesitant, stilted attempt to retain and reassemble some trace of the human form. It is impossible to replicate life as it was before tragedy, but, out of the jumble of pieces that we are left with, the task is to create something that resembles life: a second version of ourselves.

More than any of Seneca's plays, *Hercules* is preoccupied with what happens after tragedy. Here the powerful force of energy or momentum which made Hercules a hero is subverted when he murders his own family in a frenzied attack fuelled by madness. It is, however, that same force of energy which must somehow be preserved and reactivated if he is to survive beyond the immediate tragedy.

After the slaughter, Hercules falls into a deep sleep and when he eventually wakes to find his step-father Amphitryon and friend Theseus watching over him, he has no recollection of what has happened:

> AMPHITRYON: These troubles must just pass in silence.
> HERCULES: And I remain unavenged?
> AMPHITRYON: Revenge often does harm.

HERCULES:	Has anyone passively endured such troubles?
AMPHITRYON:	Anyone who feared worse.
HERCULES:	Can one fear anything, father, that is even worse or more painful than this?
AMPHITRYON:	How little of your calamity you understand!
HERCULES:	Have pity, father, I hold out my hands in supplication. What? He pulled back from my hands: the crime is lurking here. Why this blood? What of that shaft, soaked by a boy's blood. Now I see my weapons. I need not ask about the hand. Who could have bent that bow, what hand flexed the string that barely yields to me? I turn to both of you again, father is this crime mine? They are silent: it is mine.[21]

Amphitryon attempts to keep the next wave of the tragedy at bay by holding back the knowledge of what Hercules has done. But what begins as a father's attempt to counsel his son falls apart as the truth bursts out of the very silence that Amphitryon has tried to create as a protection. His counsel fails when it comes up against the enormity of the tragedy. His body cannot help revealing the truth that his brain had attempted to conceal as – despite himself – Amphitryon instinctively flinches from his son's supplicating hands. In the final line, Hercules's question 'is this crime mine?' is answered with a silence that can have no other meaning than 'it is mine'.

Unlike many of Seneca's tragedies which end with only the promise of further acts of vengeance, *Hercules* finishes with the fragile hope that the hero – with the help of his two companions Theseus and Amphitryon – will be able to heal his wounded mind and find a way to continue living.

In Act Five – in another ancient version of *sumpatheia* – Amphitryon threatens to kill himself unless Hercules refrains from suicide. Faced with Amphitryon's threat, the tragedy grinds to a halt. Repetition across the tragedies is key. Every character, across all eight plays, is caught within the same cycle of cosmic decline and each is rushing towards these points of stillness in the aftermath of repeated action:

> Stop now, father, stop, draw back your hand. Give way, my valour, endure my father's command. This labour must be added to the Herculean labours: to live. Theseus raise up my father's body, collapsed on the ground. My crime-stained hands shun contact with the one I love.[22]

As Hercules repeatedly calls for death to 'stop', the trajectory of the tragedy turns from death back towards life. The parts of Hercules that allowed him to be heroic are called into action again, but now the monster that he must slay is a psychological one. What is crucial is this shifting internal chemistry that turned a man from hero to crazed murderer: both are made of the same elemental ingredients. After the tragedy, the struggle is now to regain some version of that first formulation that allowed Hercules to survive unbearable situations. It is impossible to go backwards and retrieve an unstained version of his self: he must find a second copy of that first self and apply it now to the essential labour of living. Keeping himself alive after the tragedy will be the hardest labour of all for Hercules. Rather than a single act of strength or valour, it is a task which will demand a continuous, extended exertion of will, for while destruction can be done in a flash, survival is a long, drawn-out process.

The Stoic cosmology tells us that with every connection comes the threat of infection, and that every creative force holds the potential to become a destructive force, but the tragedies also tell us that these are the very parts of human beings – the riskiest parts on the very knife-edge between order and chaos – which must be preserved. The Stoic laws reassert themselves here at the end of the tragedy through the voice of Theseus, a man who has himself endured huge tragedy and who now guides Hercules to 'Rise up, break through adversity with your usual energy. Now regain that spirit of yours which is a match for any trouble, now you must act with great valour. Do not let Hercules give way to anger.'[23] The task of self-preservation can only begin once we have first witnessed the primal limits of self-destruction. It is through the tragedies that an audience can come to know what they – as humans – are up against and which parts of themselves most need to be preserved. The tragedies, with their original, primal forces must therefore come first and the more generalised laws and guidance of Stoicism – like that of Seneca's 124 philosophical letters – can only come second.

The Letters

Seneca's philosophical letters were written during the final years of his life, after he had retired from public life. Having served as tutor and advisor to the Roman Emperor Nero for 15 years, Seneca had become extremely well known and wealthy. He had also become entangled in an increasingly corrupt and brutal political elite. In his enforced retirement, Seneca attempted to bring his life back into line with the Stoic principles that he had been advocating throughout his professional life but perhaps not always adhering to.

The letters are addressed to a Sicilian official named Lucilius, although scholars have suggested that he is a fictional rather than a genuine correspondent as no historical evidence of Lucilius's existence has been found other than

Seneca's letters to him. In her biography of Seneca, Emily Wilson notes that, 'His name, again suspiciously, seems reminiscent of Seneca's own: Lucilius is like Seneca's own smaller, younger self. At times, Seneca seems to present Lucilius as an idealised counterpart to himself.'[24] Whether Lucilius was a real person or not, writing to him allowed Seneca to remain ostensibly within the private rather than public realm during his retirement and to be more personal than he had previously been in the tragedies or in the moral treatises that he had written earlier in his life.

Seneca presents himself as the older and wiser of the two friends in the majority of his letters. His explicit aim is to provide Lucilius with a set of useful guidelines which will help him to maintain a healthier mental life: 'There are certain wholesome counsels which may be compared to prescriptions of useful drugs; these I am putting into writing.'[25] In these letters Stoicism is used as a second-order preventative medicine, holding back the threat of contagion which proved to be so damaging in the tragedies:

> Hold fast, then, to this sound and wholesome rule of life; that you indulge the body only so far as is needed for good health. The body should be treated more rigorously, that it may not be disobedient to the mind. Eat merely to relieve your hunger; drink merely to quench your thirst; dress merely to keep out the cold; house yourself merely as a protection against personal discomfort.[26]

This programme of Stoic restraint is designed to prevent the possibility of miniature versions of the tragedies taking place. The mind must remain in control and even the smallest degree of excess cannot be tolerated. The very syntax of the letter is related to its function of prevention. Rather than, 'relieve your hunger by eating', the instruction here is to 'eat *merely to* relieve your hunger'. In each clause of both the English translation and original Latin, the preventative action precedes the effect that it aims to pre-empt: '*Cibus* famem sedet, *potio* sitim extinguat, *vestis* arceat frigus.'[27] This almost back-to-front syntax disrupts the pattern of cause and effect and demands a mental readjustment from the reader. Seneca's dynamic syntax allows concepts to be rapidly turned on their heads; false and unhelpful beliefs can be quickly replaced by or remade into new, more constructive beliefs.

The relationship between Seneca and Lucilius is not always straightforwardly that of a teacher and student or of comforter and comforted. Against hubris and against the borrowed authority of teaching a version of himself, Seneca occasionally steps down from his position of authority and repositions himself not as doctor but as his own patient, not as teacher but as his own student and not as wise philosopher but as a man struggling to meet his own demands. It is in these places that the dynamic of the letters changes. Cracks appear in the surface veneer of Stoic restraint and Seneca's own psychological struggles can be glimpsed. In these places where the individual is revealed within the general, tensions are shown to exist between the philosophy of Stoicism and the psychology of the man attempting to comply with that philosophy.

While it is helpful to have frameworks and maps that provide a general route or strategy for healthy thinking, the really useful parts of the letters are often paradoxically where the framework doesn't quite accommodate reality, where something bursts out from deeper within or when the strategy is derailed, and Seneca admits his contradictions, failures and struggles rather than always trying to have a solution. Without these cracks, the letters can be smoothed too easily into something like what has become the generic counsel of CBT. In Letter LXVIII Seneca deviates from the conventional pattern of him imparting advice on his struggling friend. Here he rejects the idea that he can help Lucilius and instead attempts to pause and find a place to 'lie quiet' and repair himself:

> What, then, am I myself doing with my leisure? I am trying to cure my own sores. If I were to show you a swollen foot, or an inflamed hand, or some shrivelled sinews in a withered leg, you would permit me to lie quiet in one place and to apply lotions to the diseased member. But my trouble is greater than any of these, and I cannot show it to you. The abscess, or ulcer, is deep within my breast. [...] There is no reason why you should desire to come to me for the sake of making progress. You are mistaken if you think that you will get any assistance from this quarter; it is not a physician that dwells here, but a sick man.[28]

Seneca is at his best when he rejects or rather transmutes the doctor/invalid dynamic and instead moves fluidly between the two roles: sometimes he is one, sometimes he is both, and at other times he is neither. Then the reader sees both the need for counsel and the underlying condition that struggles to follow it, in dialogue. So in Letter XIII Seneca again takes off his public mask and writes:

> There are more things, Lucilius, likely to frighten us than there are to crush us; we suffer more often in imagination than in reality. I am not speaking with you in the Stoic strain but in my milder style. For it is our Stoic fashion to speak of all those things, which provoke cries and groans, as unimportant and beneath notice; but you and I must drop

such great-sounding words, although, Heaven knows, they are true enough.[29]

This is the shift from public philosophy to personal psychology. The 'Stoic strain' is a fragile and finely balanced web of preconditions, and there is always potential difficulty in bridging the gap between general solutions and personal, specific experiences. The letters exist on one 'plane' but beneath them, bubbling under the surface, are powers and problems akin to the dangerous forces and resistances that explode in the tragedies. The letters need to be interpreted in terms of an extra dimension of shifting relationships, and not simply taken as abstract and programmatic counsel.

Prior to writing the letters to Lucilius and during a period of forced exile in Corsica that lasted from AD 41 to AD 49, Seneca wrote a series of three 'consolations'. Two of these texts – 'The Consolation to Marcia' and 'The Consolation to Polybium' – were addressed to members of the Roman elite whose children had died. They provide an outline of Stoic guidance on grief but were also written in the hope of gaining favour with influential figures who may have been able to help Seneca after he had been cast out of Rome, accused of committing adultery with Emperor Caligula's sister. But the third consolation was written to Seneca's own mother Helvia, not as with the others to give her comfort or guidance following a bereavement, but rather to ease her suffering during his own exile. In this letter, personal tragedy, individual psychology and general philosophy intersect as Seneca attempts to put Stoicism into practice. Now Seneca is both his mother's comforter and the cause of her distress and this paradox is at the heart of the text, where Seneca is always at his best when he is two-sided:

> Although I consulted all the works written by the most famous authors to control and moderate grief, I couldn't find any example of someone who had comforted his own dear ones when he himself was the subject of their grief. So in this unprecedented situation I hesitated, fearing that I would be offering not consolation but further irritation. Consider, too, that a man lifting his head from the very funeral pyre must need some novel vocabulary not drawn from ordinary everyday condolence to comfort his own dear ones. But every great and overpowering grief must take away the capacity to choose words, since it often stifles the voice itself.[30]

Seneca was living through his own tragedy now and as all personal tragedies feel on the inside, this experience was 'unprecedented'. None of the general and theoretic 'works written by the most famous authors to control and moderate grief' offer any assistance to him in this moment. Seneca requires 'some novel vocabulary' rather than generic words of hope or condolence. 'Everyday' language proves inadequate when faced with the messy, painful reality of actual life. Neat Stoic maxims cannot work here for they would appear too straightforwardly reductive. Instead, Seneca needs a way of communicating with his mother which acknowledges the duality of their current relationship and which will allow him to comfort her both despite and because of the fact that he is also the cause of her suffering.

As in *Hercules*, where the counsellors Theseus and Amphitryon fall silent in the face of tragedy, 'overpowering grief' silences Seneca. Tragedy renders us mute, removing 'the capacity to choose words'. However, despite Seneca's initial sense of inarticulacy and hesitancy he is able to fashion a letter of consolation to his mother. Seneca's approach – like that adopted from him by CBT – is not to try to change his situation, but instead to change the way that he and his mother think about his situation. He describes his letter as his mother's 'treatment'[31] and as such it is an early model of therapy. The consolation contains a description of the long chain of losses that Seneca's mother has suffered throughout her life, beginning with the loss of Helvia's own mother who died while giving birth to her. Like Hercules's step-father Amphitryon for whom 'the end of one trouble is the stepping stone to the next',[32] Helvia's life appears to have been an interminable cycle of sorrow.

Instead of becoming a victim of the tragic momentum, Helvia must have a way of thinking about her past suffering that will help her now to face her present suffering. Not by getting rid of it but by being it, changing its shape and using it as best she can. As his mother's counsellor, it is Seneca's job to provide her with the new helpful thought that she herself – stuck within her own predicament – might not have been able to create for herself. The paradox of this letter is that Seneca has not only caused the suffering that he must now counsel his mother through, but that he must counsel her through a predicament that he too is trapped within. The letter is an explicit attempt to reprogramme Helvia's thoughts, but in the writing of it, Seneca was also rewiring his own thoughts:

> So this is how you must think of me – happy and cheerful as if in the best of circumstances. For they are best, since my mind, without any preoccupation, is free for its own tasks.[33]

In the first sentence Seneca instructs his mother to think of him '*as if* in the best of circumstances', but in the second sentence the wishful thinking of 'as if' becomes a reality: 'for they *are* best'. This shift demonstrates on the page the way in which an opinion can determine reality and thus define the subsequent emotional response. If Seneca or his mother permit themselves to face his exile with the wrong opening thought – that Seneca is unhappy and miserable and in the worst of circumstances – then further negative emotions will duly follow.

Seneca finds counsel for himself in the primary chemistry and physics of the Stoic cosmology rather than the compact, second-order maxims of more conventional, 'everyday' Stoic philosophy. What he needs is a different perspective:

> How silly then to imagine that the human mind, which is formed of the same elements as divine beings, objects to movement and change of abode, while the divine nature finds delight and even self-preservation in continual and very rapid change.[34]

Seneca is always at his most powerful when he is speaking of 'the same elements' and seeking ways to recombine them. By finding a way to reconcile his particular position in the word – alone, uncertain and involuntarily detached from his community – with the wider universe beyond his single, particular self, Seneca was able to comfort himself and then go on to at least try to comfort his mother:

> So, eager and upright, let us hasten with bold steps wherever circumstances take us, and let us journey through any countries whatever: there can be no place of exile within the world since nothing within the world is alien to men. From whatever point on the earth's surface you look up to heaven the same distance lies between the realms of gods and men. Accordingly, provided my eyes are not withdrawn from that spectacle, of which they never tire; provided I may look upon the sun and the moon and gaze at the other planets; provided I may trace their risings and settings, their periods and the causes of their travelling faster or slower; provided I may behold all the stars that shine at night […] provided I can keep my mind always directed upwards, striving for a vision of kindred things – what does it matter what ground I stand on?[35]

The mother and son are reunified as Seneca begins to write in the first-person plural, 'let us hasten'. Here is the healthy version of the cosmology, rather than the fractured and infected cosmos of the tragedies where the system has failed. Individuals are able to reconnect the circuitry between one another and plug into the wide expanse beyond them, to think further than the limits of their own internal psychologies and to escape the limitations of the everyday, small world. The tensions of the cosmos are still visible here in the repeated formulation, 'provided I may' or 'provided I can', for the success of this system is dependent on a series of conditions or provisions which must be met. There is a fragility built into this worldview, and health and sickness, consolation and sorrow are all finely balanced. By mentally positioning himself within the cosmos, Seneca rejects the constraints and difficulties of this one particular spot of earth that he has been exiled to and enters into a vision of a much larger common space.

Notes

1 Jules Evans, *Philosophy for Life and Other Dangerous Situations* (London: Rider Books, 2012), pp. 3–4; hereafter cited as 'Evans'.
2 Ibid., p. 60.
3 Lucilius Annaeus Seneca, *Epistulae Morales*, trans. Richard M. Gunmere, The Loeb Classical Library, 3 vols (Cambridge: Harvard University Press, 2006), ii, Letter LXXVIII, p. 189; hereafter cited as *Epistles*.
4 Carl Baker, 'Mental Health Statistics for England: Prevalence, Services and Funding', House of Commons Briefing Paper, 25 April 2018.
5 Evans, p. 8.
6 Mind, 'We Need to Talk: Getting the Right Therapy at the Right Time' (2010), https://www.mind.org.uk/media/280583/We-Need-to-Talk-getting-the-right-therapy-at-the-right-time.pdf, accessed 12 February 2015.
7 Joanna Cates, 'Cognitive Behavioural Therapy Is Not Always the Answer for Anxiety and Depression', *Huffington Post*, 10 March 2015, https://www.huffingtonpost.co.uk/joanna-cates/cognitive-behavioural-not-always-the-answer_b_6814562.html, accessed 20 March 2015.
8 Tom J. Johnsen and Friberg Oddgeir, 'The Effects of Cognitive Behavioural Therapy as an Anti-Depressive Treatment Is Falling: A Meta-Analysis', *Psychological Bulletin* 141(4) (2015), pp. 747–68.
　Lars-Goran Ost, 'Efficacy of the Third Wave of Behavioural Therapies: A Systematic Review and Meta-Analysis', *Behaviour Research and Therapy* 46 (2008), 296–321.
9 Evans, p. 11.
10 Alasdair MacIntyre, *After Virtue* (Notre Dame: University of Notre Dame, 1984), p. 2.
11 Thomas G. Rosenmeyer, *Senecan Drama and Stoic Cosmology* (Berkeley: University of California Press, 1989), p. 8; hereafter cited as 'Rosenmeyer'.
12 T. S. Eliot, 'Seneca in Elizabethan Translation', in *Essays on Elizabethan Drama* (New York: Harcourt, Brace, 1956), pp. 3–55 (p. 3).
13 Brad Inwood, *Reading Seneca: Stoic Philosophy at Rome* (Oxford: Clarendon Press, 2005), pp. 5–6.
14 *Epistles*, i, XXXIII, p. 237.
15 Lucilius Annaeus Seneca, 'Thyestes', in *Four Tragedies and Octavia*, trans. E. F. Watling (Harmondsworth: Penguin, 1966), pp. 43–96 (p. 81); hereafter cited as *Thyestes*.
16 Ibid., p. 66.
17 Rosenmeyer, p. 107.
18 Ibid., p. 111.
19 *Thyestes*, p. 87.

20 Lucilius Annaeus Seneca, 'Phaedra', in *Four Tragedies and Octavia*, trans. E. F. Watling (Harmondsworth: Penguin, 1966), pp. 97–152 (p. 108).
21 Lucilius Annaeus Seneca, 'Hercules', in *Eight Tragedies*, trans. John G. Fitch, The Loeb Classical Library, 2 vols (Cambridge: Harvard University Press, 2002), i, pp. 36–159 (p. 101); hereafter cited as *Hercules*.
22 Ibid., p. 157.
23 Ibid., p. 153.
24 Emily Wilson, *The Greatest Empire* (Oxford: Oxford University Press, 2014), p. 181.
25 *Epistles*, i, VIII, 37.
26 Ibid., i, VIII, 39.
27 Ibid., i, VIII, 38.
28 Ibid., ii, LXVIII, 49.
29 Ibid., i, XIII, 75.
30 Lucilius Annaeus Seneca, 'Consolation to Helvia', in *On the Shortness of Life*, trans. C. D. N. Costa (London: Penguin, 2004), pp. 34–67 (p. 34); hereafter cited as *Helvia*.
31 Ibid., p. 37.
32 *Hercules*, p. 65.
33 *Helvia*, p. 67.
34 Ibid., p. 42.
35 Ibid., pp. 45–46.

Chapter 2

THERAPY AND THE ESSAY: MONTAIGNE, AFTER SENECA

A Case History

The French aristocrat Michel de Montaigne (1533–1592) devoted himself to public service as a magistrate, counsellor and Mayor of Bordeaux during the period of political and religious upheaval in France marked by the civil war that raged intermittently from 1562 to 1598. In 1571 – at the age of 38 – Montaigne retired from public life, set up a library in the tower of his chateaux, and focused on studying ancient philosophy and writing a book of essays. Montaigne was a particularly keen student of Seneca and was described by his contemporary, Estienne Pasquier as 'another Seneca in our language'.[1] The first half of this chapter will examine Montaigne as a reader of Seneca, considering how he put the principles of Stoicism into practice, testing them against the reality of his own experiences and adapting them to better serve and suit himself. As he wrote in the essay 'On Some Lines of Virgil', 'My philosophy lies in action.'[2] The second half of the chapter examines whether Montaigne's *Essays* offer up a particular model of self-help, concluding that they do contain a valuable therapeutic model, but one which is distinctly different from conventional modern self-help therapy.

Montaigne's self-enforced retirement followed the example of Seneca who had himself retired from his public role as advisor to the Roman Emperor Nero towards the end of his life and who, in retirement, had written his series of letters to Lucilius. In these epistles, Seneca had advised his friend to follow his lead and 'withdraw into yourself, as far as you can'.[3] As Montaigne retreated to his library he was trying to put Seneca's advice into practice: 'It seemed to me then that the greatest favour I could do for my mind was to leave it in total idleness, caring for itself, concerned only with itself, calmly thinking of itself'.[4] However, in reality he found himself struggling to achieve anything close to the Stoic ideal of tranquillity, as his mind immediately 'bolted off like a runaway horse'.[5] The discordancy between the Stoic theory of retirement and Montaigne's own lived experience was an early indication for him that philosophy was something that had to be made and moulded afresh by each individual through the act of living. It was mental and not public action to which his retirement was dedicated.

Writing in his essay 'On Solitude', Montaigne uses Seneca's advice on retirement as a starting point, but then goes on to add the caveats that he has learned through years of troubled experience:

> Withdraw into yourself, but first prepare yourself to welcome yourself there. It would be madness to entrust yourself to yourself, if you did not know how to govern yourself. There are ways of failing in solitude as in society.[6]

'But' is always an important word for Montaigne and here the sharp second thought allows him to launch on past Seneca's initial advice. In practice the Stoic maxim can only be a starting point. After the first shift of withdrawal from the public realm into the private space, there must be a second move, developing from the private sphere into the individual space.

In 1580 – nine years after retiring – Montaigne published the first edition of his *Essays*, consisting of 94 chapters split into two volumes. He wrote in the first person, in French rather than Latin, and covered a whole host of varied themes, for as he would later assert, 'All topics are equally productive to me. I could write about a fly!'[7] Montaigne called these short improvised bursts of writing 'essais' or 'attempts', inventing the essay as a form of relatively unpremeditated thinking. Time and mood took the place of a prior sense of assumed importance or a definitive commitment to hierarchical size. After their first publication, Montaigne continued to work on his *Essays*: a second edition was printed in 1582, and in 1588 a radically altered third edition was produced. This version of the *Essays* contained a third volume consisting of 13 new chapters. Rather than simply adding to the length of his work over time, Montaigne also returned again and again to the original 94 essays of Books I and II, revising and adding quotations to them in light of his further thinking and reading. Approximately five hundred and fifty new quotations were inserted into the third edition of the *Essays*, along with a further six hundred additions to the text. In the four years between the publication of the third edition of the *Essays* and Montaigne's death in 1592, he continued to make changes to his book, adding one thousand new passages and making an estimated nine thousand revisions to his punctuation. The final manuscript that he had been working on up until his death is known as 'The Bordeaux Copy' and provides the source material for the posthumous editions of the *Essays* that are published today. This manuscript was the culmination of

21 years of work, yet it remained unfinished because Montaigne's method of continual revision meant that there could never be a definitive, fixed version of the *Essays*; instead it was a living text.

The *Essays* were originally conceived as a tribute to Montaigne's friend – his fellow councillor, writer and Stoic – Etienne de La Boétie, who had died in 1563. Montaigne planned to publish his friend's work, *De La Servitude Volontaire*, alongside his own writing in order to preserve the memory of La Boétie and recreate a dialogue between the two men. However, Montaigne eventually resolved not to publish his friend's work, replacing what was to be the heart of the book with his own essay 'On Friendship'. A chapter of La Boétie's sonnets was included in early editions of the *Essays* but was later struck out by Montaigne in protest at the misappropriation of his friend's memory and political ideas by radical Protestants calling for a revolt against the Catholic monarchy. Instead, Montaigne left a blank space where the sonnets had previously been printed and the statement, 'Nine and Twenty Sonnets of Etienne de la Boétie: These verses can be found elsewhere.'[8] While La Boétie's work can no longer be found within the *Essays*, his Stoic beliefs did leave an important imprint on Montaigne's life and work. Montaigne turned to ancient philosophy for comfort after the death of La Boétie. He read widely in his retirement and inscribed his favourite quotations onto the walls and beams of his study, making them a concrete part of his physical environment. The philosophers that he frequently quotes in his *Essays* became his companions in thinking and provided him with a supporting structure or scaffolding upon which to build his own work.

Montaigne has an easy personal intimacy with the material that he quotes. He assimilates his reading into his writing and blends ancient philosophy with his own thoughts to create a chorus of co-opted voices within one text. The idea of 'essaying' or 'trialling' is central to Montaigne's work. As he writes, Montaigne is putting philosophy – and in particular the philosophy of Stoicism – to the test. Over the course of the 21 years that Montaigne was writing the *Essays*, he repeatedly questions whether Stoicism is a philosophy that can work in practice. Over time, as his conclusions begin to change, he is less inclined to disguise quotations from Seneca within his writing and instead more likely to hold them up – distinctly apart from his own thoughts – so that they can be properly inspected and critiqued.

'The taste of good and evil things depends in large part on the opinion we have of them' is characteristic of the early essays of Book I in which Montaigne is largely supportive of Stoicism. He begins by thinking about the same Stoic maxim of Epictetus that Jules Evans described as being the starting point for Albert Ellis in the development of Cognitive Behavioural Therapy

(CBT), 'Men are disturbed not by things but by their opinions about them.'⁹ Montaigne measures this central tenet against his own lived experiences:

> There is an old Greek saying that men are tormented not by things themselves but by what they think about them. If that assertion could be proved to be always true everywhere it would be an important point gained for the comforting of our wretched human condition. For if ills can only enter us through our judgement it would seem to be in our power either to despise them or to deflect them towards the good: if the things actually do throw themselves on our mercy why do we not act as their masters and accommodate them to our advantage? If what we call evil or torment are only evil or torment as far as our mental apprehension endows them with those qualities then it lies within our power to change those qualities. [...] Let us see whether a case can be made for what we call evil not being evil in itself or (since it amounts to the same) whether at least it is up to us to endow it with a different savour and aspect.¹⁰

The repetition of 'if' four times in this passage shows Montaigne's sceptical mind in action, while the phrase 'let us see' marks the movement from theory to personal, practical example. Montaigne is testing the concept set out by the Greek Stoic Epictetus, for can it actually be possible in reality that a person can determine their own emotional responses by regulating their thoughts? Can the theory be translated into practice? And if it can, then why isn't that the end of all of our problems? Why do we still suffer if it is in our power to transform our suffering by changing the way we think? For the Stoics, the extent to which pain is felt is a choice; its magnitude is determined by how much mental territory it is given to exist within. While certain patterns of thought accommodate pain and give it space to grow, Stoicism was developed as a means of starving and shrinking it.

In his essay 'On Practice' Montaigne describes a riding accident that brought him close to death. Before the accident Montaigne had been intently preoccupied with his own mortality, but this experience led to a change in his thinking and was a practical reminder of what Seneca had warned of in his Epistle XIII, 'Some things torment us more than they ought; and some torment us when they ought not to torment us at all.'¹¹ For Montaigne, knowledge that is gained through chance or by accident – as happens here – seems to be a particularly important way of learning:

> Many things appear greater in thought than in fact. I have spent a large part of my life in perfect good health: it was not only perfect but vivacious and boiling over. That state, so full of sap and festivity, made thinking

of illness so horrifying that when I came to experience it I found its stabbing pains to be mild and weak compared to my fears.

Here is an everyday experience of mine: if I am sheltered and warm in a pleasant room during a night of storm and tempest, I am dumbstruck with affliction for those then caught out in the open; yet when I am out there myself I never want to be anywhere else.

The mere thought of always being shut up indoors used to seem quite unbearable to me. Suddenly I was directed to remain there for a week or a month, all restless, distempered and feeble; but I have found that I used to pity the sick much more than I find myself deserving of pity now I am sick myself, and that the power of my imagination made the true essence of actual sickness bigger by half. I hope the same thing will happen with death, and that it will not be worth all the trouble that I am taking to prepare for it.[12]

Montaigne demonstrates his characteristic mental mobility in this passage as he builds a case for Stoicism out of his own 'everyday experiences' and thus translates reality back into philosophy. The riding accident demonstrated to him the disparity between the fearful expectations he had supposed absolute and the sudden upsetting reality of experience. His previous state of health meant that he was both physically and emotionally distanced from illness, leaving space for his imagination to create something much worse than reality. While previously, fear, dread and 'the power of my imagination' even in health had warped his perceptions and magnified certain unknowns, making the thought of sickness seem 'bigger by half'. Montaigne learns through experience to measure the world more accurately. The ability to rescale experiences in order to give them their correct weight and significance is an important part of the attitude that Montaigne cultivated. A vital element of this system of weights and measures is Montaigne's humour; the lightness of his tone and wry, carefree approach to the world helps to lighten and to shrink potentially large, heavy problems. Wry humour, born of accidents, serves as an alternative to and a defence against tragic fear and dread.

In the 'Apology for Raymond Sebond', Montaigne directs his mocking humour towards – among others – Seneca and the Stoics themselves. This is the longest essay that Montaigne ever wrote and marks a distinct break with Stoic philosophy. It can be read as Montaigne's manifesto for scepticism or as Donald Frame describes it, 'a declaration of intellectual independence'.[13] In 1569, Montaigne had translated Raymond Sebond's fourteenth-century text *Theologica Naturalis* from Latin into French at the request of his father. Sebond had written the book with the aim of proving the existence of God, but his attempt to reconcile philosophy and theology had proven controversial and in 1595 its prologue was placed on the Pope's list of banned books. In his 'Apology for Raymond Sebond' Montaigne does not take long to deviate from the task of defending the text and its author, and the essay instead quickly becomes 'a devastating critique of all dogmatic philosophy'[14] which therefore included criticism of Sebond himself.

In the final passage of 'The Apology for Raymond Sebond', Montaigne takes one particular quotation from Seneca's *Naturales Quaestiones* and – as he has done so often in the *Essays* – puts it to the test:

> To that very religious conclusion of a pagan I would merely add one more word from a witness of the same condition, in order to bring to a close this long and tedious discourse which could furnish me with matter for ever. 'Oh what a vile and abject thing is Man,' he said, 'if he does not rise above humanity.'
>
> A pithy saying; a most useful aspiration, but absurd withal. For to make a fistful bigger than the fist, an armful larger than the arm, or to try and make your stride wider than your legs can stretch, are things monstrous and impossible. Nor may a man mount above himself or above humanity: for he can see only with his own eyes, grip only with his own grasp. He will rise if God proffers him – extraordinarily – His hand; he will rise by abandoning and disavowing his own means, letting himself be raised and pulled up by purely heavenly ones.
>
> It is for our Christian faith, not that Stoic virtue of his, to aspire to that holy and miraculous metamorphosis.[15]

Montaigne dismantles Seneca's argument with three concise clauses which mimic the Roman philosopher's own succinct style: 'A pithy saying; a most useful aspiration, but absurd withal.' The first three editions of the *Essays* were published with the gentler alternative of 'There is in all his Stoic school no saying truer than that one: *but* to make a fistful bigger than a fist.' But after 1588, this initially hesitant critique of Seneca was substituted by Montaigne's final crisp verdict. The confidence of the three new clauses correspond with Montaigne's growing scepticism. Rather than using Seneca for support, here the voices of the two men are distinctly separate. Montaigne deconstructs Seneca's theory by separating the Stoic's theoretical man into his physical parts; by giving him a 'fist', an 'arm', a 'stride' and a 'grasp' he demonstrates what it would mean in practice for a man 'to rise above humanity'. For Montaigne, not only would it be impossible for an individual to single-handedly exceed the physical capacities of his species, it would be 'monstrous' or inhuman to reject our natural boundaries and try to become something beyond our own natural limits. This is the kind of philosophy that would lead to a state of constant disappointment and repentance, for every attempt to stretch beyond the physical and biological parameters of the human species is doomed to fail.

Rather than setting himself up for failure or regretting his insufficiencies, Montaigne is interested in a philosophy that will make his life more able to be lived. To read Montaigne's *Essays* is to meet somebody who has achieved ease with his own self, who can nonchalantly dismiss a precept with a shrug and relax within his own skin. This is not however a thoughtless version of nonchalance, much here depends on tone, for it is as though tone is the almost unconscious physical accompaniment to what is thought.

In his essay 'On Vanity' – also in Book III – Montaigne deviates from his central theme to discuss his travels around France. His physical freedom of movement corresponds with his mental mobility and provides in this passage a model or template of a particularly sane kind of non-linear progress that is itself explicitly against preset templates. Montaigne's *Essays* offer a model of healthy thinking, even while existing as they do in defiant opposition to the possibility of universally applicable templates for living:

> I, who most often travel for my own pleasure, am not all that bad a guide. If it looks nasty to the left I turn off to the right; if I find myself unfit to mount the saddle, I stop where I am. By acting thus I really do see nothing which is not as pleasant and agreeable to me as my home. It is true that I always do find superfluity superfluous and that I am embarrassed by delicacy, even, and by profusion. Have I overlooked anything which I ought to have seen back there? Then I go back to it: it is still on my road. I follow no predetermined route, neither straight nor crooked.[16]

Montaigne is not constrained by straight lines or preset routes; if there is danger ahead, he simply turns off in a different direction. There is no obligation to follow a certain path, he is guided by an internal compass which serves him. There is no need to endure and maintain a damaging straight route. The flexibility required to change direction is something to be nurtured.

Montaigne has no difficulty in looping back to repeat or remake his path, hence his revisions of the *Essays*. He goes back again and again to build up layers of experience just as in the *Essays* he loops back into earlier attempts at writing to consider again something he may have overlooked at first or not explored to its full depth. But importantly, he also gives himself the time to move away from certain places – often for many years – before returning again to add new layers of thought. As he declared in the essay 'On Vanity', 'I make additions not corrections.'[17] Montaigne's natural changeability contains within it something subtly constant and is all the more constant for not being under fixed mental control.

The additions made to the essay 'On Friendship' – Montaigne's ode to Etienne de La Boétie in Book I – show this process in action. In the Bordeaux copy of the *Essays*, which Montaigne was working on up until his death, he returned to one passage in the twenty-eighth essay of Book I and added the following words in italics to the original text:

> In the friendship which I am talking about, souls are mingled and confounded in so universal a blending that they efface the seam which joins them together so that it cannot be found. If you press me to say why I loved him, I feel that it cannot be expressed *except by replying: 'Because it was him: because it was me.'* Mediating this union there was, beyond all my reasoning, beyond all that I can say *specifically* about it some *inexplicable* force of destiny.[18]

It was at least eight years after the publication of the first edition of the *Essays* and over twenty-five years after La Boétie's death that Montaigne was able to complete his sentence and answer the question of 'Why I loved him'. Saul Frampton goes further in his examination of Montaigne's final manuscript when he notes that 'each part of the addition [was] written in a different pen'.[19] Frampton breaks down what at first appears to be one addition into its three component parts. From the initial full stop after 'I feel that it cannot be expressed' Montaigne first of all makes an opening for himself, deleting the full stop and reigniting the thought by inserting 'except'. He writes 'except by replying' in one colour ink, 'because it was him' in another and 'because it was me' in a third shade, indicating that each small segment was written at a different time as the thought continued to germinate mid-articulation. The bursts of clarity within these short sentences are the closest that Montaigne gets to some kind of end point or realisation, but the process of revision that he follows in writing, namely his constant looping back into the text, mean that these moments of crystallisation are scattered throughout the *Essays*. The clarity, when it surfaces, is not an answer to the question of 'Why I loved him', but an acceptance of the felt unknowable that existed between the two friends, as the two words, 'specifically' and 'inexplicable' themselves add.

An important feature of Montaigne's sanity is his capacity and willingness to go backwards and to think again by making additions to old thoughts. In order to do this he needs a language which will allow him to return to, re-open and re-energise old thoughts. In 'On Repentance' he writes about the value of the specific terms which allow him to do this important work of revision:

> You make me hate things *probable* when you thrust them on me as things *infallible*. I love terms which soften and tone down the rashness of what we put forward, terms such as 'perhaps', 'somewhat', 'some', 'they say', 'I think' and so on. And if I had had any sons to bring up I would have trained their lips to answer with inquiring and undecided expressions such as, 'What does this mean?', 'I do not understand that', 'It might be so', 'Is that true?' so that they would have been more likely to retain the manners of an apprentice at sixty than, as boys do, to act as learned doctors at ten.[20]

Montaigne avoids the false language of certainty by using a set of terms that instead introduces a helpful uncertainty and flexibility into his thought process. These words are a set of tools for developing a healthier way of thinking, 'softening' rigid straight lines, 'toning down' black-and-white absolutism and instead creating space for contradiction, compromise and indecision in the very midst of the route. This is a vocabulary for changing the way of thinking that must be learned and practised. Having a syntactic language enabling the expression of doubt or contradiction – not a set of nouns but a series of functional route-seeking adverbs and conjunctions – makes it possible to have doubts and to be contradictory. Without a linguistic mechanism to help call forward these layers of feeling from the unconscious or implicit mind, it is impossible for them to exist in the conscious world. Montaigne was engaged in a lifelong apprenticeship, and part of the sanity of the *Essays* is due to the fact that he never stopped being willing to rethink and rework his ideas and thus he never reached – or even tried to reach – a conclusion. That is his creative and buoyant scepticism.

Montaigne's Model of Self-Help

The programme of exercises typically contained within self-help books lead readers – theoretically – in a straight line from sickness to health. The imperative, instructive tone that they adopt establishes a sense of the counsellor–patient dynamic within the mind of the solitary reader and helps to impose a particular therapeutic framework. Warren Boutcher writes in *The School of Montaigne in Early Modern Europe* that the *Essays* have 'recently been rediscovered as a kind of self-help book that is relevant to our time'.[21] Yet, in his *Essays* Montaigne refuses to be explicitly instructive or to comply with any kind of permanently set framework. His tone is instead wryly comical, and it is this humour which, as Alexander Welsh describes in *The Humanist Comedy*, allows him to create a certain degree of mental 'leeway'[22] for himself. It is Montaigne's capacity to create mental leeway, humour being only one of his methods for doing so, which is perhaps his most important contribution to psychology. It is his most valuable modification of the otherwise seemingly constrictive philosophy of Stoicism and the nuanced, discretionary quality most lacking in conventional self-help.

Marion Milner, a writer who later became a psychoanalyst, was reacting against the constraints of textbook psychology when, in 1926, she began keeping a diary. In *A Life of One's Own* (1934) she went on to analyse her own diary writing experience:

> Of course there were books on psychology, handbooks telling one how to be happy, successful, well-balanced, thousands of words of exhortation about how one ought to live. But these were all outside me; they seemed too remote, they spoke in general terms and it was hard to see how they applied in special cases; it was so fatally easy to evade their demands on oneself. Was there not a way by which each person could find out for himself what he was like, not by reading what other people thought he ought to be, but directly, as directly as knowing the sky is blue and how an apple tastes, not needing anyone to tell him? Perhaps, then, if one could not write for other people one could write for oneself.[23]

Milner was looking for a genuinely self-directed therapy rather than one which was imposed upon her from the outside. As she explains in *A Life of One's Own*, her diary writing project was inspired by reading Montaigne's *Essays*:

> I must have known vaguely what lay ahead of me, for I still have a crumpled piece of paper with a quotation which I had copied out, and which I remember carrying about in my pocket at the time:
>
>> [...] Really she is the strangest creature in the world, far from heroic, variable as a weathercock, 'bashful, insolent; chaste, lustful; prating, silent; laborious, delicate; ingenious, heavy; melancholic, pleasant; lying, true; knowing, ignorant; liberal, covetous, and prodigal' – in short, so complex, so indefinite, corresponding so little to the version which does duty for her in public, that a man might spend his life in merely trying to run her to earth.[24]

Milner is quoting an essay on Montaigne written by Virginia Woolf and published in *The Common Reader* in 1925. In turn, Woolf is quoting from Montaigne's essay 'On the inconstancy of the self':

> Every sort of contradiction can be found in me, depending upon some twist or attribute: timid, insolent; chaste, lecherous; talkative, taciturn; tough, sickly; clever, dull; brooding, affable; lying, truthful; learned, ignorant, generous, miserly and then prodigal – I can see something of all that in myself, depending on how I gyrate; and anyone who studies himself attentively finds in himself and in his very judgement this whirring about and this discordancy. There is nothing I can say about myself as a whole simply and completely, without intermingling and admixture. The most universal article of my own logic is DISTINGUO.[25]

This essay was first published in 1580, yet Montaigne returned to it at the end of his life to add more to his list of contradictory characteristics. In the Bordeaux copy of the *Essays* he inserted the words, 'chaste, lecherous', 'learned, ignorant', 'generous, miserly and then prodigal'. The revisions that Montaigne made add further complexity to his already rich catalogue of personality traits, suggesting that as time passed he became to himself ever harder to pin down. Each contradictory pair is divided by only a comma; this removes any value judgement from the list and indicates how easy it is to shift from one state to its opposite. The final trio of traits that Montaigne added to this passage break up the pattern of pairs and move him even further from a binary understanding of human behaviour. The movement from 'generous' to 'miserly and then prodigal' defies conventional patterns of progression and instead follows a backwards-forwards motion that ends with Montaigne swinging towards wasteful extravagance rather than settling at a balanced Aristotelian middle ground. Montaigne's 'own logic' is determined by his own personal preference, signalled here by the Latin term *distinguo* that is used in formal debates to declare that a distinction has been made. Montaigne's additions defy the idea that mental clarity is associated with a minimalist stripping back or that contradiction and complexity signify a chaotic mind. The density of ideas that is created within the *Essays* by this gradual process of revision helps to demonstrate just how much is really contained within a person, and by extension just how much is at stake for a person in the act of living. Montaigne gives himself permission to wander as he thinks. He eschews maps or guidelines and as such his work offers up a model of a non-linear process that is markedly different to that provided by CBT self-help books and which perhaps more closely resembles the thinking shapes of psychoanalysis.

Sigmund Freud first read Montaigne's *Essays* in 1914 as war broke out in Europe and his annotated copy of the text can be found today in The Freud Museum. The *Essays* would have offered Freud a model of self-directed analysis for they contain 'the first sustained representation of human consciousness in Western literature',[26] or as Montaigne put it himself in the essay 'On Repentance', 'No man ever went more deeply into his matter'.[27] In *Freud: The Mind of the Moralist*, Philip Rieff highlights the 'genuine affinity between psychoanalysis and the psychological theories of Stoicism',[28] and positions Freud – alongside Montaigne – within a long tradition of thinkers that were inspired by Stoicism: 'The Stoic imagination [...] produced a number of psychologists – Montaigne, Burton, Hobbes, La Rochefoucauld – with whom it would be apt and even historically sound to compare to Freud'.[29] Rieff argues that it is Freud's commitment to honest self-examination through writing that links him to Montaigne: 'I know of only one writer who, in a mood or urbanity not unlike Freud's, may be said to have resolved the problem of being honest about himself: Montaigne.'[30] Freud's psychoanalytic work can be considered as an evolution of what Montaigne began when he retired from public life, turned inwards and made himself into his own subject matter. For in doing so, Montaigne began to translate the generalised theories of philosophy into something personal, specific and practical, and as such moved from philosophy into something that would come to be termed as psychology. By taking Stoicism personally and applying it to his own individual self, Montaigne demonstrated the *differences* both between and within individuals, and between general rules and particular practices.

In an interview with *The Paris Review*, the psychoanalyst and essayist Adam Phillips spoke of the relationship between psychoanalysis and literature, and more specifically, made a connection between psychoanalysis and the essay form that he himself has admired in Montaigne: 'Psychoanalytic sessions are not like novels, they're not like epic poems, they're not like lyric poems, they're not like plays – though they are rather like bits of dialogue from plays. But they do seem to me to be like essays [...] There is the same opportunity to digress, to change the subject, to be incoherent, to come to conclusions that are then overcome and surpassed, and so on [...] Essays can wander, they can meander'.[31] Montaigne makes no attempt to think or to write in progressive sequence, for his content – namely his own psychological matter – cannot be arranged in a single, linear form. As he writes in the essay 'How we weep and laugh at the same thing', 'We deceive ourselves if we want to make this never-ending succession into one continuous whole.'[32]

In an interview with *The Economist*, Adam Phillips again discussed characteristics of psychoanalysis which are akin to those of literature: 'It is as though Freud invented a setting or a treatment in which people could not exactly speak the poetry that they are, but that they could articulate themselves as fully as they are able.'[33] Montaigne developed a process of revision that was entirely unrepentant and which allowed him to articulate himself – in all his multiplicity – in full. His *Essays* defy conventional hierarchies of correction which would insist that mistakes are a source of shame and that first thoughts, once contradicted or superseded by a second thought, must be got rid of. He shows how it is possible to go backwards in a way that is healthy rather than regressive or ruminative. In particular, it is Montaigne's sense of constructive uncertainty which allows him to loop backwards again and again, opening up more thinking space for himself and reactivating formerly closed off lines of thought. The psychoanalyst Susie Orbach discusses the importance of a similar kind of constructive uncertainty in her book *In Therapy: The Unfolding Story*:

> Psychoanalysis and psychological theories of development see the capacity to hold complexity in mind – which is to say, when thinking is not arranged in banishing binaries [...] Complexity is essential to thought. There is rarely one story, one subjectivity, one way to look at and evaluate things [...] Complexity and category-making are the dialectical prerequisites of being human. We all struggle with the tension between the two poles of questioning and certainty. Out of that tension comes an enormous creativity.[34]

Montaigne's *Essays* provide a clear model of this creativity in action. The importance of this cannot be overstated for it is very difficult to even begin to imagine doing or being something without access to an external template that proves that it is possible: Montaigne is the external template that defies any other fixed template. His portrayal of individual psychology in action demands to be met with ways of thinking and versions of therapy which go beyond universal cures or overgeneralised theories.

Chapter 6 of this book will – in part – look at exactly what does happen when a group of individuals are asked to write diaries arising out of their reading in the act of becoming personal essayists. But it would be to take Montaigne too literally, too slavishly, if, like Marion Milner, everyone was required to write. *The Essays* cannot show us in steps how to attain the healthy attitude that Montaigne has cultivated because his writing is so emphatically individual and unreplicable, but he has shown that it is possible to carve out an individual space and to develop individual thinking patterns that serve to make life much more bearable.

Notes

1 Donald Frame, *Montaigne's Essais – A Study* (Upper Saddle River, NJ: Prentice-Hall, 1969), p. 97; hereafter cited as 'Frame'.
2 Michel de Montaigne, *The Complete Essays*, trans. M. A. Screech (London: Penguin Classics, 1991), Book III, Essay 5, p. 950; hereafter cited as *Essays*.
3 *Epistles*, i, VII, p. 35.
4 *Essays*, I, 8, p. 31.

5   Ibid.
6   Ibid., I, 39, p. 277.
7   Ibid., III, 5, p. 990.
8   Ibid., I, 29, p. 221.
9   Evans, p. 4.
10 *Essays*, I, 14, p. 52.
11 *Epistles*, i, XIII, p. 75.
12 *Essays*, II, 6, p. 418.
13 Frame, p. 31.
14 Ibid., p. 24.
15 *Essays*, II, 12, p. 683.
16 Ibid., III, 9, p. 1114.
17 Ibid., III, 9, p. 1091.
18 Ibid., I, 28, pp. 211–12.
19 Saul Frampton, *When I Am Playing with My Cat, How Do I Know She Is Not Playing with Me* (London: Faber & Faber, 2011), p. 27; hereafter cited as 'Frampton'.
20 *Essays*, III, 11, p. 1165.
21 Warren Boutcher, *The School of Montaigne in Early Modern Europe*, 2 vols (Oxford: Oxford University Press, 2017), ii, p. 459.
22 Alexander Welsh, *The Humanist Comedy* (New Haven, CT: Yale University Press, 2014), p. 97.
23 Marion Milner, *A Life of One's Own*, (Harmondsworth: Penguin, [1934] 1952), p. 33.
24 Ibid., pp. 31–32.
25 *Essays*, II, 1, p. 377.
26 Frampton, p. 7.
27 *Essays*, III, 2, p. 908.
28 Philip Rieff, *Freud: The Mind of the Moralist* (London: Methuen, 1965), p. 17; hereafter cited as 'Rieff'. The authorship of this book has since been credited to Rieff's then wife Susan Sontag.
29 Ibid., p. 17.
30 Ibid., p. 66.
31 Adam Philips, 'The Art of Nonfiction No. 7', interview by Paul Holdengraber, *Paris Review*, 208 (2014), https://www.theparisreview.org/interviews/6286/adam-phillips-the-art-of-nonfiction-no-7-adam-phillips, accessed 15 April 2016.
32 *Essays*, I, 38, p. 265.
33 London, E. H., 'The Q&A: Adam Phillips. Poetry as Therapy', *The Economist*, 29 March 2012, https://www.economist.com/blogs/prospero/2012/03/qa-adam-phillips, accessed 15 April 2016.
34 Susie Orbach, *In Therapy: The Unfolding Story* (London: Profile Books, 2018), pp. 83–84.

Chapter 3

THERAPY AND POETRY: WORDSWORTH, AFTER SENECA

Wordsworth and Seneca

William Wordsworth was 21 years old when he first travelled to France in November 1791. He discovered a country that had been radically transformed by a revolution that was still unfolding, and remained there for over one year. Jane Worthington argues that Wordsworth developed a particular interest in and understanding of Roman philosophy – and specifically Stoicism – while living in France. In *Wordsworth's Reading of Roman Prose* she describes how the culture and philosophy of the Roman Republic had gained a new significance in revolutionary France: 'The heroic figures of Rome were regularly set up as models of virtuous conduct. French republicans were constantly urged to imitate Roman simplicity of manners.'[1] Worthington argues that in France, Wordsworth 'learned that history, and particularly the ancient history of Rome, could be made to serve present ends. History had come to life.'[2]

While in France, amidst a new world of freedom, Wordsworth formed a relationship with a woman called Annette Vallon, with whom he had a daughter named Caroline. However, in December 1792, just before the Reign of Terror took hold of the country and war was declared between England and France, Wordsworth returned home, leaving Annette and Caroline behind. Immediately after returning from France, Wordsworth struggled to find relief from his own guilt, grief and sense of disillusionment in the revolution, in an intermingling of private and political feelings. In 1795 he began work on a text that was referred to until its eventual publication 48 years later simply as 'a tragedy'. What eventually became known as *The Borderers* is a relentlessly bleak drama, which followed the template laid down by Seneca in that it served as an initial holding ground for the trauma – both individual and national – that Wordsworth had experienced in France.

The Borderers is a closet drama that was never intended to be acted out on a stage but exists in a strange in-between space between private and public discourse. As Byron said of his own closet drama *Cain*, it is 'mental theatre'.[3] *The*

Borderers belongs to a cluster of plays written by Romantic poets in response to the French Revolution: Coleridge's *The Fall of Robespierre* (1794) and *Osorio* (1797), Shelly's *Prometheus Unbound* (1820) and *The Cenci* (1819) and Byron's *Cain* (1821). Karen Raber establishes a link between these plays and the closet dramas of the English Civil War, the Restoration and the Renaissance. The Renaissance poets, in particular Coleridge's favourite Samuel Daniel, are 'often called "neo-Senecan" because they take as their model the domestic tragedies of the Latin poet Seneca'.[4] Raber argues that during periods of instability or revolution, closet drama and specifically tragedy provided a more private space for writers to explore the psychological impact of political upheavals than the stage could afford. In the Fenwick note of 1843, Wordsworth explicitly sets out his aim in writing the tragedy: 'To preserve in my distinct remembrance what I had observed of transition of character and the reflections I had been led to make during the time I was witness of the changes through which The French Revolution passed.'[5]

The Borderers is concerned with psychological rather than physical movement, mental transitions and incomplete internal changes which, privately existent only fleetingly between definite points of public action, are so difficult to observe. As Mortimer – the tragedy's main character – says as he stands on the cusp of committing a terrible crime, 'There is something / Which looks like a transition in my soul, / And yet it is not'.[6] In *The Borderers* Wordsworth is concerned with identifying those points of transition which do exist, though lost in the moment of their very conversion into abrupt event. As Rivers, the villain of the tragedy, states in Act III:

> Action is transitory, a step, a blow –
> The motion of a muscle – this way or that –
> 'Tis done – and in the after vacancy
> We wonder at ourselves like men betrayed.[7]

It was within that 'after vacancy' that Wordsworth had found himself writing *The Borderers*.

The tragedy is set in thirteenth-century England during the Baronial Revolts which turned the north of the country into a strange and lawless no man's land. Wordsworth uses this historical setting as a testing ground, conducting an experiment to re-examine – within the controlled space of a five-act tragedy – his experiences of the Revolution and the effects of a lawless vacuum on human psychology. Wordsworth writes in the Fenwick note: 'As to the scene and period of action, little more was required for my purpose than the absence of established law and government, so that the agents might be at liberty to act on their own impulses.'[8] 'At liberty' hints at a more problematic freedom than the Liberté lauded in the slogans of the French Revolution.

There are three acts of desertion or betrayal in this tragedy. The first takes place in Act III when Mortimer abandons an old blind man called Herbert on a heath, having been manipulated by Rivers into believing him to be an imposter, posing as the father of the woman Mortimer loves. He leaves him 'where no foot of man is found, no ear / Can hear his cries'.[9] But the tragedy's real psychological starting point and original model of betrayal is revealed in Act IV when Rivers tells the retrospective story of how, when sailing back from Palestine, he had been persuaded by the rest of the ship's crew to turn against his captain and abandon him on a desert island. It is this act which is replicated in different forms – and each time with different configurations of guilt throughout the tragedy.

> RIVERS: One day at noon we drifted silently
> By a bare rock, narrow and white and bare.
> There was no food, no drink, no grass, no shade,
> No tree nor jutting eminence, nor form
> Inanimate, large as the body of man,
> Nor any living thing whose span of life
> Might stretch beyond the measure of one moon;
> To dig for water we landed there – the captain
> And a small party of which myself was one.
> There I reproach'd him for his treachery
> His temper was imperious, and he struck me –
> A blow! I would have killed him, but my comrades
> Rush'd in between us – They all hated him –
> And they insisted – I was stung to madness –
> That we should leave him there, alive – we did so.[10]

There is a terrible simplicity to Rivers's final three words, 'we did so', for like the firing of a starting pistol, they initiate the tragic momentum of the whole play. 'Action is transitory', but there is then an after-sense of contagion running through the tragedy as different characters not only repeat the same acts but also repeat the same words and syntactical forms, unconsciously demonstrating how the driving mental structures behind those acts have spread between them. Mortimer's construction, 'no foot of man is found, no ear / Can hear his cries', finds its root here in Rivers's own repetition of the words 'no' and 'nor' which strip away all life from this place, before ending ironically with that very word 'alive'.

In his preface to *The Borderers*, Wordsworth writes of the strange forward-backward process that recurs when somebody commits to and pushes on with a terrible action:

> In a course of criminal conduct every fresh step that we make appears a justification of the one that preceded it, it seems to bring back again the moment of liberty and choice; it banishes the idea of repentance, and seems to set remorse at defiance. Every time we plan a fresh accumulation of our guilt, we have restored to us something like that original state of mind, that perturbed pleasure, which first made the crime attractive.[11]

Repetition is here a way of returning to the first moments, just before a crime, not out of some desire to repent or make amends, but rather as a means of reviving the first sense of relish at the act, unaffected by the thoughts of remorse or repentance which come later.

Wordsworth explains that one of his central concerns when writing *The Borderers* was 'the position in which the persons in the drama stood relatively to each other'.[12] As Rivers continues to tell his story, Mortimer interjects to blend his own fresh experiences into the narrative:

RIVERS:	'Twas a spot –
	Methinks I see it now – how in the sun
	Its stony surface glittered like a shield
	It swarmed with shapes of life, scarce visible;
	And in that miserable place we left him –
	A giant body mid a world of beings
	Not one of which could give him any aid,
	Living or dead.
MORTIMER:	A man by men deserted,
	Not buried in the sand – not dead or dying,
	But standing, walking – stretching forth his arms:
	In all things like yourselves, but in the agony
	With which he called for mercy – and even so,
	He was forsaken.
RIVERS:	There is a power in sounds:
	The groans he uttered might have stopped the boat
	That bore us through the water.[13]

Mortimer enters into Rivers's memory, chorically adding to the narrative despite not having experienced this specific 'spot' nor having previously heard the story. His own recent memories of abandoning Herbert merge together with Rivers's memories from a more distant place and time. When Mortimer describes 'the agony / With which he called for mercy', the echo of Herbert calling out on the heath, 'Oh! Mercy! Mercy!'[14] reverberates through the tragedy and joins with the cries of the abandoned captain to create one awful sound.

In contrast to Rivers's indifference, Mortimer comes to represent remorse in all the force of momentary action becoming fact, shorn of excuse, 'I led him to the middle of this heath / I left him without food and so he died.'[15] But then the third character, Robert – a poor cottager living with his wife in the only house on the heath – complicates the dialectic by inhabiting the space between remorse and indifference. It was Robert's own choice to leave Herbert to die and yet his past experience of tyranny and the lasting damage that it has inflicted on his character provide him with a degree of mitigating innocence. As Robert is travelling home he discovers Herbert close to death. He leaves him because he is afraid of being blamed for murder if the man were to then die in his own home. Robert's paranoia is a result of having been falsely imprisoned, 'his confinement / Has made him fearful, and he'll never be / The man he was'.[16] The line ending that dissects 'be' and 'the man' reinforces Robert's diminished state.

The ongoing rhythm of the tragic momentum is related to the forces of Senecan tragedy that run on and on and on, repeating and layering tragedy upon tragedy as contagion takes effect. So it is that Mortimer cries 'Oh monster! Monster! There are three of us, / And we shall howl together'[17] This trio of men, who at different times and in different contexts have committed the same sin of abandonment, are pulled back together; all three are monstrous distortions of men who – sharing their crime – can now only howl like wild animals.

After the Tragic

There is a fine line between being at risk of contagion and not risking anything because of its threat, and in the immediate post-revolutionary period of *The Borderers*, this was the predicament that Wordsworth found himself grappling with. During the French Civil Wars of the sixteenth century, Montaigne had responded to the threat of infection by withdrawing from public life and advocating an inward individualism. In his essay 'On Solitude', he writes:

> Contagion is particularly dangerous in crowds. Either you must loathe the wicked or imitate them […] Sea-going merchants are right to ensure that dissolute, blasphemous or wicked men do not sail in the same ship with them, believing such company to be unlucky.[18]

In *The Borderers*, the story of Rivers's corruption at sea exemplifies the dangers of contagion within the closed confines of a ship, acting as a microcosm of the wider dangers within society that Montaigne experienced during the French Civil Wars and which Wordsworth also faced during the French Revolution. In 'On Solitude' Montaigne is borrowing from Seneca's epistle VII 'On Crowds':

> Do you ask me what you should regard as especially to be avoided? I say, crowds; for as yet you cannot trust yourself to them with safety. I shall admit my own weakness, at any rate; for I never bring back home the same character that I took abroad with me. Something of that which I have forced to be calm within me is disturbed; some of the foes that I have routed return again [...] To consort with the crowd is harmful [...] Certainly, the greater the mob with which we mingle, the greater the danger.[19]

And yet for all the madness of zealotry that Wordsworth had faced during the French Revolution, he had concerns about complete withdrawal: his characteristic mental position is poised between separation and connection. This stance coloured Wordsworth's translation of Senecan thought in the poems that he wrote after *The Borderers* and ultimately led him away from the Stoic principle of withdrawal and towards a version of transmutation which finds its most notable expression in his poem 'The Ruined Cottage'.

But between 1802 and 1809 Wordsworth wrote a series of poems that Jane Worthington has described as his most explicitly 'Stoic'.[20] These include 'Resolution and Independence' (1802), 'The Character of the Happy Warrior' (1806) and 'Ode to Duty' (1804), which begins with an epigraph from Seneca's epistle CXX: 'I am no longer good through deliberate intent, but by long habit have reached a point where I am not only able to do right, but am unable to do anything but what is right.'[21] Coleridge scornfully remarked that 'you may get a motto for every sect in religion or line of thought in morals or philosophy from Seneca; but nothing is ever thought out by him.'[22] But the explicit link to Seneca at the beginning of 'Ode to Duty' was a signal of Wordsworth's growing emotional engagement with Stoicism.

'The Character of the Happy Warrior' was written in 1806 as a memorial to Lord Nelson, a hero of the Napoleonic wars who had been killed a year earlier in the Battle of Trafalgar. In his notes to the poem Wordsworth wrote that it was not only Lord Nelson who had been the inspiration behind the poem's Stoic model of control, 'many elements of the character here portrayed were found in my brother John, who perished by shipwreck as mentioned elsewhere. His messmates used to call him "The Philosopher."'[23] The poem is at once a public memorial to a national figurehead and an act of private remembrance. It is here that a subtly different form of Stoicism emerges in the man who

> doomed to go in company with Pain,
> And Fear, and Bloodshed, miserable train!
> Turns his necessity to glorious gain;
> In face of these doth exercise a power
> Which is our human nature's highest dower:
> Controls them and subdues, transmutes and bereaves
> Of their bad influence, and their good receives:
> By objects, which might force the soul to abate
> Her feeling, rendered more compassionate;
> Is placable – because occasions rise
> So often that demand such sacrifice;
> More skilful in self-knowledge, even more pure,
> As tempted more; more able to endure,
> As more exposed to suffering and distress;
> Thence, also, more alive to tenderness.[24]

'Controls them and subdues' seems like a familiar expression of Stoic order and restraint, but 'transmutes and bereaves', which connects back to 'turns', is more unexpected. Instead of submitting to 'necessity', the Happy Warrior is able mentally to transform his predicament to one of 'glorious gain'. He shifts away from the frugal, bare existence typical of Stoicism by changing the very form of his pain and fear. The rhyming line endings, 'pain' / 'gain', 'bereave' / 'receive', 'distress' / 'tenderness', demonstrate a corresponding transmutation of feeling. While Stoicism often seems to be a process of bereavement and self-deprivation, here the movement from 'bereaves' to 'receives' is a surprising change. The latter gain is a result of the former loss.

Transmutation is the key to Wordsworth's further development of a broadly Stoic quietism. While for Seneca and the Stoics dangerous passions needed to be discarded or 'banished', Wordsworth saw feelings of loss and pain as having a value that should not be wasted, but rather, converted into a form of aid. Within seven lines of this poem the word 'more' is repeated seven times, but the 'mores' are not simple additions: they are changes and result from unexpected shifts. The double 'more' at the centre of line 24, separated by a semicolon, is the place of transmutation where temptation is converted to endurance – 'As tempted more; more able to endure' – and culminates in the distinctly un-Stoic, 'Thence, also, more alive to tenderness', where 'tenderness' is the final 'glorious gain'. It is a risk to expose a soft, sensitive delicacy, but in order to receive back the tenderness of others it is a necessary risk.

Wordsworth offers an alternative kind of defence to that offered by Stoicism and it comes not from withdrawal but from becoming *more* receptive, sensitive and permeable to feelings. It is as if removing the armour could be a more effective defence, as it instead allows for the growth of the skin.

The Excursion

The Excursion (1814) is the culmination of this phase of adapted Stoicism and is the only poem of any great length written by Wordsworth that was published during his lifetime. Composed primarily between 1806 and 1809 and originally intended to form one part of Wordsworth's never-completed masterpiece *The Recluse*, it was begun in response to Coleridge's demand to 'write a poem in blank verse, addressed to those, who, in consequence of the complete failure of the French Revolution, have thrown up all hopes of the amelioration of mankind'.[25] This section will trace the progress of the particular model of Stoic-therapy that is offered up within the text and consider how the poem was used both by Wordsworth and subsequent readers as a form of therapy.

The Excursion follows a pedlar and a poet as they walk together over the course of five days through the Lake District, encountering on the way an old recluse who joins them in their walk. The pedlar has been described by Bruce Graver as one of Wordsworth's 'clearest representations of the Stoic sage'.[26]

In Books III and IV of the poem – entitled 'Despondency' and 'Despondency Corrected' – the pedlar attempts to counsel the depressed recluse using a distinctly Stoic model of therapy. In Book IV Wordsworth incorporates eight lines from Samuel Daniel's sixteenth-century poem 'To the Lady Margaret Countess of Cumberland' into his own text. This fragment itself ends with a two-line quotation from Seneca's *Naturales Quaestiones*, the same quotation that Montaigne critiqued in his 'Apologie for Raymond Sebond':

> Knowing the heart of man is set to be
> The center of this world, about the which
> These revolutions of disturbances
> Still roll; where all th' aspects of misery
> Predominate; whose strong effects are such
> As he must bear, being pow'rless to redress:
> *And that unless above himself he can*
> *Erect himself, how poor a thing is man.*[27]

Jane Worthington suggests that Wordsworth was the first to identify this part of Daniel's poem as belonging to Seneca, a sign for her that 'his knowledge of Seneca was as wide as it was thorough'.[28] In his notes to the first edition of

The Excursion, Wordsworth quoted an additional four stanzas from Daniel's poem, writing, 'The whole poem is very beautiful. I will transcribe four stanzas from it, as they contain an admirable picture of the state of a wise man's mind in a time of public commotion.'[29] While Montaigne called into question the possibility of contorting the self into something beyond its own physical limits, for Wordsworth that transmutation almost to the point of self-transcendence is exactly what must be done in order to preserve some degree of central calm at the core of the self in protection against the encroaching agitation of external forces.

Energy is neither created nor destroyed, it can only be transferred from one form to another. Within the poetry of Wordsworth, feelings seem to act in a similar way. They transmute into different forms: they are transmitted between people and, more strangely, between people and places in ways radically different from the mere repetition of contagion in *The Borderers*. To arrive at the realisation of the possibility of transmutation, Wordsworth had to find forms of repetition that were not wholly destructive, not seeking to inhibit the painful material but delivering it again and again for revision and reuse.

The first book of *The Excursion*, also known as 'The Ruined Cottage', is one of the best demonstrations of Wordsworth's commitment to preventing suffering from serving only as mere waste and will form the basis of the reading experiments detailed in Chapters 5 and 6. In his essay on 'Wordsworth's Ethics', the Victorian critic Leslie Stephen – who himself attested to the psychological benefits of reading Wordsworth – describes the poet's commitment to the prevention of emotional waste: 'Wordsworth's favourite lesson is the possibility of turning grief and disappointment into account. He teaches in many forms the necessity of 'transmuting' sorrow into strength […] the waste of sorrow is one of the most lamentable forms of waste'.[30]

The Excursion is made up of a series of conversations between a gradually increasing circle of people. The different sets of relationships that develop between a shifting group of characters provide an alternative to those of *The Borderers*, marked and brought together by contagion. In the midst of the trauma of Book III as the recluse speaks of his dead wife, the presence of the silent, listening minds of his two companions – the pedlar and the poet – create the very earliest possibility of healing:

> You never saw, your eyes did never look
> On the bright form of Her whom once I loved: –
> Her silver voice was heard upon the earth,
> A sound unknown to you; else, honoured Friend!
> Your heart had borne a pitiable share
> Of what I suffered, when I wept that loss,
> And suffer now, not seldom, from the thought

> That I remember, and can weep no more.
> Stripped as I am of all the golden fruit
> Of self-esteem; and by the cutting blasts
> Of self-reproach familiarly assailed;
> Yet would I not be of such wintry bareness
> But that some leaf of your regard should hang
> Upon my naked branches: lively thoughts
> Give birth, full often, to unguarded words;
> I grieve that, in your presence, from my tongue
> Too much of frailty hath already dropped;
> But that too much demands still more.[31]

The relationship between the different pronouns of this passage creates a circuit that runs across and down the lines. The accusatory 'you' and 'your' of the opening line stand in contrast to the repeated and capitalised 'Her' of the beloved wife. There is a huge disconnect between all that the recluse has gone through ('I loved', 'I suffered', 'I wept', 'I remember') and his companions who did not know the woman and therefore can never comprehend the tragedy of her absence. With each 'I' the recluse sinks deeper into his depression. The presence of the poet and pedlar does however now offer the recluse the chance of plugging back into the mental circuitry of a group: 'Yet would I not be of such wintry bareness / But that some leaf of your regard should hang / Upon my naked branches.' The back-to-front syntax of these two lines reflects how difficult it is for the recluse to articulate or even to imagine the possibility of feeling better and yet also his unwillingness to surrender. He needs the 'regard' of another mind outside of himself to do the work of esteeming himself that he is not able to do. Although located prior to the explicit counsel of 'Despondency Corrected', this passage feels like a version of counselling, and is more successful due to the silence of the addressees. The presence of the listening companions draws the recluse's words out of him with a silent force that overpowers his own reticence to reveal his emotional fragility. The syntax of the final two lines acts as a formula for a particularly Wordsworthian version of therapy. 'Too much' + 'too much' = 'but [...] still more' is a distinct departure from Stoic principles of emotional detachment, bareness or curtailment, into a working-through and a revision.

In Book IV, the pedlar intentionally takes on the role of counsellor, dominating the dialogue and offering the recluse a version of therapy rooted in conventional Stoic principles:

> There is a luxury in self-dispraise;
> And inward self-disparagement affords

> To meditative spleen a grateful feast.
> Trust me, pronouncing on your own desert,
> You judge unthankfully: distempered nerves
> Infect the thoughts: the languor of the frame
> Depressed the soul's vigour. Quit your couch –
> Cleave not so fondly to your moody cell;
> Nor let the hallowed powers, that shed from heaven
> Stillness and rest, with disapproving eye
> Look down upon your taper, through a watch
> Of midnight hours, unseasonably twinkling
> In this deep Hollow, like a sullen star
> Dimly reflected in a lonely pool.
> Take courage, and withdraw yourself from ways
> That run not parallel to nature's course.[32]

The idea that 'distempered nerves / Infect the thoughts' recurred throughout Seneca's philosophical letters. The pedlar's tone, as from an early version of self-help, instructs the recluse to 'trust me' and 'take courage' and warns against the self-indulgence of continued self-criticism, which 'affords / To meditative spleen a grateful feast'. This inward looking, self-perpetuating depression is one version of emotional wastage, but the pedlar's explicit counsel, which attempts to 'correct' the recluse's mood, does not work. In his response the recluse undercuts what he perceives to have been overly simplistic advice:

> "But how begin? And whence? 'The mind is free –
> Resolve,' the haughty moralist would say,
> 'This single act is all that we demand.'
> Alas! Such wisdom bids a creature fly
> Whose very sorrow is, that time hath shorn
> His natural wings! – To friendship let him turn
> For succour; but perhaps he sits alone
> On stormy waters, tossed in a little boat
> That holds but him, and can contain no more.[33]

For the recluse, instructions like 'resolve' or 'take courage' are inadequately glib. Any suggestion that 'a single act' is 'all' that is needed to get him out of his depression feels like a bitter mockery of a predicament that has robbed him of his 'natural' wings. He cannot fly, he sits. Reducing the size of the task that he is facing is not helpful: he is already in a 'small' world with 'but' himself, alone. The final image of the recluse 'tossed in a little boat / That holds but him, and can contain no more' recalls the syntax of the passage in Book

III where, 'Too much of frailty hath already dropped; / But that too much demands still more'. But his difficulty now is that he has no physical capacity or mental space for the 'still more' that is needed and his therapist-companion is offering him in this instance even less.

The titles 'Despondency' and 'Despondency Corrected' suggest a sequential movement from ill health to well-being, but in reality such a linear pathway towards recovery could not hope to succeed if Wordsworth was to remain true to his own rules of living. Accordingly, the recluse must veer repeatedly towards and then away from the healthier 'corrected' way of thinking towards which the pedlar is trying to steer him. In his preface to the 1814 edition of *The Excursion* Wordsworth acknowledges the deficiency of the pedlar's counsel. As *The Excursion* was only ever supposed to be one part of the longer poem *The Recluse*, Wordsworth always intended for the character's recovery to occur not in Book IV – 'Despondency Corrected' – but much later:

> It was my wish, and I might say intention, that we should resume our wanderings, and pass the Borders into his native country, where as I hoped, he might witness, in the society of the Wanderer, some religious ceremony [...] which [...] might have dissolved his heart in tenderness, and so have done more towards restoring the Christian faith in which he had been educated [...] than all that the Wanderer and Pastor, by their several effusions and addresses, had been able to effect.[34]

Had Wordsworth ever been able to finish the poem, it would have been some form of direct but chance encounter that would have given the recluse his best hope of recovery. By recalling his non-tragic past this live experience would have allowed undercurrents of feeling to re-emerge from within him, unlike the unsuccessful attempts at consciously directive therapy in Book IV which tried to impose a cure upon him from the outside.

Wordsworth's childhood was marked by the death of his mother when he was eight years old and of his father five years later. In 1805, when Wordsworth was 35 years old, his beloved older brother John died in a shipwreck and in 1812 two of his children died within the space of six months. While *The Excursion* was primarily composed between 1806 and 1809, it was as a grieving father that Wordsworth turned back to the poem for support in 1813 and made further revisions to the text. He wrote as a defence against his own chronic grief, against the stagnating paralysis suffered in this poem by the characters of Margaret and the recluse, following their own multiple bereavements. In January 1813, a few weeks after their second bereavement, Wordsworth's sister Dorothy wrote, 'William has begun to look into his poem *The Recluse* within the last two days and I hope that he will be better for it'.[35]

Like Coleridge 14 years earlier, Dorothy believed that this poem could do some good. Editors of the Cornell edition of *The Excursion* have identified that it was in early 1813 that Wordsworth returned specifically to Books III and IV of the poem. In lines added to Book III after January 1813 Wordsworth writes about the sudden deaths of the recluse's own two children:

> – With even as brief a warning – and how soon
> With what short interval of time between
> I tremble yet to think of – our last prop,
> Our happy life's only remaining stay –
> The Brother followed; and was seen no more!³⁶

In these stuttering lines, without his usual syntax, Wordsworth was writing his own grief into the poem. The line endings cut short each unit of sense, reflecting the structural breakdown of the family unit and of the poet's own mental state.

For many subsequent readers, and in particular his Victorian readers, Wordsworth's poetry became an instrument for finding a way through difficulties. Matthew Arnold wrote of 'Wordsworth's healing power'³⁷ and John Ruskin described using Wordsworth's poetry 'as a daily text book from youth to age'.³⁸ In his autobiography, first published in 1873, John Stuart Mill described how reading Wordsworth helped him through a period of mental crisis:

> What made Wordsworth's poems a medicine for my state of mind, was that they expressed, not mere outward beauty, but states of feeling, and of thought coloured by feeling, under the excitement of beauty [...] I needed to be made to feel that there was real, permanent happiness in tranquil contemplation. Wordsworth taught me this, not only without turning away from, but with a greatly increased interest in the common feelings and common destiny of human beings.³⁹

William James, one of the founders of the discipline of psychology who himself suffered repeated psychological crises throughout his life, attested to the personal therapeutic benefit of reading Wordsworth's poetry and in particular of reading *The Excursion*. On the 1st of February 1870, he wrote in his diary: 'Today I about touched rock-bottom.'⁴⁰ It was however directly after this lowest of points that his first biographer Ralph Bardon Perry recorded a period of partial recovery in James's lifelong struggle with depression. This recovery was in part fuelled by the books William James was reading at the time. In a letter of 1873, James's father writes of a recent and dramatic improvement in his son's mental state: 'He came in here the other afternoon when I was sitting alone, and after walking the floor in an animated way for a moment, exclaimed "Dear me! What a difference there is between me now and me last spring [...] now feeling my mind so cleared up and restored to sanity. It is the difference between life and death" [...] I ventured to ask what specifically in his opinion had promoted the change. He said several things: the reading of Renouvier (specially his vindication of the freedom of the will) and Wordsworth, whom he has been feeding on for a good while.'[41] David E. Leary has identified that it was specifically Book IV of *The Excursion*, 'Despondency Corrected', that James found particularly helpful to him:

> He was reading and re-reading Wordsworth's long poem *The Excursion* especially the section on "Despondency Corrected". He left that work – as Mill had – with an enhanced sense that human cognition entails what Wordsworth called a "marriage" of mind and matter; a union of the subjective and objective brought about by the mind's "excursive power" to "walk around" phenomena, viewing them this way and that, from one vantage point and another.[42]

In his criticism of *The Excursion*, William Hazlitt argued that rather than portraying a series of different characters, the poem was made up of 'soliloquies of the same character, taking different views of the subject'.[43] The pedlar was after all the man that Wordsworth had imagined he might have become, the poet was not dissimilar to the man Wordsworth was at the time that he was writing *The Excursion* and the recluse – suffering in the wake of the failed French Revolution and grieving the loss of his family – was a character who shared much of Wordsworth's own trauma. Whether the poem's central characters are considered as distinct individuals, different facets of the same person, or both, they allowed Wordsworth to shift between different mental positions as he wrote. In turn, the poem's interlocking characters demand a certain mental mobility from the reader and it is this that proved useful to William James, helping him to get unstuck from the fixed psychological state of 'rock bottom' that he had found himself in.

Another troubled reader – who, like so many others, found guidance in the poetry of Wordsworth – wrote an anonymous letter under the pseudonym 'Mathetes' to Coleridge's magazine *The Friend*. In this letter the 24-year-old John Wilson laid out his admiration for Wordsworth. In anxious concern for the progress of his generation he called on the poet to come forward and accept the role of teacher, guide and protector of their fragile minds, 'If a teacher should stand up in their generation, conspicuous above the multitude in superior power [...] to his cheering or summoning voice all hearts would turn.'⁴⁴ In his response to Mathetes's letter, also published in the magazine, Wordsworth refused the role that his young admirer had proposed and questioned the assumption that the transfer of knowledge was best achieved through premeditated and explicit teaching. Instead, Wordsworth encouraged a transaction that relied as much on the mind of the student as the teacher:

> There is a life and spirt in knowledge which we extract from truths scattered for the benefit of all, and which the mind, by its own activity, has appropriated to itself – a life and spirit, which is seldom found in knowledge communicated by formal and direct precepts [...] I trust that the assistance which my Correspondent has done me the honour to request will in course of time flow naturally from my labours, in the manner that will best serve him.⁴⁵

For Wordsworth, help works best when it occurs on a subliminal level, almost by psychologically syntactic stealth rather than through straight lines of directed transmission. Help that is not known to be needed, or help that is not known to be being given, or help that is directed at one person but deflected into another are permitted and it is these implicit, almost accidental kinds of teaching and learning that Wordsworth supports.

In his 'Answer to Mathetes' Wordsworth goes on to reject straight-line versions of progress and in doing so casts off the anxieties that false, linear templates enforce. He describes progress as a subliminal phenomenon that combines backwards and forwards motion:

> The progress of the species neither is nor can be like that of the Roman road in a right line. It may be more justly compared to that of a river, which both in its small reaches and larger turnings is frequently forced back towards its fountains, by objects which cannot otherwise be eluded or overcome; yet with an accompanying impulse that will ensure its advancement hereafter, it is either gaining strength every hour, or conquering in secret some difficulty, by a labour that contributes as effectually to further it in its course, as when it moves forward uninterrupted in a line, direct as that of the Roman road with which we began the comparison. [...] It suffices to content the mind, though there may be an apparent stagnation, or a retrograde movement in the species, that something is doing which is necessary to be done, and the effect of which will in due time appear; – that something is unremittingly gaining, either in secret preparation or in open and triumphant progress.⁴⁶

If a reader were to trace the track of the recluse's mind as he proceeds through the course of *The Excursion* – as if he or she were tracing the route that the men follow in their journey – it would be a line that moves backwards more frequently than forwards, that stops and refuses to go onwards or attempts to veer back on itself before surging forwards only to then come to an abrupt halt. In Wordsworth's redefinition of progress, these moves all belong to the indistinct and unknowable process that he can only pin down as far as to say 'something is doing which is necessary to be done'. The 'is doing' only emerges when 'done' and perhaps long after that. The pedlar's too linear corrective passages attempt to carry the recluse too directly out of his despondency and therefore actually sidestep this unidentifiable but crucial interior preparatory work of preconscious 'doing' that must come first. Wordsworth's is a model of progress that is particularly important to the argument of this book as it exists as an antidote to the overly linear, reductive pathways to recovery that are commonly prescribed by modern psychological therapies.

Despite the failure of the pedlar's attempts at correction in Book IV, there are several places within *The Excursion* where more successful forms of therapy take place almost by accident. These are places which are distinctly non-linear and which are instead characterised by circular movement, reflection, rebounds, turns and returns. For example, in Book IV it is the poet rather than the recluse who receives the benefit of the pedlar's therapy as if by deflection. He is able to gain benefit from words that were not intended for or directed at him, but which were unknowingly needed by him, in a way that the recluse is not able to:

> The words he uttered shall not pass away
> Dispersed, like music that the wind takes up
> By snatches, and lets fall, to be forgotten;
> No – they sank into me, the bounteous gift
> Of one whom time and nature had made wise.[47]

In the downward shift of 'they sank into me' the pedlar's spoken words become heavy and permanent, as if converted into a more solid currency that can be put to later use. In the silent give and take of this passage, something of real value is transferred between the three individual but somehow connected main characters and thus preserved intact.

A further example from Book IV occurs as the pedlar remembers listening to the cry of a solitary raven echoing through the mountains. As he recalls the gradations of silence created by the bird as it circled over the valley, the poem moves from the mode of surface dialogue and linear exchange that has hitherto dominated it, and shifts instead to a different kind of language that belongs at the very edge of the unspoken and unwritten:

> Within the fabric of this circuit huge,
> One voice – the solitary raven, flying
> Athwart the concave of the dark blue dome,
> Unseen, perchance above all power of sight –
> An iron knell! With echoes from afar
> Faint – and still fainter – as the cry with which
> The wanderer accompanies her flight
> Through the calm region, fades upon the ear,
> Diminishing by distance till it seemed
> To expire; yet from the abyss is caught again,
> And yet again recovered![48]

In the shift from 'faint' to 'still fainter' the limits of sound and distance are stretched as though an analogue to the creation of memory itself. The echo is momentarily lost in the pause at the end of the line between 'it seemed' and 'To expire', but with each line the pedlar is attuning himself to the silence and becomes able to catch the sound again and again, even when it seems to have been lost. Non-linear progress is a particularly literary feature of Wordsworth's philosophy due to its specific connection to his use of lineation. This passage provides a model of the kind of non-linear and barely perceptible progress that Wordsworth outlined in his reply to Mathetes, its patterns of turns and returns leading to the final recovery of the last line. The sequence of recovery is 'yet [...] again / And yet again'.

The Latin word for a line of poetry – *versus* – originates from the word for 'a furrow', while *verto* – the corresponding verb – describes the action of the plough as it turns at the edge of the field to begin each new furrow.[49] In the Roman mind poetry is therefore connected – if only subconsciously – to movement across a physical space, the marking out of a distinct pattern onto the land and to a repeated pattern of turns and returns that connect together a series of straight lines. This is cultivation and culture. Wordsworth composed much of his poetry as he walked outdoors and there is a relationship between the rhythms of the poet's stride, the pathways that he followed as he walked, and the mental structure of linear turns and returns within his poetry.

In a letter to John Thelwall written in 1804, Wordsworth identified line endings as places of particular concern and power for him:

> As long as blank verse shall be printed in lines, it will be physically impossible to pronounce the last words or syllables of the lines with the same

indifference as the others, i.e. not to give them an intonation of one kind or another, or to follow them with a pause, not called out for by the passion of the subject, but by the passion of metre merely.[50]

By creating a gap in the circuitry of the poem, line endings trigger an electrical surge amid temporary silence or hesitation that in the midst of formulation rather than at its end cannot fail to have some kind of effect – whether conscious or unconscious – on the mind of the reader. Wordsworth took full advantage of the opportunity that line endings provide for rewiring the mind as we would now put it, and this may be one reason for the particular therapeutic power of his poetry. It was not, however, until the mid-twentieth century that critics such as William Empson, Donald Davie, Christopher Ricks and Herbert Lindenberger specifically began to study Wordsworth's use of lineation and to build the argument that it was a central component of his literary language.

In *Articulate Energy* (1955), Donald Davie argues that 'this is poetry where the syntax counts enormously, counts for nearly everything'.[51] In his 1971 essay 'A Pure Organic Pleasure from the Lines', Christopher Ricks locates in the line endings a holding place for 'what the poet values, as well as the instrument by which his values are expressed'.[52] William Empson wrote extensively on Wordsworth's use of the single word 'sense' in his book *The Structure of Complex Words* (1951), noticing that three quarters of the instances of the word in *The Prelude* were located at line endings and arguing that this meant that it was held 'slightly apart from the stock phrase it comes in, so that some wider meaning for it can be suggested'.[53] Line endings function as junction points that disrupt straight line thinking and trigger what Davie described in relation to Milton as a 'flicker of hesitation'[54] in the reader's mind as they hang momentarily in the gap, uncertain of quite where the turn into the next line will take them. Again this under-sense is to do with something other than simple, conscious sense, final ends or directed goals and outcomes.

In Book V of the 1805 *Prelude,* as Wordsworth watches a boy mimicking the hooting of an owl, his use of lineation helps to expand space, creating width and depth that stretches both inwards into the body and outwards into the landscape:

                And when it chanced
That pauses of deep silence mocked his skill,
Then sometimes in that silence while he hung
Listening, a gentle shock of mild surprise
Has carried far into his heart the voice
Of mountain torrents.[55]

The line break between 'hung' and 'listening' famously creates a moment of mental suspension, slowing the pace of time and creating a holding place for thought. This gap feels like an extended physical realisation of the 'flicker of hesitation' and is reinforced by the subsequent line which ends with the word 'surprise'. Silence becomes a 'deep' space or a substance that a person can be 'in' – can 'sink' into. It is in this silent space – as the boy listens intently for the returning calls of the owls – that he is able to tune into another previously unnoticed layer of sound, 'the voice of mountain torrents'. The horizontal span of the word 'far' corresponds with the vertical depth of the silence in which the boy first hung. Thomas De Quincey wrote of the same lines: 'This very expression, "far", by which space and its infinities are attributed to the human heart, and to its capacities of re-echoing the sublimities of nature, has always struck me with a flash of sublime revelation.'[56]

In the final book of *The Excursion*, as the much enlarged group of travellers – which now includes the pastor and his family as well as the poet, pedlar and recluse – all walk down to a lakeside, one of the pastor's daughters begins to sing. Her voice sinks into the hearts of the collective group with a vertical inward movement that is akin to the horizontal shift inwards of *The Prelude* so admired by De Quincey:

> That lovely Girl supplied a simple song,
> Whose low tones reached not to the distant rocks
> To be repeated thence, but gently sank
> Into our hearts; and charmed the peaceful flood.[57]

The line break after that Wordsworthian verb 'sank' extends the interior space into which the song can travel down into, revealing an internal landscape that is as expansive as that of the mountains and lakes on the outside. It recalls the place in Book IV when the pedlar's words of counsel 'sank into' the mind of the poet, rather than being wasted 'like music that the wind takes up / By snatches, and lets fall, to be forgotten'. The preservation of such therapeutic material is a collective human endeavour, and in both these cases more than one mind is needed to provide a home or a holding place for words that contain the potential for healing. They become lodged in deep places where they are needed, if not necessarily known to be needed, and where they in turn can be protected and stored wholly intact.

It is in the second half of *The Excursion* – located after the poem's core book of counsel 'Despondency Corrected' – that a second attempt is made at alleviating the recluse's depression. Within the enclosure of the churchyard and now in the company of the pastor, the poem's forward movement is replaced by a long period of stillness, interrupted only as the recluse asks to hear the stories of the men and women buried there. It is these stories, or spoken epitaphs, which provide the group with a more solid form of counsel – grounded in live experience – than that which the pedlar had been able to offer in the earlier books of the poem. These oral epitaphs retain the physical qualities of their stone counterparts and the pastor's words are marked out as different from the kinds of speech that have thus far filled the poem. These are not 'fruitless [...] abstractions' but 'solid facts' and 'plain pictures' that have a particularly permanent value, or which hold in memory some kind of foundational truth.

It was F. W. H. Myers, the psychologist and poet born in the Lake District in 1843 – seven years before the death of Wordsworth – who developed the idea of the 'subliminal' to describe the domain beneath the threshold of consciousness. Myers was a friend of and influence on William James and in 1881 wrote a book on William Wordsworth. In *Human Personality and Its Survival of Bodily Death*, published posthumously in 1907, Myers writes of the possible transfer or surfacing of material from the subliminal layers of the mind and into the consciousness: 'I conceive that there may be, not only co-operations between these quasi-independent trains of thought, but also upheavals and alternations of personality of many kinds, so that what was once below the surface may for a time, or permanently rise above it.'[58] Myers believed that material that the subconscious was holding in storage could be pulled back up to the surface in time of need and put to conscious work. In the churchyard books of *The Excursion* an attempt is made to get at those buried resources.

Wordsworth wrote three essays on the subject of epitaphs. The first was initially published in *The Friend* on the 22nd of February 1810 alongside Coleridge's poem 'The Tombless Epitaph' and Wordsworth's own translations of the epitaphs of the sixteenth-century Italian Poet Gabriello Chiabrera. This essay was republished in 1814 alongside *The Excursion* as a footnote to Books VI and VII, the section entitled 'The Churchyard in the Mountains'. In doing so Wordsworth repurposed the essay as a companion and aid to reading this part of the poem. After the failure of the pedlar's words to effect real psychological change in 'Despondency Corrected', this second attempt at counsel by the pastor tunes into the primary language of the epitaph as if looking now for a quality within written language that when spoken will make up for some deficiency in the pedlar's earlier words. The epitaph is a model of bareness, which, as Wordsworth wrote in his first 'Essay Upon Epitaphs', 'should speak, in a tone which shall sink into the heart'.[59] It is again the vital therapeutic word 'sink into' that bears weight but allows for slowness rather than immediate feeling.

One of the stories that the pastor tells in Book VI is of a young mother called Ellen who, having been forced to leave her newborn baby and take on a job nursing the children of another family, becomes caught in a paralysing grief when her own child dies. Abandoned by her baby's father and in turn abandoning the child to its death, Ellen is one of Wordsworth's many tragic mothers:

> You see the Infant's grave; and to this spot,
> The mother, oft as she was sent abroad,
> On whatsoever errand, urged her steps:
> Hither she came; here stood, and sometimes knelt
> In the broad day, a rueful Magdalene!
> So call her; for not only she bewailed
> A mother's loss, but mourned in bitterness
> Her own transgression; penitent sincere
> As ever raised to heaven a streaming eye!
> – At length the parents of the foster child,
> Noting that in despite of their commands
> She still renewed and could not but renew
> Those visitations, ceased to send her forth;
> Or, to the garden's narrow bounds, confined.
> I failed not to remind them that they erred;
> For holy Nature might not thus be crossed.[60]

Ellen's stolen visits to the churchyard 'in broad day' contrast with the restorative and tranquil pockets of shade – particularly within the churchyard – that provide shelter throughout the poem for the group of travellers. Here, Ellen is exposed to the light of the sun and finds no comfort from returning again and again to the spot where her baby is buried, 'she still renewed and could not but renew / Those visitations'. Ellen is part of a pattern of grief that runs through the poem and which includes Margaret, the recluse and Wordsworth himself, writing as he was out of his own need to mourn the deaths of two of his own children and yet somehow avoid the unresolved grief that the lives of these dead mothers warn against. As the pastor speaks it is as if in composing Ellen's epitaph he is attempting for a second time to realign her disturbed life and allow the grief that was restricted while she lived to play out now in full.

In his essay 'Remembering, Repeating and Working Through', Freud describes the way in which patients undergoing psychoanalysis often unwittingly re-enact their memories:

> The patient does not remember anything of what he has forgotten and repressed, but acts it out. He reproduces it not as memory but as an action; he repeats it, without, of course, knowing that he is repeating it […] As long as the patient is in treatment he cannot escape from his

compulsion to repeat; and in the end we understand that this is his way of remembering.[61]

It is the job of the analyst to unpick the memories stored within these repetitions and re-enactments and to then lead the patient towards the hoped for third mental stage of 'working through'. Wordsworth's repetitions and revisions similarly reveal traces of his own traumas, and were also the means by which he too managed to attain that third stage of mental repair.

It is in the silent aftermath of Ellen's story that the priest's epitaph is shown to be doing its work on the group, as if in secret:

> The Vicar ceased; and downcast looks made known
> That each had listened with his inmost heart.
> For me, the emotion scarcely was less strong
> Or less benign than that which I had felt
> When seated near my venerable Friend,
> Under those shady elms, from him I heard
> The story that retraced the slow decline
> Of Margaret sinking on the lonely heath,
> With the neglected house to which she clung
> – I noted that the solitary's cheek
> Confessed the power of nature – Pleased though sad,
> More pleased than sad, the grey-haired Wanderer sate.[62]

The feelings transmitted by the pastor are absorbed by each member of the group separately, but it is the pedlar who is able to transmute what he has received into the blended feeling of 'Pleased though sad / More pleased than sad'. This composite emotion requires the syntax of poetry to exist for it defies linear either/or frameworks of thinking. The pedlar retains a sadness that cannot but deduct something from his pleasure, a pleasure which in turn is adding something to his sadness.

In this passage the poet recalls the corresponding spot in Book I where he had heard the poem's original template of unresolved and unhealthily ruminating grief. His remembrance of Margaret here is part of the poem's long effort – which began in 'The Ruined Cottage' – to prevent her life and suffering from being wasted:

> At this the Wanderer paused;
> And, looking up to those enormous elms,
> He said, "'Tis now the hour of deepest noon.
> At this still season of repose and peace,

This hour when all things which are not at rest
Are cheerful; while this multitude of flies
With tuneful hum is filling all the air;
Why should a tear be on an old Man's cheek?
Why should we thus, with an untoward mind,
And in the weakness of humanity,
From natural wisdom turn our hearts away;
To natural comfort shut our eyes and ears;
And, feeding on disquiet, thus disturb
The calm of nature with our restless thoughts?"[63]

Wordsworth was trying not to diminish his sense of loss or to turn his losses into gains, but instead to create sorrow that was not wholly sorrow to hear of, for the human value buried within its pain. In *The Master and His Emissary*, Iain McGilchrist warns that 'Error arises from "either/or" thinking (it must be pleasure or it must be pain), coupled with sequential analysis (if both are present, one must give rise to the other, presumably pain to pleasure). The option that both emotions might be caused at the same moment by the very same phenomenon is excluded.'[64] Without a framework that allows for something other than either/or thinking, the spectrum of blended, reciprocal emotions that Wordsworth shows to be so necessary and internally beneficial to us are wasted. The experimental work of Chapters 5 and 6 will in part aim to explore whether Wordsworth's poetry does offer modern readers such a framework for more non-linear, non-binary thinking patterns to develop.

Notes

1. Jane Worthington, *Wordsworth's Reading of Roman Prose* (Hamden, CT: Archon Books, 1970), p. 8; hereafter cited as 'Worthington'.
2. Ibid., p. 11.
3. Lord Gordon George Byron, *Life, Letters and Journals of Lord Byron*, ed. Thomas Moore (London: John Murray, 1892), p. 525.
4. Karen Raber, 'Closet Drama', in *The Oxford Encyclopaedia of British Literature*, ed. David Scott Kastan (Oxford: Oxford University Press, 2006), pp. 28–32 (p. 28).
5. William Wordsworth 'The Fenwick Note', in *The Borderers*, ed. Robert Osborn (Ithaca, NY: Cornell University Press, 1982), pp. 814–15 (p. 815); hereafter cited as Fenwick.
6. William Wordsworth, *The Borderers*, ed. Robert Osborn (Ithaca, NY: Cornell University Press, 1982), Act II, Scene i, ll. 91–93; hereafter cited as *Borderers*.
7. Ibid., III, v, ll. 60–63.
8. Fenwick, p. 814.
9. *Borderers*, III, iii, ll. 128–29.
10. Ibid., IV, ii, ll. 22–30.

11 William Wordsworth, 'Preface to *The Borderers*', in *The Prose Works of William Wordsworth*, ed. W. J. B. Owen and Jane Worthington Smyser, 3 vols (Oxford: Clarendon Press, 1974), i, pp. 76–80 (p. 79); hereafter cited as *Prose*.
12 Fenwick, p. 814.
13 *Borderers*, IV, i, ll. 22–51.
14 Ibid., III, iv, l. 141.
15 Ibid., V, ii, ll. 169–70.
16 Ibid., III, ii, ll. 20–22.
17 Ibid, V, ii, ll. 55–57.
18 *Essays*, I, 39, p. 267.
19 *Epistles*, i, VII, pp. 29–31.
20 Worthington, p. 60.
21 *Epistles*, iii, CXX.
22 Samuel Taylor Coleridge, *Specimens of Table Talk of the Late Samuel Taylor Coleridge*, ed. Henry Nelson Coleridge, 2 vols (London: John Murray, 1835), i, p. 181.
23 Christopher Wordsworth, *Memoirs of William Wordsworth*, ed. Henry Reed, 2 vols (Boston, MA: Ticknor, Reed and Fields, 1851), i, p. 299.
24 William Wordsworth, 'The Character of the Happy Warrior', in *Wordsworth's Poetical Works*, ed. Ernest de Selincourt and Helen Derbyshire, 5 vols (Oxford: Clarendon Press, 1940–49), iv, ll. 12–26, pp. 86–87; hereafter cited as *Wordsworth's Poetical Works*.
25 Samuel Taylor Coleridge, *Collected Letters of Samuel Taylor Coleridge*, ed. Earl Leslie Griggs, 6 vols (Oxford: Clarendon Press, 2000), i, p. 527.
26 Bruce Graver, 'Wordsworth and the Stoics', in *Romans and Romantics*, ed. Timothy Saunders et al. (Oxford: Oxford University Press, 2012), pp. 146–59 (p. 149).
27 William Wordsworth, *The Excursion*, ed. Sally Bushell, James A. Butler and Michael C. Jaye (Ithaca, NY: Cornell University Press, 2007), Book IV, ll. 327–34; hereafter cited as *Excursion*.
28 Worthington, p. 45.
29 *Excursion*, p. 301n6.
30 Leslie Stephen, 'Wordsworth's Ethics', in *Hours in a Library* (1829), 3 vols (London: Smith, Elder, 1892), ii, pp .270–307 (pp. 299–300).
31 *Excursion*., III, ll. 484–501.
32 Ibid., IV, ll. 475–90.
33 Ibid., IV, ll. 1077–85.
34 *Excursion*, 'Preface to the edition of 1814', p. 1224.
35 Dorothy Wordsworth, *The Letters of William and Dorothy Wordsworth, The Middle Years: Part II, 1812–20*, ed. Ernest de Selincourt, 2nd edition, rev. Mary Moorman and Alan G. Hill (Oxford: Clarendon Press, 1970), p. 84.
36 *Excursion*, III, ll. 654–58.
37 Matthew Arnold, 'Memorial Verses', in *Matthew Arnold Selected Poems*, ed. by Miriam Allott (Oxford: Oxford University Press, [1850] 1995), l. 63, p. 96.
38 John Williams, *Wordsworth Translated* (London: Continuum, 2009), p. 127.
39 John Stewart Mill, *Autobiography*, (Oxford: Oxford University Press, [1873] 1971), p. 89.
40 Ralph Bardon Perry, *The Thought and Character of William James*, 2 vols (London: Humphrey Milford, 1935), i, p. 322.
41 Ibid., p. 339.
42 David E. Leary, 'Instead of Erklaren and Verstehen: William James on Human Understanding', in *Historical Perspectives on Erklaren and Verstehan*, ed. Uljana Feest (Berlin: Max Planck Institute for the History of Science, 2007), pp. 121–40 (p. 124).

43 William Hazlitt, 'On Mr Wordsworth's *The Excursion*', in *William Wordsworth: A Critical Anthology*, ed. Graham McMaster (Harmondsworth: Penguin, [1814] 1972), pp. 114–20 (p. 116).
44 'Letter of Mathetes', *Prose*, ii, p. 33.
45 'Reply to Mathetes', *Prose*, ii, p. 8.
46 Ibid., pp. 11–12.
47 *Excursion*, IV, ll. 1280–84.
48 Ibid., IV, ll. 1140–50.
49 Rosemary Huisman, *The Written Poem: Semiotic Conventions from Old to Modern English* (London: Cassell, 1999), p. 108.
50 William Wordsworth, *The Letters of William and Dorothy Wordsworth, The Early Years, 1787–1805*, ed. Ernest de Selincourt, 2nd edition, rev. Chester L. Shaver (Oxford: Clarendon Press, 1967), p. 434.
51 Donald Davie, *Articulate Energy* (London: Routledge, 1955), p. 111.
52 Christopher Ricks, 'Wordsworth: "A Pure Organic Pleasure from the Lines"', in *William Wordsworth: A Critical Anthology*, ed. Graham McMaster (Harmondsworth: Penguin, 1972), pp. 505–34 (p. 507).
53 William Empson, *The Structure of Complex Words* (London: Chatto & Windus, 1977), p. 289.
54 Donald Davie, 'Syntax and Music in *Paradise Lost*', in *The Living Milton*, ed. Frank Kermode (London: Routledge, 1960), pp. 70–84 (p. 73).
55 *Prelude*, V, ll. 404–9.
56 Thomas de Quincey, *Recollections of the Lakes and the Lake Poets*, ed. David Wright (Harmondsworth: Penguin, [1839] 1970), p. 161.
57 *Excursion*, IX, ll. 534–37.
58 F. W. H. Myers, *Human Personality and Its Survival of Bodily Death*, (New York: Dover, [1903] 2005), p. 27.
59 'Essay Upon Epitaphs I', *Prose*, ii, p. 57.
60 *Excursion*, VI, ll. 1004–19.
61 Sigmund Freud, 'Remembering, Repeating and Working Through', in *The Standard Edition of the Complete Psychological Works of Sigmund Freud*, ed. by James Strachey, 24 vols (London: Hogarth Press, [1814] 1953–74), xii, pp. 145–56 (p. 150); hereafter cited as 'Remembering, Repeating and Working Through'.
62 *Excursion*, VI, ll. 1074–85.
63 Ibid., I, ll. 630–43.
64 Iain McGilchrist, *The Master and His Emissary: The Divided Brain and the Making of the Western World* (New Haven, CT: Yale University Press, 2009), p. 362.

Chapter 4

THERAPY AND THE NOVEL: GEORGE ELIOT, AFTER WORDSWORTH

George Eliot and William Wordsworth

In *Wordsworth and the Victorians*, Stephen Gill describes George Eliot as 'Wordsworth's ideal reader',[1] so in-tune was she to the poet's ideas. In turn, while working on *Silas Marner*, George Eliot imagined Wordsworth as her own ideal reader, admitting in a letter to her publisher that 'it was not a story she believed anyone would be interested in, but myself, (since William Wordsworth is dead)'.[2]

This chapter begins by exploring the connections between George Eliot and Wordsworth, focusing in particular on her earliest works –*Scenes of Clerical Life*, *Adam Bede*, *The Mill on the Floss* and *Silas Marner* – which can be read as prose translations of Wordsworth's poetry. A second relationship – that of George Eliot with the new discipline of psychology – is then examined, with particular consideration given to the ways in which her realist novels can be regarded as literary translations of this new science.

The sense of concordance that George Eliot felt towards Wordsworth was a steady feature of her life, from her youth, when she first read his poetry. In 1839, on her twentieth birthday, the then Mary Ann Evans wrote of her admiration for 'our incomparable Wordsworth' in a letter to a friend, remarking that, 'I have been so self-indulgent as to possess myself of Wordsworth at full length, and I thoroughly like much of the contents of the first three volumes […] I never before met with so many of my own feelings, expressed just as I could like them.'[3] In Wordsworth she had found a compatriot in feeling. Margaret Hamans states, 'Had there been no Wordsworth, Eliot would still have discovered for herself what are commonly taken to be their shared beliefs in the value of childhood and rural life and in the necessity of constant interchange between feeling and knowledge.'[4] She argues that Wordsworth's poetry deals in foundational truths which belong deep within human roots and are already known at some level by many of his readers. The relationship between Wordsworth and George Eliot is therefore not simply one of linear transfer or passive inheritance from the poet to the novelist, and is all the more Wordsworthian in nature because of this. For as we have seen, Wordsworth did not believe in mimetic followers, or in the possibility of a literal handing on of messages and meanings. Nonetheless, his work as summarised in the 'Preface to Lyrical Ballads' did create a revolution in relation to art's relation to common life. In that sense George Eliot was indeed his prose successor in the name of realism – in its aspirations in both depicting and in turn having an effect upon ordinary existence.

In her first three novels, *Adam Bede*, *The Mill on the Floss* and *Silas Marner*, George Eliot announced herself as a descendent of Wordsworth and committed herself to the principles that he set out in the great preface to the second edition of *Lyrical Ballads*: 'The principal object then proposed in these poems was to choose incidents and situations from common life, and to relate or describe them, throughout, as far as was possible in a selection of language really used by men.'[5] George Eliot shared Wordsworth's conception of what literature 'really' should be for and what it should contain. Prior to writing her first novel she had asserted her own belief in the importance of ordinary lives and voices in her collection of short stories *Scenes of Clerical Life*: 'Depend upon it, you would gain unspeakably if you would learn with me to see some of the poetry and the pathos, the tragedy and the comedy, lying in the experience of a human soul that looks out through dull grey eyes, and that speaks in a voice of quite ordinary tones.'[6]

George Eliot published *Adam Bede* in 1859, yet set her novel sixty years earlier in 1799. Her characters are therefore contemporaries of the younger Wordsworth and inhabit the same world as the characters of his early poems. Wordsworth and Coleridge published their first edition of *Lyrical Ballads* in 1799 and in *Adam Bede*, Captain Arthur Donnithorne offers his opinion of the revolutionary collection of poems. In doing so, he becomes one of the part-disparaging, part-baffled readers that Wordsworth addresses in his preface, 'they will look around for poetry, and will be induced to inquire by what species of courtesy these attempts can be permitted to assume that title'[7]:

> I've got a book I meant to bring you god mamma. It came down in a parcel from London the other day. I know you are fond of queer wizard-like stories. It's a volume of poems, *Lyrical Ballads*: most of them seem to be twaddling stuff: but the first is in a different style – *The Ancient Mariner* is the title. I can hardly make head or tail of it as a story, but it's a strange striking thing.[8]

Arthur's dismissive comments mark him out as non-Wordsworthian. This is an early warning sign within the novel. His inability to grasp the meaning and value of these poems of ordinary people foreshadows his later inability to see his lowly lover Hetty as much more than an exciting amusement.

Significantly, George Eliot read *The Excursion* twice while writing *Adam Bede* and begins the novel with an epigraph from Book VI of the poem:

> So that ye may have
> Clear images before your gladden'd eyes
> Of nature's unambitious underwood
> And flowers that prosper in the shade. And when
> I speak of such among the flock as swerved
> Or fell, those only shall be singled out
> Upon whose lapse, or error, something more
> Than brotherly forgiveness may attend.[9]

After Shakespeare, Wordsworth was the writer that George Eliot most commonly drew upon for epigraphs and mottos for her novels. By collecting together the guiding voices of those authors who had come before her and placing them within her work in this way, she builds the sense that her novels are part of a much larger collective endeavour at thinking. By beginning her first novel with these lines from *The Excursion*, George Eliot places her story within the same half-obscured shade inhabited by the ordinary people who meant so much to Wordsworth. These lines are spoken by Wordsworth's pastor as he guides the pedlar, poet and recluse around his churchyard, telling the stories of the people buried there, including that of Ellen the young woman deserted by her lover when pregnant and now buried alongside her dead child. The story of Ellen resonates with that of Hetty in *Adam Bede*, a young woman also abandoned by her lover when pregnant, and eventually sentenced to death for the murder of her new born baby. 'Something more' than merely 'forgiveness' was needed in such extremity.

George Eliot's second novel, *The Mill on the Floss*, was published in 1860 and has been described as 'her most Wordsworthian novel'.[10] The story of Maggie Tulliver explores the deep-rooted ties that are forged in childhood and which continue, amid disruption, to resonate throughout adulthood. In *The Mill on the Floss*, George Eliot takes what Wordsworth identified in 'Intimations of Immortality' as 'those first affections / Those shadowy recollections' which 'Are yet the fountain-light of all our day / Are yet a master-light of all our seeing'[11] and charts their growth and development over time within Maggie Tulliver's mind, beyond those first stages.

The novel begins with a neo-Wordsworthian narrator – akin to George Eliot herself – standing on a bridge beside the river Floss, looking across at the mill that Maggie and her family once lived in, remembering and calling back into being the past world in which the events of the novel, that are yet to be told, take place:

> Just by the red-roofed town the tributary Ripple flows with a lively current into the Floss. How lovely the little river is, with its dark, changing wavelets! It seems to me like a living companion while I wander along the bank and listen to its low, placid voice, as to the voice of one who is deaf and loving. I remember those large dipping willows. I remember the stone bridge. And this is Dorlcote Mill. I must stand a minute or two here on the bridge and look at it, though the clouds are threatening and it is far on in the afternoon. Even in this leafless time of departing February it is pleasant to look at – perhaps the chill damp season adds a charm to the trimly kept, comfortable dwelling-house, as old as the elms and chestnuts that shelter it from the northern blast.[12]

This wandering narrator is reminiscent of both the poet and the pedlar in 'The Ruined Cottage', two characters who are moved by the specific power of the place in which they find themselves, to tell stories of the past. The epigraph to *Adam Bede* explicitly positioned that novel within the 'shade' of 'nature's unambitious underwood', and here, on the opening page of *The Mill on the Floss*, the narrator's gaze falls upon 'the elms and chestnuts' which 'shelter' the family home, placing the novel within that same Wordsworthian space. The river is a continuous force that runs throughout the novel, spanning past and present. In this place these basic elements of water, stone and trees constitute a language that provides a direct route back into the past. With each repetition of 'I remember', deeply held feelings are surfacing, the past is reclaiming this space and reasserting its claim on this person's emotions, creating in this pause an almost trance-like state of contemplation, 'I must stand a minute or two here on the bridge and look at it'.

In the same way, the childhood experiences of Maggie and Tom Tulliver have a foundational power and leave an imprint on them that is distinctly Wordsworthian:

> Life did change for Tom and Maggie, and yet they were not wrong in believing that the thoughts and loves of these first years would always make part of their lives. We could never have loved the earth so well if we had had no childhood in it – if it were not the earth where the same flowers come up again every spring that we used to gather with our tiny fingers as we sat lisping to ourselves on the grass, the same hips and haws on the autumn hedgerows, the same redbreasts that we used to call 'God's birds' because they did no harm to the precious crops. What

novelty is worth that sweet monotony where everything is known and loved because it is known?

The wood I walk in on this mild May day, with the young yellow-brown foliage of the oaks between me and the blue sky, the white star-flowers and the blue-eyed speedwell and the ground ivy at my feet – what grove of tropic palms, what strange ferns or splendid broad-petalled blossoms, could ever thrill such deep and delicate fibres within me as this home scene? These familiar flowers, these well remembered bird-notes, this sky with its fitful brightness, these furrowed and grassy fields, each with a sort of personality given to it by the capricious hedgerows – such things as these are the mother tongue of our imagination, the language that is laden with all the subtle inextricable associations the fleeting hours of our childhood left behind them.[13]

Maggie's childhood relationships – both with people and the natural world – form a template or touchstone which inform the rest of her life. The small details of the natural world, which return again and again, become lodged in the psyche, 'the same flowers that come up again every spring [...] the same hips and haws on the autumn hedgerows, the same redbreasts'. The repetitions of nature provide a child with the first model of continuity within change and as such, one of their first models of love. These tiny details of nature are experienced in childhood on a grander scale, felt as they are with 'tiny fingers'. They become an integral part of each person and are the building blocks out of which personal thinking can develop, 'such things as these are the mother tongue of our imagination, the language laden with all the subtle inextricable associations'. The shift in this passage from the specifics of Tom and Maggie's childhood experiences back to the wider, plural perspective of the voice which opened the novel, leads to this general and distinctly Wordsworthian principle of the rooted growth of the human imagination.

But as George Eliot's characters change from children into adults, Wordsworth's elemental view of the world comes under strain. The foundations that were laid in Maggie's childhood are tested, and the original template of love that she learnt from nature as a child is overwhelmed by a tangle of complicated and competing forces and feelings. George Eliot's prose representation of the thick, complex density of adult life is a departure from Wordsworth's bareness of expression and is a characteristic which takes her deeper into the realm of inner psychology. Yet still in this shift George Eliot does not relinquish or replace Wordsworth's primary forces. They remain embedded within her characters, struggling for the expression of their birthright, but becoming messily compounded with all the accumulated matter of adult life.

So it is that in Book 3, entitled 'The Great Temptation', Maggie tries to disentangle herself from an impossible love affair with Stephen Guest. He is a man expected to marry Maggie's cousin Lucy, and Maggie is herself virtually engaged to her childhood friend Phillip Wakem – this is the crucial second stage in love and life:

> She was silent for a few moments, with her eyes fixed on the ground; then she drew a deep breath and said, looking up at him with solemn sadness, 'Oh, it is difficult – life is very difficult! It seems right to me sometimes that we should follow our strongest feeling; but then, such feelings continually come across the ties that all our former life has made for us – the ties that have made others dependent on us – and would cut them in two. If life were quite easy and simple, as it might have been in paradise, and we could always see that one being first towards whom – I mean, if life did not make duties for us before love comes, love would be a sign that two people ought to belong to each other. But I see – I feel it is not so now; there are things we must renounce in life; some of us must resign love. Many things are difficult and dark to me, but I see one thing quite clearly: that I must not, cannot, seek my own happiness by sacrificing others. Love is natural, but surely pity and faithfulness and memory are natural too. And they would live in me still and punish me if I did not obey them.[14]

There are fleeting moments of simplicity during Maggie's childhood when it feels as if she is in paradise, such is the natural ease with which she loves her brother, her father and her cousin Lucy. But in adulthood, there are no simple relationships. The direct lines that connect people together have become tangled up and a complicated series of equations have replaced the basic bonds of Maggie's childhood: later feelings continually 'come across' the early straight lines of her relationships. Maggie cannot be a sister to Tom or a cousin to Lucy or a friend to Phillip if she is to be the wife of Stephen. Those first three relationships are so deeply rooted in her childhood, they form the very foundations upon which her life has been built, that to jeopardise them would be to put her own psyche in jeopardy. While Stephen tries to argue that their love should have a natural supremacy over the conflicting claims of other people's feelings, for Maggie, love does not exist in isolation. There are relations and claims 'before love comes'. In the adult realm her love for Stephen is bisected by pity and faithfulness for Lucy and Phillip, and these feelings are as equally rooted in nature as love itself and therefore equally impossible for Maggie to dismiss. 'Love is natural', but in the adult world of George Eliot's prose, the sentence cannot end there, and 'but surely […] too' insists that the full difficulty of incompatible realities be faced. This is a sign of George Eliot's need for a complex syntax.

George Eliot and the New Discipline of Psychology

George Eliot was closely associated with a group of prominent thinkers who, in the second half of the nineteenth century, played an important role in the development of the newly emerging discipline of psychology. Alexander Bain was a leading mathematician, linguist and empirical philosopher who published *The Senses and the Intellect* (1855), *The Emotions and the Will* (1859) and founded the psychology journal *Mind* in 1876. Bain was an associate of John Stuart Mill, George Eliot and her partner George Henry Lewes, and a leading proponent of the formal study of everyday human behavioural patterns and experiences. He wrote for the Millite *Westminster Review*, a radical magazine which from 1851 to 1854 was effectively edited by Mary Ann Evans before she became George Eliot. Herbert Spencer was a philosopher, biologist, political theorist, editor of *The Economist* and friend of George Eliot. He also wrote for *The Westminster Review* and published *The Principles of Psychology* (1885) in which he argued that the mind was subject to the laws of nature and should be studied as part of a broader biological and evolutionary framework. George Henry Lewes was a literary critic and scientist who wrote the five-volume study *Problems of Life and Mind*, the final two volumes of which were edited by George Eliot after her partner's death.

The careers of each of these three individuals spanned across different specialities, contributing to the still relatively uncircumscribed nature of psychology as it took on an emergent identity in the nineteenth century. Rick Rylance in *Victorian Psychology and British Culture* summarises, 'Economists, imaginative writers, philosophers, clerics, literary critics, policy makers, as well as biomedical scientists contributed to its formation. It was an unshapely, accommodating, contested, emergent, energetic discipline filled with dispute and without settled lines of theory or protocols for investigation.'[15]

George Eliot played an important role in shaping this still porous field of human enquiry while also absorbing elements of the new scientific language back into her own novels, famously described by herself as 'experiments in life'.[16] Sally Shuttleworth sets out George Eliot's unique position at the time, at the junction between scientific and literary thinking, 'She brought to her writing a breadth of knowledge of contemporary social and scientific theory unmatched by any of her peers. Scientific ideas did not merely filter through into the metaphors and images of her work; in constructing her novels she engaged in an active dialogue with contemporary scientific thought.'[17]

In a letter to her publisher written in 1860, George Eliot described writing *The Mill on the Floss* in order to meet her own need for 'a widening psychology'.[18] The novel demonstrates just what was at stake during these early stages in the development of a language for the half-hidden mind. Maggie battles against and suffers under the narrow, straight-lined rigidity of those around her, particularly her brother Tom. She is confined by his mental smallness, which cannot see beyond black and white binaries and which crushes all the complicated compounds of Maggie's emotional life. For Maggie, who is a version of George Eliot's own childhood self, psychology is not an abstract, theoretical discipline, but rather an urgently needed tool for living. George Eliot writes in defiant opposition to the restrictively narrow ways of thinking that dominate in the outside world and which leave Maggie ostracised by society and disowned by her brother in Book 7:

> All people of broad, strong sense have an instinctive repugnance to the men of maxims; because such people early discern that the mysterious complexity of our life is not to be embraced by maxims, and that to lace ourselves up in formulas of that sort is to repress all the divine promptings and inspirations that spring from growing insight and sympathy.[19]

As a novelist, George Eliot's most important contribution to the urgent struggle for a wider psychology was the development of a syntax complex enough to trace the intricacies of both conscious and subconscious mentality with self-checking movement between particular and general, general and particular. For while general maxims attempt to superimpose a narrow set of principles onto people, George Eliot's syntax instead allows the full complexity of individual lives to emerge.

In chapter 5 of Book 5, Tom discovers that his sister has been secretly meeting with Philip Wakem, the son of the hated lawyer who is blamed for the bankruptcy of the Tulliver family. After the initial awful confrontation where Maggie is forced by her moralistic brother to renounce Philip, all of her compressed feelings burst out of her:

> Tom and Maggie walked on in silence for some yards. He was still holding her wrist tightly as if he were compelling a culprit from the scene of action. At last Maggie with a violent snatch drew her hand away, and her pent-up, long-gathering irritation burst into utterance.
>
> 'Don't suppose that I think you are right, Tom, or that I bow to your will. I despise the feelings you have shown in speaking to Philip; I detest your insulting unmanly allusions to his deformity. You have been reproaching other people your whole life; you have been always sure you yourself are right; it is because you have not a mind large enough to see that there is anything better than your own conduct and your own petty aims.'

'Certainly,' said Tom coolly. 'I don't see that your conduct is better, or your aims either. If your conduct, and Philip Wakem's conduct, has been right, why are you ashamed of its being known? Answer me that. I know what I have aimed at in my conduct, and I've succeeded; pray, what good has your conduct brought to you or anyone else?'

'I don't want to defend myself,' said Maggie, still with vehemence; 'I know I've been wrong – often, continually. But yet, sometimes when I have done wrong, it has been because I have feelings that you would be the better for, if you had them.'[20]

Maggie condemns Tom's small-mindedness and through a process of complex checks and balances, shows her own need for a larger mental capacity that at once can take in the mind of somebody outside of her, whom she loves, and criticises, and feels criticised by, and still can transcend that other's narrowness, without herself having Tom's assurance of self-justification. Tom tries to take back control of his sister as 'culprit' and reimpose the hard logic of what Maggie sees as a language of reproach and certainty. The syntactical hinge 'but yet' opens up a space for Maggie to think within that is so much wider than Tom's narrow 'If […] why' formulation allows. It is George Eliot's syntax, at once despite and because of the character's felt flaws, which enables Maggie to have the vitally important, complicated final thought of, 'sometimes when I have done wrong it has been because I have feelings that you would be the better for, if you had them'. This thought cuts across Tom's narrow rules and discovers a link between 'wrong' and 'better' that his mind could never have found.

In the nineteenth century there was a collective and profound mental shift away from religious frameworks of thinking. It was as if psychology had to become instead the holding ground for human needs and difficulties in the post-religious space. One of the primary challenges that the new psychologists faced was how to rehome the old forms of truthfulness and counsel that had been embedded for millennia within religious practice and to develop secular translations of or alternatives to those religious rituals such as confession and prayer which had previously served such a crucial psychological purpose.

In *Adam Bede*, the gap that has been created by the shift from formal religion to modern psychology is felt keenly when Arthur visits the pastor Mr Irwine in an attempt to confess his relationship with Hetty. In place of the old confession box, Arthur finds himself seated informally at the modern breakfast table:

> Still, there was this advantage in the old rigid forms, that they committed you to the fulfilment of a resolution by some outward deed: when you have put your mouth to one end of a hole in a stone wall and are aware that there is an expectant ear at the other end, you are more likely to say what you came out with the intention of saying than if you were

seated with your legs in an easy attitude under the mahogany with a companion who will have no reason to be surprised if you have nothing particular to say.[21]

There is for Arthur now no formal discipline, no ritual commitment to continue with what he had intended:

> Arthur was anxious not to imply that he came with any special purpose. He had no sooner found himself in Mr Irwine's presence than the confidence which he had thought quite easy before, suddenly appeared the most difficult thing in the world to him, and at the very moment of shaking hands he saw his purpose in quite a new light. How could he make Irwine understand his position unless he told him those little scenes in the wood; and how could he tell them without looking like a fool? And then his weakness in coming back from Gawain's, and doing the very opposite of what he intended! Irwine would think him a shilly-shally fellow ever after. However, it must come out in an unpremeditated way; the conversation might lead up to it.[22]

'No sooner [...] than' Arthur walks into the meeting with Mr Irwine, he begins his attempt mentally to extricate himself from his inner promise. It becomes not theological but psychological, not binding in advance but shiftable 'at the very moment'. The familiar, casual atmosphere of the breakfast table makes it both harder for Arthur to confess and easier for him to avoid confession, for 'how could he make Irwine understand his position unless he told him those little scenes in the wood'. It is these small details, delivered with the secrecy of free indirect discourse, that pile up in a series of repeated 'ands' that take Arthur further and further away from the sticking point until the big admission is made impossible for him. 'Unless', 'until', 'without' are little flinching words struggling against seeing it through to the truth. It is this change of scale, when the big is lost within the small, and the small needs to be seen in the light of the big that is hidden within it, that constitutes George Eliot's contribution to realist psychology. And it is a contribution that can see psychology itself as a terrifying alternative to older versions of truth. God is not real for Arthur in this moment, and instead he faces only the relaxed physical form and the outstretched hand of Irwine, banishing the thought of any reality which is not there immediately present.

Arthur turns from inner truth to evasive social appearance. The indistinct, hidden movement of Arthur's mind – backwards and away from the helping hand that is stretched out before him – marks a turning point in his life. It is only George Eliot, outside his mind, but also able to enter into it, who can see this almost imperceptible movement and recognise what is at stake. It is only George Eliot, sited outside of time, who is able to see the span of Arthur's life and trace backwards to this indistinct place where an instinctive reaction – or is it inaction – changes his course.

Two hundred pages later – after Hetty has been arrested for the murder of her newborn child – Irwine sees in retrospect the earlier lost opportunity for Arthur to confess. In the light of the unfolding tragedy, Irwine is now able to see what had previously been obscured, namely the internal struggle that had played out within Arthur as he had stood before him at the breakfast table:

> It was a bitter remembrance to him now – that morning when Arthur breakfasted with him, and seemed as if he were on the verge of a confession. It was plain enough now that he had wanted to confess. And if their words had taken another turn … if he himself had been less fastidious about intruding on another man's secrets … it was cruel to think how thin a film had shut out rescue from all this guilt and misery. He saw the whole history now by that terrible illumination which the present sheds back upon the past.[23]

George Eliot forces her characters to have these second moments of 'terrible illumination'. That almost imperceptible turning point when Arthur shrank back from confession cannot be left to pass unnoticed even when it is too late: there is a turning back now instead, in hindsight. Consequences will always return, especially if in the first instance characters seem to have managed to avoid them. George Eliot's use of forward-backward switches is one way in which she attempts to foster in her reader's minds that crucial mental foresight in which her characters are often psychologically lacking. It is as if unable to help her characters, George Eliot instead offers to her readers in the outside world that which might have prevented or mitigated the internal tragedies of the novels.

What George Eliot requires from herself and from her readers is the almost impossible demand on unsupported human nature to face squarely this post-religious dilemma without resorting to fantasies of easy cure:

> I might refashion life and character entirely after my own liking; I might select the most unexceptional type of clergyman and put my own admirable opinions into his mouth on all occasions. But it happens, on the contrary, that my strongest effort is to avoid any such arbitrary picture, and to give a faithful account of men and things as they have mirrored themselves in my mind. The mirror is doubtless defective; the outlines will sometimes be disturbed, the reflection faint or confused; but I feel as

much bound to tell you as precisely as I can what that reflection is, as if I were in the witness-box narrating my experience on oath.[24]

Realism is not simply an aesthetic or intellectual choice for George Eliot, nor is it an easy choice. It takes George Eliot's 'strongest effort' to fulfil her responsibility to tell the truth about human life, and in particular the parts of life about which human beings struggle the most to tell the truth. In the midst of judgement she forgives her characters what they cannot be, but she cannot allow herself to evade what they cannot face. It is both despite and because of her characters' frequent inability to act as witnesses to their own lives that George Eliot's testimony cannot ever falter: she *hears* what it is her characters cannot say, save subconsciously, unconsciously, despite themselves. It is not as critics have sometimes argued previously – that she simply lays down explanatory and didactic explanations alongside her characters, as though she were herself no more than another version of those men of maxims she hates.

All this is the work of translation by the figure called George Eliot in the midst and at the apex of the novels – a super-mind seeming to transcribe the unspoken inner processes of her creatures into a language of seriousness that they themselves dared hardly admit or confess to. Feuerbach's *The Essence of Christianity*, translated by Mary Ann Evans before ever she became George Eliot, is the great work concerning the processes of translation. There Feuerbach wrote, 'Religion is human nature reflected, mirrored in itself.'[25] It was he who saw in the unconscious human creation of God precisely the creative process that was key to the creative power of George Eliot herself: 'Man – this is the mystery of religion – projects his being into objectivity, and then again makes himself an object to this projected image of himself thus converted into a subject.'[26] What George Eliot did was to take the step into secular consciousness: to project out of her experience and imagination the creation of characters who seemed to become, at best, autonomous in respect of their creator; then to receive back from them the thoughts they did not want, the thoughts they made her have in their place, such that George Eliot becomes the inner God of the novel.

In Book 3, chapter 6 of *The Mill on the Floss*, this process of two-way mirroring or projection and interjection, is manifest. Here the teenage Maggie sits crying after another disagreement with her brother:

> In books there were people who were always agreeable or tender, and delighted to do things that made one happy, and who did not show their kindness by finding fault. The world outside the books was not a happy one, Maggie felt; it seemed to be a world where people behaved the best to those they did not pretend to love and that did not belong to them.

And if life had no love in it, what else was there for Maggie? Nothing but poverty and the companionship of her mother's narrow griefs – perhaps of her father's heart-cutting childish dependence. There is no hopelessness so sad as that of early youth, when the soul is made up of wants and has no long memories, no superadded life in the life of others, though we who look on think lightly of such premature despair as if our vision of the future lightened the blind sufferer's present.

Maggie in her brown frock, with her eyes reddened and her heavy hair pushed back, looking from the bed where her father lay to the dull walls of this sad chamber which was the centre of her world, was a creature full of eager, passionate longings for all that was beautiful and glad; thirsty for all knowledge; with an ear straining after dreamy music that died away and would not come near to her; with a blind, unconscious yearning for something that would link together the wonderful impressions of this mysterious life and give her soul a sense of a home in it.

No wonder, when there is this contrast between the outward and the inward, that painful collisions come of it.[27]

George Eliot shifts into free indirect discourse in the sentence, 'And if life had no love in it, what else was there for Maggie?' The question half expresses what Maggie feels in the despair of her young inner psyche and half consists of what George Eliot feels in her accompanying cry of sympathy – the two sit alongside each other. Free indirect discourse is a mode which allows George Eliot to blend her own mind with Maggie's and to bridge the gap between Maggie 'in the book' and the novelist representing in her readers 'the world outside the books'.

It is George Eliot's ability to move in and out and across different mental planes in her writing that gives her the 'superadded life' that Maggie lacks. As she wrote in a letter to her friend John Sibree, 'Creation is the superadded life of the intellect: sympathy, all embracing love, the superadded moral life.'[28] But rather than a linear progression from childish experience to adult explanation, there must be another turn, back again into the thick of the child's experience. Again, this is the Wordsworthian law, to counterbalance the danger of the adult mode taking the child's reality too lightly. But it also exists to put the adult thoughts back to use within Maggie's predicament: If Maggie has an ear romantically straining after the music that might make life more complete, if she blindly yearns to see the links that would hold life together as a whole, then the mature version of that ear is George Eliot's, hearing those inner cries, and the mature version of that occluded vision is the attempt by George Eliot to steer a complex syntax through the twists and turns of life's passage.

In the final sentence of the passage there is a further turn, back to the adult voice of George Eliot the psychologist, 'No wonder, when there is this contrast between the outward and the inward, that painful collisions come of it'. This final thought is not superimposed by the wiser adult voice, it emerges out of the process of feedback between child and adult mental positions that came before it and is an adult version of the initial childish sense of discrepancy felt by Maggie between what is 'in books' and in 'the world outside books'.

I am arguing that since the modern switchover from religion to psychology, certain gaps have been left unfilled, certain human needs have been left unmet, and it is the arts – and here specifically literature – that can in some way fill those gaps, spanning as it does the space between religion and psychology. It is the novel itself that George Eliot is offering up as a secular version of the confession or witness box. For although the presence of George Eliot alongside her characters cannot possibly be known by the characters themselves and cannot enter the book to help them, that presence affects a different community – the community of readers. It is the creation of George Eliot herself that is the greatest creation of her novels. For this is the embodiment of the idea that there is someone who listens to human characters, who tries to speak to their thoughts, despite the characters themselves not knowing of course of her existence.

George Eliot and Spinoza

In 1856, Mary Ann Evans finished working on a translation of the seventeenth-century philosopher Baruch Spinoza's *Ethics*, although it remained unpublished until 1978. Her partner George Henry Lewes published articles on Spinoza in *The Westminster Review* (1843) and *The Fortnightly Review* (1866).

Spinoza's *Ethics* sets out a philosophy of the emotions, written in the style of a geometric treatise. In it he acknowledges 'only three primitive, or primary emotions, namely, pleasure, pain and desire'.[29] In a 48-point list of 'definitions of the emotions' he then classifies all of the secondary feelings compounded out of these three primary elements:

14. Confidence is pleasure arising from the idea of something past or future, concerning which all cause of doubt is removed.
15. Despair is pain arising from the idea of something past or future, concerning which all cause of doubt is removed.[30]

There is a logical exactness to Spinoza's definitions which turns the emotions from vague or messy personal sensations into distinctly knowable phenomena. Each point in his list is like a mathematical equation for the creation of an emotion. There is something austerely comforting in recognising that emotions too must comply with a kind of logic and consequently, by analysis, can be brought under a degree of control. For Mary Anne Evans it must have felt like a turn inside-out, from the near chaos of subjective experience to the possibility of a more objective understanding. That possibility itself enabled and demanded a more impersonal form of mind to work within and upon the realm of personal experience.

If the whole range of our emotions can be understood as a series of compounds that are created by adding to or subtracting from the basic original building blocks of pleasure, pain and desire, it begins to be easier to see how one feeling could be turned into another.

Spinoza's *Ethics* challenges the restrictive binary categories of negative and positive, good or bad emotions:

> As to good and evil, they also indicate nothing positive in things considered in themselves, and are simply modes of thought or notions which we form from a comparison of individuals. For one and the same thing can be at the same time good, bad, evil and indifferent [...] By good I understand that which we certainly know to be useful to us. By evil I understand that of which we certainly know that it hinders us from participating in some good.[31]

Spinoza is neutrally concerned with the human usefulness of thoughts and feelings in terms of 'conatus' – survival and flourishing. Emotion is 'a confused idea': rational thought helps to undo the psychological confusion and make the idea within the emotion become what he calls 'adequate', that is, clear not confused, actively thinkable rather than passively suffered. Otherwise, we are stuck with 'inadequate ideas' which are not useful to us: 'As long as the human mind perceives things from the common order of nature, it does not have an adequate, but only a confused and mutilated knowledge of itself, of its own body, and of external bodies.'[32] Inadequate ideas prevent us from attaining any true understanding of our lives. Without adequate ideas, our emotions remain as things which happen to us, that we must suffer rather than understand or in any way master.

Spinoza's philosophy is related to Stoic thought, in that it demonstrates how it is possible to alter the character of the mind by taking control of the emotions. In *Spinoza and the Stoics*, Fermin DeBrabander states that 'Spinoza's most notable Stoic trait is his psychotherapy.'[33] He argues that Spinoza shares the Stoic belief that 'The passions, i.e. irrational judgements, are in our power to manipulate, and consequently [...] therapy involves their manipulation.'[34] But while Stoic manipulation would generally mean discarding emotions, Spinoza's *Ethics* shows how emotions can be deconstructed and then reconfigured, turning irrational emotional matter into something vital that can serve us.

While Spinoza had an important impact on Victorian freethinkers such as George Eliot, James Froude, Matthew Arnold and William Hale White, his work gained further influence near the end of the nineteenth century when it was read by Sigmund Freud and became highly valued by the psychoanalysts of the early twentieth century. Spinoza is not mentioned directly in any of Freud's published writing, but he was given the title of 'the philosopher of psychoanalysis'[35] by Freud's contemporary Lou Andreas – Salomé. In *Emotion, Thought and Therapy*, Jerome Neu argues that 'Spinoza provides a philosophical foundation for much in Freud'[36] namely how it might be possible to change the composition of our emotions through the two-stage process that forms the basis of modern psycho-dynamic treatments, 'making the unconscious conscious may be compared in some ways with transforming confused ideas into adequate ones. Correcting our understanding can contribute to correcting our emotional disorders.'[37]

In addition to Freud's reading of Spinoza, it is important to note that Freud also read and gifted copies of George Eliot's novels to his family and friends. In a letter written in 1885 to his then fiancé Martha, he described having his four-volume copy of *Middlemarch* on his desk as he worked. Freud told his friend and fellow psychoanalyst Ernest Jones that *Middlemarch* had 'illuminated important aspects of his relations with Martha'.[38]

In a letter to her friend Charles Bray, George Eliot wrote of her own sense that a conventional translation could never be an adequate means of expressing Spinoza's philosophy:

> What is wanted in English is not a translation of Spinoza's works, but a true estimate of his life and system. After one has rendered his Latin faithfully into English, one feels that there is another yet more difficult process of translation for the reader to effect, and that the only mode of making Spinoza accessible to a larger number is to study his books, then shut them, and give an analysis. For those who read the very words Spinoza wrote there is the same sort of interest in his style as in the conversation of a person of great capacity who has led a solitary life and who says from his own soul what all the world is saying by rote; but this interest hardly belongs to a translation.[39]

The 'yet more difficult process of translation' that is required to be done is the translation of Spinoza's theory into modified practice. It was through George Eliot's realist novels that she was able to create a different kind of translation of Spinoza's philosophy, in which his geometric definitions were transformed into the imaginative depiction of real people, in real minds and real bodies.

Middlemarch is perhaps the best example of George Eliot's implicit translation of Spinoza's philosophy into realist fiction due to the dense mass of human life that it contains and the broad spectrum of emotions that its characters experience. In *Middlemarch*, the capacity of different characters to think adequately varies wildly. The young, newly married doctor Tertius Lydgate is one example of a character who often struggles in this respect.

In chapter 64 Lydgate is overcome by debt and unable to face the reality of his marriage after an argument with his wife Rosamond:

> His marriage would be a mere piece of bitter irony if they could not go on loving each other. He had long ago made up his mind to what he thought was her negative character – her want of sensibility, which showed itself in disregard both of his specific wishes and his general aims. The first great disappointment had been borne: the tender devotedness and docile adoration of the ideal wife must be renounced, and life must be taken up on a lower stage of expectation, as it is by men who have lost their limbs. But the real wife had not only her claims, she had still a hold on his heart, and it was his intense desire that the hold should remain strong. In marriage, the certainty, 'She will never love me much,' is easier to bear than the fear, 'I shall love her no more.' Hence, after that outburst, his inward effort was entirely to excuse her, and to blame the hard circumstances which were partly his fault.[40]

The two utterances, 'She will never love me much,' and 'I shall love her no more' belong to Lydgate's subconscious mind and are embedded here within George Eliot's free indirect discourse. They have never been spoken by him and he would never want to hear them out loud, but some deeper part of his mind has already weighed them against one another and chosen the disappointment of 'never [...] much' over the worse pain of 'no more'. When her characters are unable to think the necessary and saving thoughts for themselves, George Eliot must intervene and, in the detached mind-space created by free indirect discourse, enable thoughts to exist that characters cannot bear to have for themselves. The degree to which characters are consciously involved in the thinking that takes place through free indirect discourse varies, but throughout the novel it provides a model of what the kind of semi-detached clarity of thought that Spinoza advocated might look like. This becomes in George Eliot's work not a reductive, cold or narrow kind of rationalism however: in many cases, free indirect discourse reveals more thoughts than can be easily held within one single mind. Free indirect discourse becomes here a holding ground for thoughts that are too painful to be put to use by a character and yet too important to remain obscured and unused within their subconscious. If Lydgate were to read this passage he would have to look at and hear from the outside the voices of his deepest interior as it balances the two terrible choices of 'She will never love me much,' and 'I shall love her no more'. It would hurt him to see secret psychological thinking turned into written thought and made visibly substantive on the page. But Lydgate is unable to look in at himself and his wife from the outside, while he is in the thick of the trouble itself. This inability is at once a form of survival by the perseverance of 'conatus' and even so a form of continued and distorted inner suffering. That doubleness is George Eliot's domain.

The psychoanalyst Christopher Bollas writes in *The Mystery of Things* that

> Self-experiencing is a palimpsest of many elements: conscious thought, inarticulate forming ideas on the margins of consciousness, unconscious disseminations, images which pass by in incomplete form, polysemous words pregnant with meanings, somatic drives, body memories, body attitudes and intersecting engagements. It seems to help us to think some of this to bifurcate the mind in two: a thinking part that addresses a naïve self as listener and a listening-experiencing self that emotionally and intuitively tests thoughts.[41]

Free indirect discourse reveals some of the different layers of that palimpsest. It allows for 'inarticulate forming ideas' within a character to surface and be formed instead by the consciousness of the author. It also demonstrates some of the saturated thickness of thoughts as they really exist but in a way we can rarely manage to get hold of in their entirety. A 'thinking part' addresses a naive listening self, which then becomes – through the process of listening – what is effectively a third experiencing self that puts the initial thoughts to the test. But few characters in *Middlemarch* besides Dorothea Brooke can manage this process. Instead, it is the author and the reader who must take on these different mind roles. George Eliot translates Lydgate's rough, deep approximations of feeling into language that can be seen and listened to, if not by Lydgate himself then instead by the reader who must then stand in for the character's absent 'listening-experiencing self'.

Dorothea is the one character in *Middlemarch* who is able to think more adequately. She is the character most able to exist simultaneously within her predicament and also to step outside of it. In chapter 42, after a dispute with her husband, she gradually shifts from a position of childish, frustrated pain: 'What have I done – what am I – that he should treat me so? He never knows what is in my mind – he never cares. What is the use of anything

I do? He wishes he had never married me'[42] to one of disinterested 'resolved submission'. During this transition, free indirect discourse is transformed by George Eliot to create a means for Dorothea to move consciously from inside her troubles to a view of them as though from without. As night falls, the real shift in thinking happens for Dorothea and she reclaims that 'best soul' which she has had to lock away within the pain of her marriage. The stillness turns into a fuller motionlessness:

> Dorothea sat almost motionless in her meditative struggle, while the evening slowly deepened into night. But the struggle changed continually, as that of a man who begins with a movement towards striking and ends with conquering his desire to strike. The energy that would animate a crime is not more than is wanted to inspire a resolved submission, when the noble habit of the soul reasserts itself. That thought with which Dorothea had gone out to meet her husband – her conviction that he had been asking about the possible arrest of his work, and that the answer must have wrung his heart, could not be long without rising beside the image of him, like a shadowy monitor looking at her anger with sad remonstrance. It cost her a litany of pictured sorrows and of silent cries that she might be the mercy for those sorrows – but the resolved submission did come; and when the house was still, and she knew that it was near the time when Mr Casaubon habitually went to rest, she opened her door gently and stood outside in the darkness waiting for his coming upstairs with a light in his hand.[43]

That is the role of thought: to transform as far as it can the quantum of sheer life energy that can take one form or another. 'Resolved submission' may not be the magical thinking of a cure but is not just submission here either. It is an active rather than a passive act, returning to the situation from a higher level of resolution, one that demands as much force and effort as an angry attack would have cost Dorothea. '*That* thought *with which* Dorothea had gone out to meet her husband' has become an autonomous thing here, produced by her mind but now somehow apart from her. It is this imaginative 'conviction that he had been asking about the possible arrest of his work, and that the answer must have wrung his heart' that guides her now towards the state of 'resolved submission' that Spinoza would surely deem to be a more adequate mode of thinking.

It is the thought which must come first and which creates her – the thinker – rather than her self, rashly, angrily and narrowly determining her thoughts as she did in the immediate aftermath of the argument with her husband. The adequate thought now guards over the other parts of Dorothea's own mind, acting as a 'monitor'. The 'monitor' is like the role that George Eliot herself takes on within the novel, on behalf of her characters, yet here Dorothea is able to do it for herself and in so doing achieves something like the perspective of the novelist, seeing as though from the outside right into herself. This is an important mental evolution for Dorothea and it is particularly important for George Eliot to pick up and hold onto the good things like this that her characters' brains and minds can manage. She must make sure that the good thought is not wasted or left hidden in the unconscious. George Eliot – and more broadly literature – must offer a holding-place that can turn individual mental evolutions into the possibility of communal human blueprints for thinking.

A Case History: Daniel Deronda and Gwendolen Harleth

Diagnosis

A number of literary critics and psychologists have studied Gwendolen Harleth as a psychological case history and interpreted her relationship with Daniel Deronda as a therapeutic exchange. The psychiatrist T. S. Clouston (1840–1915) drew one of the earliest definitions of female adolescence from the character of Gwendolen and wrote of George Eliot: 'This authoress is by far the most acute and subtle psychologist of her time, and certainly the character I have mentioned is most worthy of study by all physicians who look on the mind as being in their field of study or sphere of action.'[44] In 1999, the literary critic Bernard J. Paris guest edited an issue of *The American Journal of Psychoanalysis* which explored psychoanalytic approaches to George Eliot and contained two essays on *Daniel Deronda* by the psychoanalysts Carl Rotenberg and Margot Waddell. In Rotenberg's essay he diagnoses Gwendolen as suffering from 'foreboding, depression, dream-like states, symptomatic impulses to destructive acting out, murderous dreams, obsessive-compulsive symptoms, manifest anxiety, and obsessional self-recrimination'.[45] He asserts that 'George Eliot was a proto-psychologist who, decades prior to the development of psychoanalysis, had a remarkable understanding of how a treatment relationship works'.[46] This final section of the chapter will look in greater detail at how the 'treatment relationship' between Daniel and Gwendolen functions and what it tells us about George Eliot's own particular model of what we have come to think of as therapy.

In *Daniel Deronda* Gwendolen suffers greatly from what Spinoza would have termed 'inadequate thinking'. Her psychological predicament is laid bare in the places in the novel where the dissonance between who she is and how she sees herself becomes most apparent. When the wooden panel in the drawing room covering a ghostly portrait suddenly flies open while Gwendolen is in the middle of a group performance of a scene from *The Winter's Tale*, her terrified shrieks reveal a part of her character that does not correspond with her norm:

> She wondered at herself in these occasional experiences, which seemed like a brief remembered madness, an unexplained exception from her normal life; and in this instance she felt a peculiar vexation that her helpless fear had shown itself, not, as usual, in solitude, but in well-lit company.[47]

The difference between her 'normal' public persona and this other strange thing that has come out of her is too difficult to reconcile: she can barely recognise it as belonging to herself, calling it 'itself'. It is Daniel who throughout much of the novel urges Gwendolen not to diminish her sense of what modern psychologists would call cognitive dissonance,[48] but rather to heighten it so as to widen 'the narrow round'[49] of her life and explore the conflicts within it.

Therapy

For Carl Rotenberg, the 'treatment relationship' between Daniel and Gwendolen closely resembles that of a psychoanalyst and his patient: 'In psychoanalysis, there are three aspects of the transference relationship: (1) the past repeating itself in the present relationship, (2) a newer present expressing itself in place of past relationships and (3) a damaged self-seeking transformation. All three elements are present in the Gwendolen–Daniel relationship, which has a healing effect on Gwendolen and holds out the promise of a better future for her'.[50] Margot Waddell similarly claims that the mental shifts of the novel can be mapped onto the processes of psychoanalysis:

> Through a complicated process of mental association, Deronda becomes an aspect of Gwendolen's conscience. He becomes a superego figure who fully incorporates the ego-ideal. Quite apart from what he independently stands for, Gwendolen projects onto him an area of herself which is later reintegrated only when she is ready to assimilate, or to introject, those wiser and more tolerant elements which are largely represented in his nature.[51]

However, Bernard J. Paris, also a historian of psychoanalysis, does not accept these assertions, instead arguing that 'Deronda is more like a clergyman than a therapist […] I am amazed that so many commentators have seen has ministrations as precursors of psychotherapy.'[52]

Daniel and Gwendolen do develop an unorthodox relationship which is difficult to pin down. He becomes a confident, confessor and therapist to her: a blend of priest, psychoanalyst and potential lover. However, critics of the novel are failing in their reading when they refuse to acknowledge the human multiplicity of this informal relationship, arguing that it is instead only one thing. Navigating the strange secular relationship that exists without normal boundaries or foundations becomes increasingly painful for both Daniel and Gwendolen and makes the therapeutic relationship complicated and difficult.

In her distress, after getting married to a man she had previously committed herself not to wed, and faced with his emerging cruelty, Gwendolen seeks out Daniel to help her. Entering the library in which he sits working, the room takes on the atmosphere of a confessional 'private chapel'.[53] Her own small mind is unable to think a way out of her troubles, but she looks to his larger mind to help her to have the harder thoughts that she would be unwilling to think alone:

> 'I *am* selfish. I have never thought much of anyone's feelings, except my mother's. I have not been fond of people. But what can I do?' she went on, more quickly. 'I must get up in the morning and do what everyone else does. It is all like a dance set beforehand. I seem to see all that can be – and I am tired and sick of it. And the world is all confusion to me' – she made a gesture of disgust. 'You say I am ignorant. But what is the good of trying to know more, unless life were worth more?'
>
> 'This good,' said Deronda, promptly, with a touch of indignant severity, which he was inclined to encourage as his own safeguard; 'life *would* be worth more to you: some real knowledge would give you an interest in the world beyond the small drama of personal desires. It is the curse of your life – forgive me – of so many lives, that all passion is spent in that narrow round, for want of ideas and sympathies to make a larger home for it.[54]

Gwendolen's thoughts are predetermined by her situation and have a determinedly narrow certainty. Her language is rigid and leaves her with no room to manoeuvre: 'I am', 'I have never', 'I have not', 'I must'. She is thinking in those anti-imaginative, normal terms, which sweepingly reduce 'anyone', 'everyone else' and 'all that can be' to something worthless. But Daniel demonstrates to Gwendolen how a thought that is inadequately narrowing can be turned on its head, her 'unless life were worth more?' is turned into his '*would* be worth more to you'. Daniel's syntax – in contrast to Gwendolen's – is not linear or fixed or contracting, but expansive. The final sentence of the passage is long and twisted: 'It is the curse of your life – forgive me – of so many lives, that all passion is spent in that narrow round, for want of ideas and sympathies to make a larger home for it'. It is by a syntax that *wants* a larger home for 'it', so that the thoughts can create the self rather than the normative self controlling the thoughts in a self-diminishing cycle.

Daniel's form of therapy is often riskily close to causing or exacerbating trauma, and when he speaks again after that initial aggressive jolt of judgement, his tone is softer. But he still insists that pain is an unavoidable part of the process of widening that Gwendolen must endure:

> 'Take the present suffering as a painful letting in of light,' said Deronda, more gently. 'You are conscious of more beyond the round of your own inclinations – you know more of the way in which your life presses on others, and their life on yours. I don't think you could have escaped the painful process in some form or other.'
>
> 'But it is a very cruel form,' said Gwendolen, beating her foot on the ground with returning agitation.[55]

This version of 'letting in light' is not like drawing open the curtains; it is a painful, violent tearing open. But this is what is required in order to create room for all the thought material that Gwendolen needs to have in her mind, other than her own ego. Just as unavoidable as the painful process that Gwendolen must endure is her resistance to it, and her final statement, 'But it is a very cruel form', is a return to the fixed language of childlike objection and complaint that she began with when she asked in the wrong tone 'But what can I do?' and 'But what is the good of trying to know more, unless life were worth more?'. What is present here in George Eliot's realism are the demands of what Freud was sternly to call the reality principle, namely the belief in the emergence of a governing mental capacity that works to forgo instant gratification and regulate the opposing and pre-existing 'pleasure principle'.[56]

Widening the gaps between the different parts of ourselves is counterintuitive and contrary to what modern psychological therapies might try to do in seeking to lessen cognitive dissonance. It would be easier if we could have single, consistent and fixed characters, but in the painful and even aggressive process of widening which takes place within the novel, and which at certain points of extreme crisis is as close as could possibly be to cruelty. There is no let off from suffering, only the need for its conversion:

> Turn your fear into a safeguard. Keep your dread fixed on the idea of increasing that remorse which is so bitter to you. Fixed meditation may

do a great deal towards defining our longing or dread. We are not always in a state of strong emotion, but when we are calm we can use our memories and gradually change the bias of our fear, as we do our tastes. Take your fear as a safeguard. It is like the quickness of hearing. It may make consequences passionately present to you. Try to take hold of your sensibility, and use it like a faculty, like vision.[57]

'Turn your fear into a safeguard' is an utterance Gwendolen has to hear repeated again and again in her mind through what follows until it turns from an abstract piece of advice into a part of her own mental armoury. With each repetition of Daniel's urgent words George Eliot is facing the problem – too often ignored by conventional self-help books – of what to do with counsel that you know to be theoretically valuable but do not know how to make real. As Gwendolen returns again and again to Daniel's advice, she is struggling to enact that crucial 'turn'. It is as if her mind knows that this is important counsel and yet unable to put it into action instead keeps hold of the sheer words and keeps repeating them until they can be put to use.

It is a 150 pages after Daniel first gives his advice that the pair meet again and Gwendolen admits the difficulty that she has had putting his words into reality: 'I wanted to tell you that I have always been thinking of your advice, but is it any use? – I can't make myself different, because things about me raise bad feelings – and I must go on – I can alter nothing – it is no use.'[58] Rather than the mental evolution that Daniel had proposed, Gwendolen sees only a stagnating continuation of the same patterns of behaviour playing out ahead of her. Yet, despite this insistent fixed belief that 'I can alter nothing', Daniel's advice continues to reverberate through her mind. She is 'always' thinking of it; all those verbs – 'turn', 'keep', 'use', 'change', 'take', 'make' – are gradually bedding down within her mind. Even if the conscious part of her brain thinks 'it is no use', another part of her has insisted on keeping hold of the words.

When Gwendolen finds herself confined on a yacht, sailing on the Mediterranean Sea with her detestable husband, Daniel's words circle back around her mind. It is here – in the thick of psychological struggle – that Gwendolen perhaps comes closest to what Freud – in the essay 'Remembering, Repeating and Working Through' – called the 'arduous task'[59] of 'working through':

She remembered Deronda's words: they were continually recurring in her thought – 'Turn your fear into a safeguard. Keep your dread fixed on the idea of increasing your remorse … Take your fear as a safeguard. It is like quickness of hearing. It may make consequences passionately present to you.'

And so it was. In Gwendolen's consciousness Temptation and Dread met and stared like two pale phantoms, each seeing itself in the other – each obstructed by its own image; and all the while her fuller self beheld the apparitions and sobbed for deliverance from them.

Inarticulate prayers, no more definite that a cry, often swept out from her into the vast silence, unbroken except by her husband's breathing or the plash of the wave or the creaking of the masts; but if ever she thought of definite help, it took the form of Deronda's presence and words, of the sympathy he might have for her, of the direction he might give her. It was sometimes after a white-lipped, fierce eyed temptation with murdering fingers had made its demon visit that these best moments of inward crying and clinging would come to her, and she would lie with wide-open eyes in which the rising tears seemed a blessing, and the thought, 'I will not mind if I can keep from getting wicked,' seemed an answer to the indefinite prayer.[60]

Gwendolen is trapped within the narrow physical space of a boat, stranded in the middle of a huge expanse of sea and suffering under the power of her husband. She now has lost all agency over her own life, is desperate somehow to rid herself of this life, this marriage, or even (such is the Temptation) this husband. It is now that the 'turn' begins to happen within her. With the four small words, 'And so it was', George Eliot switches into Gwendolen's suddenly heightened consciousness. 'Temptation and Dread' are two versions of her anxiety about the future. Inside her mind they have turned into weird, ghostly figures which she has to watch battling against one another. It is only when they give way to the 'form' of Deronda that she can even begin to provide her own thoughts to her cries. When Gwendolen's own thoughts are 'inarticulate prayers', Daniel's words, embedded through repetition into her own mind, give her a language and a purpose with which to go on.

The therapeutic role that Daniel fulfils for Gwendolen, and which I am arguing that George Eliot fulfils for her readers, is that he gives her thoughts that her own mind could not – while in turmoil – construct for itself. The new widening idea that guides Gwendolen must come from a demanding 'help' from the outside; this is the classic purpose of therapy and is why an analyst is needed in the therapy room to think out the thoughts about a patient's life that they cannot think for themselves.

Outcomes

The idea of a genuine future was something that George Eliot was concerned with throughout her whole career. The first original work that she planned but never managed to write was a book called *The Idea of a Future Life*, and her interest in both individual and communal futures persisted. Gillian Beer argues in *Darwin's Plots* that 'The book remained unwritten but its concerns were never abandoned [...] the topic continued to preoccupy George Eliot throughout her working life and it found its most intense form in *Daniel Deronda*.'[61] The idea of a future life can be mapped onto Freud's third stage of psychoanalysis, that of 'working through', for it is at this stage that a patient's deepest resistances – as manifested in their repetitions – can be overcome. It is these resistances which prevent the emergence of a genuine future by instead continually projecting forward a repeated version of the past.

The final page of *Daniel Deronda* contains the letter that Gwendolen sends to Daniel on his wedding day when he is to be married to another woman, and thus tentatively looks towards their own now very separate futures. That separation is crucial: again, painful and yet necessary to Gwendolen's adulthood. Critics have used this letter as evidence both of Gwendolen's growth and of her decline. For the psychoanalyst Bernard Barnett, the letter 'speaks of her determination to make a new beginning',[62] while alternatively, the literary critic Elizabeth Daniels has written that Gwendolen is 'Not free of the guilt of her past, [but] weak from the chaos of her inner turmoil, with no sustaining dream of the future [...] left in a state of collapse – a pitiable bundle of conflicts'.[63] In her essay 'The Spoiled Child: What Happened to Gwendolen Harleth?' Margaret Reimer argues that 'the conclusion of the novel gives scant evidence of transformation in Gwendolen. Despite her pledge to live and "be better", her future appears bleak'.[64] The biographer and novelist Diana Souhami published a reimagined version of *Daniel Deronda* in 2014, entitled *Gwendolen*. She concluded this novel by turning Gwendolen into a suffragette, in an attempt to give her a more conventionally satisfying future: 'Eliot abandons her and sends her back home having had a disastrous marriage and been abandoned by the man she loves. My first instinct was to try to help her [...] to rescue her. Or put her on the path to rescue.'[65] Bernard J. Paris seized upon the ending of the novel as proof that any perceived therapeutic exchange between Daniel and Gwendolen had failed: 'Deronda certainly plays an important role in Gwendolen's psychic life [...] but I do not think that he helps her to find effective coping devices or leads her in the direction of psychological health. After Grandcourt's death, Gwendolen becomes even more dependent on Deronda; and, despite her brave words, her prospects after his departure seem very bleak to me.'[66]

The novel's deliberately open ending has caused concern among critics and psychoanalysts who find it difficult to accept that we can never know with any certainty what will now happen to Gwendolen. However, this uncertainty cannot be used as evidence that Daniel's therapy has failed. For by refusing to give Gwendolen a definitive resolution or single, fixed role, George Eliot is instead giving her the difficult reality of a genuine future, one, that is to say, unknown and beyond fiction. I would argue that Gwendolen's final letter contains small but significant signs of the important mental shift that has taken place within her over the course of the novel:

> Do not think of me sorrowfully on your wedding day. I have remembered your words – that I may live to be one of the best women, who make others glad that they were born. I do not yet see how that can be, but you know better than I. If it ever comes true, it will be because you helped me. I only thought of myself, and I made you grieve. You must not grieve any more for me. It is better – it shall be better with me because I have known you.[67]

The insertion of the small words 'yet' and 'ever' turn the despair of present uncertainty ('how') into something that 'may' be, perhaps without a name, only a grammar. In her final sentence Gwendolen corrects herself from saying simply 'it is better with me', which would have been too much like an insincere reassurance out of step with the determination of the novel to transcend kindness, and a sacrilegious attempt to satisfy Daniel. Instead she adds the words 'it shall be', in recognition that she is not yet, but can envisage a future when she 'may' be. This final letter sits in stark contrast to Gwendolen's earlier assertions at the beginning of her relationship with Daniel: 'I can't make myself different [...] and I must go on – I can alter nothing.'[68] Now, by imagining him thinking of her, him not wanting her to be sorrowful, and her not wanting him to think her sorrowful, she is able to make herself less so. It is a complex to-and-fro, as complex as any syntax. Even now that he is absent, he safeguards the best part of her, as George Eliot does more widely for all of her characters. This relationship mirrors the potential therapeutic relation that exists between a book and its reader, which has been modelled throughout this book in the interlinked relationships between different readers and writers.

Rather than providing Gwendolen with an explicit cure or solution or resolution, Daniel – as George Eliot's closest representative within the novel – has given her the capacity to inhabit more complex constructions. She exists now, not as a singular, fixed entity – as the critics who are so keen to place her back within a defined role would have it – but in the grey areas of 'may', 'yet', 'if' and 'shall'. While it is perhaps easier to judge the outcomes of any therapeutic exchange in terms of conventional markers of success or failure, success cannot simply mean a score on a well-being scale. In these rigid terms, the literary model of therapy which I am advocating in this book might produce outcomes which could initially look like failure. However, despite the apparent 'bleak' uncertainty of Gwendolen's prospects, by looking at her very syntax it is possible to see how she now has the capacity for two-way blended thinking: she is seeing herself through the expansive view of a mind outside herself, absorbing back into herself an aspect of that mind, and able now to release herself from the narrowness of seeking an immediately fixed, definite solution or cure for her life.

Notes

1. Stephen Gill, *Wordsworth and The Victorians* (Oxford: Clarendon Press, 1998), p. 147; hereafter cited as *Wordsworth and The Victorians*.
2. Ibid., p. 161.
3. Thomas Pinney, 'George Eliot's Reading of Wordsworth', *Victorian Newsletter*, 24 (1963), pp. 20–22 (p. 20).
4. Margaret Homans, *Bearing the Word: Language and Female Experience in Nineteenth-Century Women's Writing* (Chicago, IL: The University of Chicago Press, 1986), p. 121.
5. 'Preface to the *Lyrical Ballads*', *Prose*, i, p. 123.
6. George Eliot, 'The Sad Fortunes of the Rev. Amos Barton', in *Scenes of Clerical Life*, ed. Graham Handley (London: Everyman, [1857] 1994), p. 41.
7. 'Preface to the *Lyrical Ballads*', *Prose*, i, p. 123.
8. George Eliot, *Adam Bede*, ed. Carol A. Martin (Oxford: Oxford World's Classics, [1859] 2001), pp. 59–60; hereafter cited as '*Adam Bede*'.
9. *Excursion*, VI, ll. 651–58.
10. *Wordsworth and The Victorians*, p. 157.
11. 'Intimations of Immortality', *Wordsworth's Poetical Works*, iv, ll.149–53, p. 283.
12. George Eliot, *The Mill on the Floss*, ed. A. S. Byatt (London: Penguin Popular Classics, [1860] 1994), p. 1; hereafter cited as '*The Mill on the Floss*'.
13. Ibid., p. 38.
14. Ibid., p. 461.
15. Rick Rylance, *Victorian Psychology and British Culture 1850–1880* (Oxford: Oxford University Press, 2000), p. 7; hereafter cited as 'Rylance'.
16. George Eliot, *The George Eliot Letters*, ed. Gordon S. Haight, 9 vols (New Haven, CT: Yale University Press, 1954–78), vi, p. 216; hereafter cited as *GEL*.
17. Sally Shuttleworth, *George Eliot and Nineteenth-Century Science* (Cambridge: Cambridge University Press, 1984), p. ix.
18. *GEL*, iii, p. 318.
19. *The Mill on the Floss*, p. 510.
20. Ibid., p. 354.
21. *Adam Bede*, p. 147.
22. Ibid., p. 153.
23. Ibid., pp. 365–66.
24. Ibid., p. 159.
25. Ludwig Feuerbach, *The Essence of Christianity*, trans. George Eliot (New York: Prometheus, [1841] 1989), p. 62.
26. Ibid., pp. 29–30.
27. *The Mill on the Floss*, p. 238.

28 *GEL*, i, p. 251.
29 Benedict de Spinoza, *Ethics*, trans. George Eliot (Salzburg: University of Salzburg, [1677] 1981), p. 141; hereafter cited as 'Spinoza'.
30 Ibid., pp. 143–44.
31 Ibid., pp. 155–56.
32 Ibid., p. 51.
33 Firmin DeBrabander, *Spinoza and the Stoics: Power, Politics and the Passions* (New York: Continuum, 2007), p. 25.
34 Ibid., pp. 25–27.
35 Lou Andreas-Salomé, *The Freud Journals*, trans. Stanley A. Leavy (London: Hogarth Press, 1965), p. 75.
36 Jerome Neu, *Emotion, Thought and Therapy* (London: Routledge and Kegan Paul, 1977), p. 151.
37 Ibid.
38 S. S. Prawer, *A Cultural Citizen of the World: Sigmund Freud's Knowledge and Use of British and American Writings* (London: Legenda, 2009), p. 73.
39 *GEL*, i, p. 321.
40 George Eliot, *Middlemarch*, ed. David Carroll (Oxford: Oxford World's Classics, [1872] 2008), p. 613; hereafter cited as *Middlemarch*.
41 Christopher Bollas, *The Mystery of Things* (New York: Routledge, 1999), pp. 79–80.
42 *Middlemarch*, pp. 399–400.
43 Ibid., pp. 400–401.
44 T. S. Clouston, *Clinical Lectures on Mental Disease* (New York: Lea Brothers, 1897), p. 592.
45 Carl T. Rotenberg, 'George Eliot – Proto-Psychoanalyst', *American Journal of Psychoanalysis*, 59(3) (1999), pp. 257–70 (p. 260); hereafter cited as 'Rotenberg'.
46 Ibid., p. 269.
47 George Eliot, *Daniel Deronda*, ed. Graham Handley (Oxford: Oxford World's Classics, [1876] 1988), p. 51; hereafter cited as *Deronda*.
48 Leon Festinger, *A Theory of Cognitive Dissonance* (Stanford, CA: Stanford University Press, 1962).
49 *Deronda*, p. 387.
50 Rotenberg, p. 266.
51 Margot Waddell, 'On Ideas of "the Good" and of "the Ideal" in George Eliot's Novels and in Post-Kleinian Psychoanalytic Thought', *American Journal of Psychoanalysis*, 59(3) (1999), pp. 271–86 (p. 277).
52 Bernard J. Paris, *Rereading George Eliot: Changing Responses to Her Experiments in Life* (Albany: University of New York Press, 2003), p. 164; hereafter cited as 'Paris'.
53 *Deronda*, p. 385.
54 Ibid., p. 387.
55 Ibid., p. 388.
56 Sigmund Freud, 'Beyond the Pleasure Principle', in *The Standard Edition of the Complete Psychological Works of Sigmund Freud*, ed. James Strachey, 24 vols (London: Hogarth Press, 1953–74), xviii, pp. 7–64.
57 *Deronda*, p. 388.
58 Ibid., p. 521.
59 '*Remembering, Repeating and Working Through*', p. 155.
60 *Deronda*, p. 577.

61 Gillian Beer, *Darwin's Plots* (Cambridge: University of Cambridge Press, 2000), p. 171.
62 Bernard Barnett, *You Ought To! A Psychoanalytic Study of the Superego and Conscience* (London: Karnac, 2007), p. 83.
63 Elizabeth Daniels, 'A Meredithian Glance at Gwendolen Harleth', in *George Eliot: A Centenary Tribute*, ed. Gordon S. Haight, and Rosemary T. Van Arsdel (London: Macmillan, 1985), pp. 28–37 (p. 35).
64 Margaret Reimer, 'The Spoiled Child: What Happened to Gwendolen Harleth?', *Cambridge Quarterly*, 36 (2007), pp. 33–50 (p. 50).
65 Cole Moreton, 'Author Diana Souhami: "Why I 'Rescued' a Character Left in the Lurch by George Eliot"', *Independent*, 13 September 2014, https://www.independent.co.uk/arts-entertainment/books/features/author-diana-souhami-why-i-rescued-a-character-left-in-the-lurch-by-george-eliot-9729873.html, accessed 11 November 2017.
66 Paris, p. 159.
67 *Deronda*, pp. 694–95
68 Ibid., p. 521.

Part II

Three Experiments

Chapter 5

EXPERIMENT ONE: A FIRST READING

Part I of this book has sought to examine the ways in which literature can serve as a repository for therapeutic thought and practice. By focusing on four representative literary models, spanning a period of two thousand years from Ancient Rome up until the nineteenth-century creation of the formal discipline of psychology, each of the previous four chapters have considered the different ways in which both readers and writers alike have used literature as a form of personal therapy.

The aim of Part II is to reactivate the arguments of Part I and demonstrate how theoretical literary study can benefit from accommodating more imaginative, empirical methodologies. For as Iain McGilchrist writes in *Against Criticism*, with specific reference to the study of Wordsworth, 'To criticise his poetry properly one would need to have a knowledge of theology, philosophy, syntax, psychology and biology, as well as a powerful enough imagination to hold them all together, and to see them finally as an aspect of the same thing'.[1]

Chapters 5 and 6 will set out the results of two practical reading experiments which demonstrate Wordsworth's poetry in action and thus illuminate its workings in ways that theoretical criticism cannot. Results of a third experimental study, based upon readers' engagement with the work of George Eliot, will follow in Chapter 7. All three experiments are designed to investigate whether personal engagement with literature can open up particular areas and ways of thinking and thus illustrate the genuine use that literary reading can have in the real world. What is offered in the following three chapters is not, of course, final proof but supportive and testing evidence in relation to emerging positions and propositions.

The following three chapters seek to meet the challenge set out by Rita Felski in *The Limits of Critique*:

> Literary theory would do well to reflect on – rather than condescend to – the uses of literature in everyday life: uses that we have hardly begun to understand. Such a reorientation, with any luck might inspire more capacious, and more publicly persuasive rationales for why literature, and the study of literature, matter.[2]

It is important to recognise that much of what takes place, and much of what is of most value in the reading process, is hidden, implicit, unquantifiable and entirely unsuitable for conventional formal study. Private reading is a secret exchange, and the therapeutic power of literature is closely tied to its ability to obliquely – rather than explicitly – hold up a mirror to human troubles. In order to study literary reading and its value, we must be careful to develop methodologies which preserve and respect the very nature and quality of the thing itself. As Terence Cave argues in *Thinking with Literature*, we must 'acknowledge the power of scientific methodologies without renouncing the ambition (some might say the duty) to devise methodologies specific to literature as an object of knowledge'.[3]

The challenge was to design a series of experimental studies which would

1. Create a space for readers to engage carefully with a complex and unfamiliar work of literature, on their own personal terms and in extended, reflective privacy, rather than as an academic or explicitly therapeutic exercise.
2. Offer a means through which first-hand acts of private reading could be captured and analysed, helping to reveal the implicit, hidden effects of reading while avoiding reductive oversimplification or narrowing categorisation.

The experimental work of Part II is informed by two models of particularly innovative literary scholarship by I. A. Richards's *Practical Criticism* (1929) and Michael Paffard's *Inglorious Wordsworths* (1973).

I. A. Richards was a highly influential Cambridge scholar and a leading proponent of New Criticism, a movement in literary theory which advocated the close analysis of literary texts. *Practical Criticism* has been described as 'the first large-scale experiment in psychology conducted to discover how real readers understand, interpret and evaluate literary texts'.[4] For his experiment, Richards handed out copies of 13 poems – stripped of all historical and biographical context – to a large group of Cambridge undergraduates and colleagues and then analysed the written responses that the students produced. Richards discovered a widespread inability to successfully 'read' poetry, and in *Practical Criticism* he outlines a series of common reading faults, highlights his participants' propensity to rely on preconceptions and 'stock responses' in their analysis of the poetry and comments on the sense of bewilderment and confusion felt by students when faced with unfamiliar material that has been stripped of all the props of context. By measuring the true state of reading at the university, Richards was able to identify some of the work that was still to be done in teaching:

> It is not inevitable, or in the nature of things, that poetry should seem such a remote, mysterious, unmanageable thing to so large a majority of

readers. The deficiencies so noticeable in the protocol writers […] are not native inalterable defects in the average human mind. They are due in a large degree to mistakes that can be avoided, and to bad training. In fact does anyone ever receive any useful training in this matter?[5]

Ninety years after *Practical Criticism*, poetry may have become even more of a 'remote, mysterious, unmanageable thing' to an even larger majority of the population than Richards found it to be.

Richards argued that while some aspects of life are suited to scientific modes of thinking, there are many others which are not, and in order to think about those grey areas of existence that do not correspond with logic and reason we need something closer to poetry:

> There are subjects – mathematics, physics and the descriptive sciences supply some of them – which can be discussed in terms of verifiable facts and precise hypotheses. There are other subjects – the concrete affairs of commerce, law, organisation and police work – which can be handled by rules of thumb and generally accepted conventions. But in between is the vast corpus of problems, assumptions, adumbrations, fictions, prejudices, tenets; the sphere of random beliefs and hopeful guesses; the whole world, in brief, of abstract opinion and disputation about matters of feeling. To this world belongs everything about which civilised man cares most. I need only instance ethics, metaphysics, morals, religion, aesthetics, and the discussions surrounding liberty, nationality, justice, love, truth, faith and knowledge to make this plain. As a subject matter for discussion, poetry is a central and typical denizen of this world.[6]

The experimental work of Part II of this book will investigate the impact that 'literary language' can potentially have on human thinking and explore the role that it can play in helping people to inhabit the grey areas that exist outside of the reach of 'everyday' language. The experimental methods of psychological science are thus being put to use here in the service of something deeper than empiricism.

Michael Paffard conceived of his book *Inglorious Wordsworths* while struggling to teach English literature – and in particular the poetry of Wordsworth – to a class of sixth-form students. Uncertain of the degree to which his pupils could relate to Wordsworth's poetry, Paffard developed a questionnaire which he eventually handed out to 500 sixth-form and undergraduate students. The aim of the survey was to find out if participants had ever experienced 'transcendental' moments that could be in any way akin to those famously described by Wordsworth in his poetry. The questionnaire itself makes no reference to

Wordsworth, instead Paffard includes a paragraph from the autobiography of the naturalist W. H. Hudson, in which he describes watching the sunset as a child, 'The sight of the magnificent sunset was sometimes more than I could endure and made me wish to hide myself away.'[7] He then asks his participants, 'Does this remind you of anything you have ever felt? If you have ever had an experience which you feel is in any way similar to the ones the writer of this passage is describing, please try to write about it on the blank page overleaf.'[8] Of the 400 questionnaires that were returned to him, 222 participants responded to this question, and it was these responses that the book goes on to analyse and catalogue in more detail.

Paffard's conclusions can be applied to a much broader range of psychological experiences than the transcendental: 'Transcendental experience demands another voice. One of the least controversial things that can be said about it is that it craves a language to express the inexpressible, a poetic, religious, extravagant language which is most effective when it is non-prosaic, non-propositional and logically odd.'[9] The reading experiments that follow will explore whether Wordsworth's poetry can offer modern readers 'another voice' with which to express thoughts and feelings that exist outside of the remit of everyday language. In doing so, these experiments will begin to set out what the syntax, language, pacing and tone of Wordsworth's poetry can actually do to and for people in practice.

In addition to the experimental models of Richards and Paffard, innovative research into reading, carried out by David S. Miall and Donald Kuiken from The University of Alberta, informed the development of my study design. Reacting against many of the post-structuralist theories that dominate literary criticism, Miall and Kuiken have adopted empirical methods for the study of real readers' responses to literature. Their work concentrates in particular on readers' reports of 'foregrounded' language (derived from the Prague School of linguisticians in the 1930s). For Miall and Kuiken, it is the 'foregrounded' sections of a text which have a particularly salient effect upon readers and are what allow the experience of reading literature to shift beyond mere browsing or scanning.[10]

Experiment One: Study Design

A group of 10 adults were recruited to take part in this study via advertisements displayed across the University of Liverpool campus. All participants were required to be at least 18 years of age and fluent in English. The final group of participants (A1–A10) were aged between 22 and 61 years and consisted of four males and six females. All recruits were invited to attend an individual one-hour session in the University of Liverpool library. During these

Table 5.1. Experiment one: Sample information

Participant Number	Age	M/F	Profession	Do You Read for Pleasure?	Do You Read Poetry?	Have You Ever Studied Wordsworth?
A1	22	M	Accounting student	Y	Y	N
A2	37	M	Politics lecturer	Y	N	N
A3	27	F	English student	Y	Y	Y
A4	45	M	Linguistics lecturer	Y	Y	Y
A5	45	F	University administrator	Y	N	N
A6	43	F	Medical education lecturer	Y	N	N
A7	45	F	Public health researcher	Y	N	N
A8	61	F	Retired youth worker	Y	Y	N
A9	46	M	English as an additional language tutor	Y	Y	Y
A10	53	F	University administrator	Y	N	N

sessions participants were asked to fill out a short survey about themselves and their reading habits[11] (see Table 5.1). They then sat alone in a private study room to audio-record themselves reading one short news article and two extracts of Wordsworth's poem 'The Ruined Cottage' (see Figure 5.1). After reading each passage in turn participants were asked to record themselves speaking freely about anything that seemed important, interesting or moving within each text.[12]

The first passage of poetry given to readers explores the emotional turmoil that the pedlar felt as a teenager. In the second extract the pedlar recounts the story of Margaret, the last inhabitant of the now ruined cottage. A short introductory summary was provided alongside each extract of poetry in order to give readers an idea of the wider context of the poem. The chosen news article gives an account of the suicide of a 92-year-old woman called Olive Cooke. It is an emotionally charged article and was selected because its themes – namely the distress, depression and death of an isolated female – correspond with those of 'The Ruined Cottage'. The poem was chosen for its bare, primary emotion, and because, as so often in Wordsworth's poetry it leaves space and silence for readers themselves to occupy. The character of the pedlar is – as

Passage One – BBC Regional News Report, 20 May 2015

Olive Cooke death: Poppy seller had depression, inquest hears

A ninety-two year-old woman who was found dead in the Avon Gorge had "long term issues with periodic depression", an inquest has heard. Olive Cooke was one of the UK's longest-serving poppy sellers and had collected money in Bristol for the Royal British Legion for seventy-six years. Media coverage of her death focussed on suggestions she had been overwhelmed by junk mail from charities. An inquest into her death was opened and adjourned until the 16th of July. Avon Coroner's Court heard that Mrs Cooke was pronounced dead at 18:20 on the 6th of May by a paramedic and was formally identified by her grandson. She had complained to her local newspaper last year about the amount of requests for donations she was receiving. A friend told the BBC that while he would not blame her death entirely on charities "pestering" her, she had been "under pressure". Coroner's officer Linda Grove told the hearing: "This lady had long term issues with periodic depression and low mood." Her family said the charity requests, while "intrusive", were not to blame for her death. They said she had left a note to explain the reasons for her death which had mentioned depression and being elderly. Mrs Cooke, from Fishponds, started selling poppies at the age of sixteen as her father was an active Royal British Legion member having served in World War One. She said it took on new meaning for her when her first husband was killed in action in World War Two.

Passage Two – Extract from 'The Ruined Cottage', *The Excursion*, Book I, ll. 280–300

And thus before his eighteenth year was told,
Accumulated feelings pressed his heart
With still increasing weight; he was
   o'er-powered
By Nature; by the turbulence subdued
Of his own mind; by mystery and hope,
And the first virgin passion of a soul
Communing with the glorious universe.
Full often wished he that the winds
   might rage
When they were silent: far more fondly now
Than in his earliest season did he love
Tempestuous nights – the conflict and
   the sounds
That live in darkness. From his intellect
And from the stillness of abstracted thoughts
He asked repose; and, failing oft to win
The peace required, he scanned the laws
   of light
Amid the roar of torrents where they send
From hollow clefts up to the clearer air
A cloud of mist that, smitten by the sun,
Varies its rainbow hues. But vainly thus,
And vainly by all other means, he strove
To mitigate the fever of his heart.

Passage Three – Extract from 'The Ruined Cottage', *The Excursion*, Book I, ll. 815–33

It would have grieved
Your very soul to see her. Sir, I feel
The story linger in my heart; I fear
'Tis long and tedious; but my spirit clings
To that poor woman: – so familiarly
Do I perceive her manner, and her look,
And presence; and so deeply do I feel
Her goodness, that, not seldom, in my walks
   A momentary trance comes over me;
And to myself I seem to muse on One
By sorrow laid asleep; or borne away,
A human being destined to awake
To human life, or something very near
To human life, when he shall come again
For whom she suffered. Yes, it would have
   grieved
Your very soul to see her: evermore
Her eyelids drooped, her eyes downwards
   were cast;
And, when she at her table gave me food,
She did not look at me.

Figure 5.1. The three passages used in experiment one

discussed in Chapter 3 – Wordsworth's most explicit representation of a Stoic sage. The poem therefore shares a certain amount of the Stoic DNA of a modern CBT (Cognitive Behavioural Therapy) self-help book. The question here is whether, once distilled through the mind of the poet, it can have any comparable therapeutic effect on readers.

After each session, audio recordings were fully transcribed and double-checked for accuracy. All transcripts were coded and initial sets of categories and themes were then formed. Thematic analysis was selected as the primary analytical methodology due to its flexibility and capacity to 'potentially provide a rich, detailed, yet complex account of data'.[13] However, in order to collect as much varied evidence as possible, and in line with the analytical approach devised by researchers at The University of Liverpool's Centre for Research into Reading, Literature and Society (CRILS), the analytical methodology remained rooted in the techniques of close literary analysis and was informed throughout by the analytical techniques of linguistic studies. This blended approach resulted in the identification of four main themes:

1. Summary Mode versus Active Reading
2. Distraction versus Emotional Focus
3. Certainty versus Imaginative Uncertainty
4. Looking on the Bright Side versus Looking Back and Thinking Again

Summary Mode versus Active Reading

It was clear from an initial reading of the transcripts that participants typically spoke for longer about each of the passages of poetry than the news article. The average length of responses to passage one was 240 words, while responses to passages two and three averaged at 367 and 449 words, respectively. A paired t-test was conducted in order to compare the length of participant responses to the two types of text. For the purpose of the test, responses to passages two and three were combined, due to the fact that the combined length of the two poetry extracts was roughly equal to the length of the single news article. A statistically significant difference was found between the length of the news article responses ($M = 240.3$) and the poetry responses ($M = 850.2$) ($t(9) = -5.3094$, $p < 0.0004878$).

While it was to be expected that participants would have more to say about the two distinct poetry stimuli than the single news article, the difference in the length of the two sets of transcripts can partly be accounted for by the large amount of direct quotations that participants used when talking about the poetry. Direct quotations appeared to help participants to focus on specific details within the poetry. This means that the transcripts relating to the poetry extracts are not only greater in length, but also have a specific quality. In contrast, the shorter responses to the news article tend to contain general, conclusive statements which mirror the summary mode of the article itself. The following two examples from participant A6 illustrate the difference between the 'summary mode' typically adopted in response to the news article and the more expansive thinking that is produced in response to the poetry due to 'active reading' of the texts. First, having read the news article, participant A6 stated:

> So overall, I remember the story from the time, although I remember it in a slightly different way, and it's a sad story. Obviously the media angle – being the way that she was pestered and put under pressure – that was the main focus. (A6)

The combination of 'overall' and 'obviously', which here lead onto the conclusive, 'that was the main focus', are suggestive of a detached summary mode which centres around the presentation of the story in the media, somewhat at the expense of the actual real person contained within the story itself. After reading the second extract of poetry, the same participant responded with a detailed commentary which incorporated direct quotations from the text:

> Coming back to the actual text of the poem, so it's opening and it's saying immediately, 'It would have grieved / Your very soul to see her' so you would have been … her grief is so obvious, she must have been ravished by it. So again that creates a picture in my mind of this poor woman in her cottage having been abandoned, looking a right old state. So yeah, that's really sad. She is described as a 'poor woman', she looks destroyed. (A6)

Direct quotations seem to draw readers back into the text while simultaneously allowing them to move on into places of greater imaginative depth, as here where the participant begins to see 'a picture in my mind' of Margaret, and shifts to speaking about her in the present tense, 'she *looks* destroyed'. The literary material appears to evoke the cognitive capacity of mental imagery in a way that the non-literary text did not. This reader has become imaginatively present within the story by returning to 'the actual text'. No comparable mental shift occurs in any of the responses to the news article. The unexpected use of the word 'ravished' at the centre of this example demonstrates how the use of quotations from the text, interwoven alongside the reader's own voice, can trigger the use of different, unusual vocabulary and syntax. Readers not only borrow or recycle the vocabulary of the poetry; in cases like this they pull

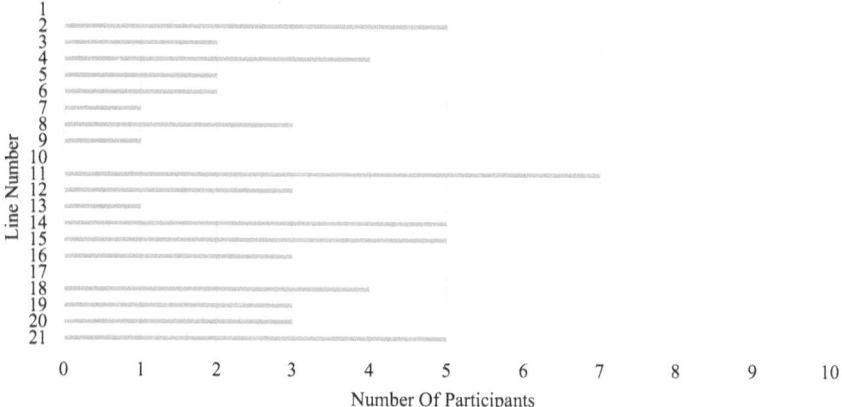

Figure 5.2. Graph showing the most frequently quoted lines of poetry extract one

words out of their own minds that they would perhaps be unlikely to use in normal, everyday speech and which are not found in responses to the news article. The argument posited here is that it is the poetry that seems to be demanding a more varied vocabulary.

Having identified that the length – and to some extent the depth – of some of the responses to the poetry were due to the frequency of participants' use of direct quotations, it was important to explore which sections of the poetry extracts readers were selecting to quote. A graph was drawn to show the number of participants who directly quoted from each line of the first extract of poetry (see Figure 5.2). Figure 5.3 indicates – through font size – exactly where the most frequently quoted sections of each line of poetry were.

The prominent sections of the text form a map of interconnections down the lines. There is some sense of commonality in the choices that each individual participant made. For example, the first two words of line 11 – 'Tempestuous nights' – were significant for seven of the ten participants. The group as a whole appeared to share an understanding of where certain pulse points or places of particularly powerful meaning were within the text.

In a number of responses, participants did not seem to quote from the text in a regular, sequential order. To gain a clearer understanding of each participant's reading pattern, the order in which they quoted from different line numbers of each extract of poetry was recorded. For example, participant A2 quoted from the following lines in the following order in his response to the first extract of poetry (Table 5.2).

> Accumulated feelings pressed his heart
>   still increasing weight
>   turbulence
>   mystery and hope
>   passion
>   glorious universe
> Full often wished he that the winds might rage
>   far more fondly now
>
> **Tempestuous nights**
>   intellect
>   abstracted thought
>   **failing oft to win**
> **The peace required**
>   the roar of torrents
> **A cloud of mist**
>   rainbow
> **And vainly by all other means**
> **To mitigate the fever of his heart.**

Figure 5.3. The most frequently quoted sections of poetry extract one

Table 5.2. The order of direct quotations in participant A2's response to poetry extract one

Quotation Number	Line Number	Quotation
1	6	The first virgin passion of a soul
2	7	Communing with the glorious universe
3	20	Strove
4	21	To mitigate the fever of his heart
5	11	Tempestuous nights
6	15	Scanned the laws of light
7	14	He asked repose

Each individual reading pattern was then plotted on a graph (Figure 5.4):

- Participant A1 was the one reader who clearly worked steadily through the poem, making regular stops, to produce a detailed but linear close reading of the text.
- Participants A2, A3, A4, A5 and A6 all jump vertically and horizontally across the lines.
- The graphs for participants A7, A8, A9 and A10 are reflective of the lower levels of direct engagement with the text in these four responses.
- Comparable analysis of responses to the news article would not be possible due to the near total absence of direct quotations from the text in this set of responses.

Participant A6 reflected on her non-linear approach to reading the text:

> I feel that I'm not quite reading it right, but I don't know why I should feel that really. I can read it in any way I wish to. I could do it a sentence at a time in quite a clinical way, but I think … I think … It's quite a powerful piece of writing, and some of the words used like 'pressure on his heart', 'turbulence', 'tempestuous nights', it's quite dramatic isn't it? As I'm doing this now my eyes are going to different parts of it and picking different things out and again I'm thinking maybe I should be more systematic, go line by line, rather than picking things out instantly, but I think that's just how I read, I'm trying to get a feel for it. (A6)

This reader's initial hesitancy, expressed here in the opening sentence, is quickly and usefully discarded as she realises that in the privacy of her own company, 'I can read it any way I wish to.' In part, readers A2, A3, A4, A5 and A6 appear to be casting about as they jump through the lines, looking for anchors that will help them to understand the meaning of the text. However, as they move instinctively up and down the lines, readers appear to be tuning into the internal, non-linear circuitry of the poetry, where meaning is not created simply 'line by line' but in the transfer of feeling vertically and diagonally across the lines. For example, there is a connection between line 2, 'Accumulated feeling pressed his heart' and line 21, 'To mitigate the fever of his heart' that is picked up on by participant A4. A number of participants also instinctively link together the word 'turbulence' in line 4 with 'tempestuous' in line 11. Once this connection is made it helps to unlock the wider meaning of the passage and the relationship between external turmoil and internal, psychological unrest. Participant A5 for example, pairs these two words together twice in her response:

110   RETHINKING THERAPEUTIC READING

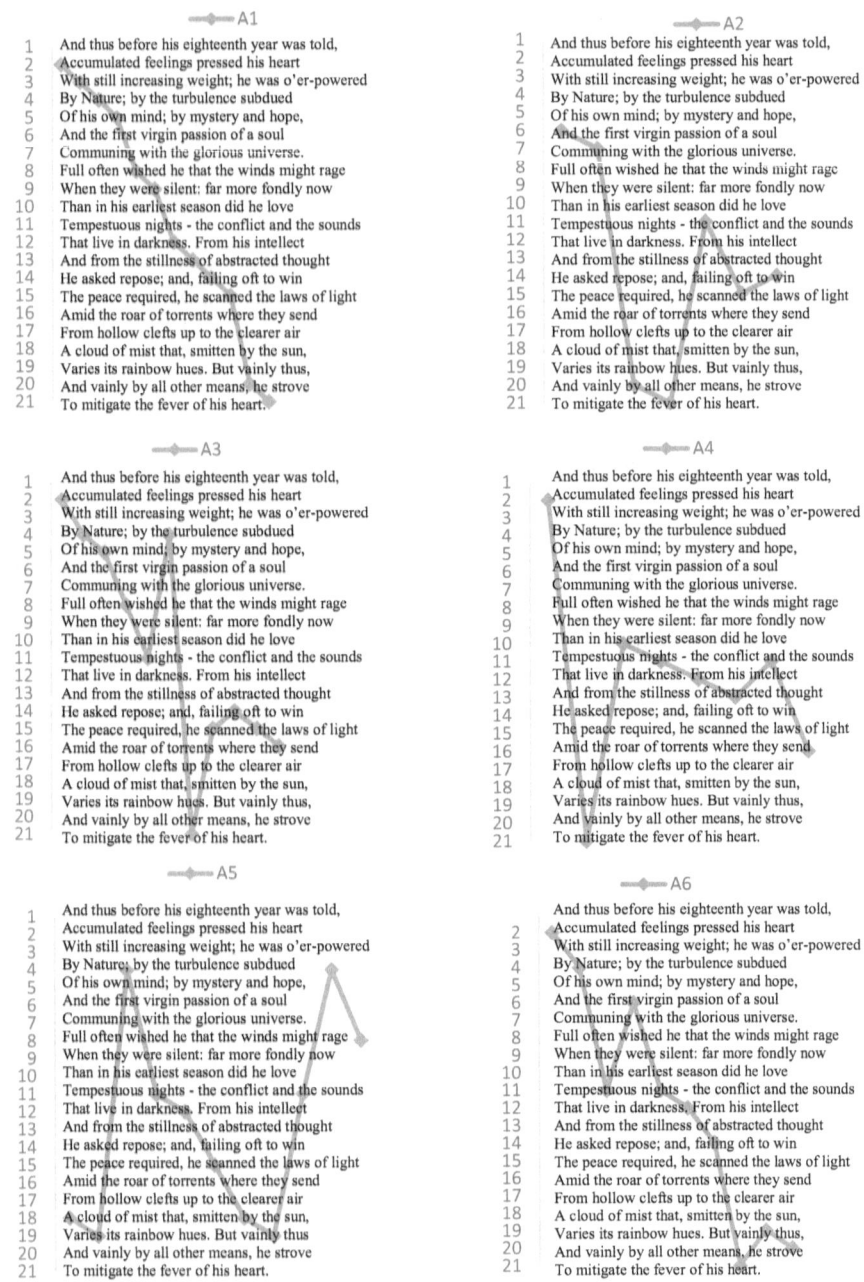

●━━━ A1

1 And thus before his eighteenth year was told,
2 Accumulated feelings pressed his heart
3 With still increasing weight; he was o'er-powered
4 By Nature; by the turbulence subdued
5 Of his own mind; by mystery and hope,
6 And the first virgin passion of a soul
7 Communing with the glorious universe.
8 Full often wished he that the winds might rage
9 When they were silent: far more fondly now
10 Than in his earliest season did he love
11 Tempestuous nights - the conflict and the sounds
12 That live in darkness. From his intellect
13 And from the stillness of abstracted thought
14 He asked repose; and, failing oft to win
15 The peace required, he scanned the laws of light
16 Amid the roar of torrents where they send
17 From hollow clefts up to the clearer air
18 A cloud of mist that, smitten by the sun,
19 Varies its rainbow hues. But vainly thus,
20 And vainly by all other means, he strove
21 To mitigate the fever of his heart.

●━━━ A2

1 And thus before his eighteenth year was told,
2 Accumulated feelings pressed his heart
3 With still increasing weight; he was o'er-powered
4 By Nature; by the turbulence subdued
5 Of his own mind; by mystery and hope,
6 And the first virgin passion of a soul
7 Communing with the glorious universe.
8 Full often wished he that the winds might rage
9 When they were silent: far more fondly now
10 Than in his earliest season did he love
11 Tempestuous nights - the conflict and the sounds
12 That live in darkness. From his intellect
13 And from the stillness of abstracted thought
14 He asked repose; and, failing oft to win
15 The peace required, he scanned the laws of light
16 Amid the roar of torrents where they send
17 From hollow clefts up to the clearer air
18 A cloud of mist that, smitten by the sun,
19 Varies its rainbow hues. But vainly thus,
20 And vainly by all other means, he strove
21 To mitigate the fever of his heart.

●━━━ A3

1 And thus before his eighteenth year was told,
2 Accumulated feelings pressed his heart
3 With still increasing weight; he was o'er-powered
4 By Nature; by the turbulence subdued
5 Of his own mind; by mystery and hope,
6 And the first virgin passion of a soul
7 Communing with the glorious universe.
8 Full often wished he that the winds might rage
9 When they were silent: far more fondly now
10 Than in his earliest season did he love
11 Tempestuous nights - the conflict and the sounds
12 That live in darkness. From his intellect
13 And from the stillness of abstracted thought
14 He asked repose; and, failing oft to win
15 The peace required, he scanned the laws of light
16 Amid the roar of torrents where they send
17 From hollow clefts up to the clearer air
18 A cloud of mist that, smitten by the sun,
19 Varies its rainbow hues. But vainly thus,
20 And vainly by all other means, he strove
21 To mitigate the fever of his heart.

●━━━ A4

1 And thus before his eighteenth year was told,
2 Accumulated feelings pressed his heart
3 With still increasing weight; he was o'er-powered
4 By Nature; by the turbulence subdued
5 Of his own mind; by mystery and hope,
6 And the first virgin passion of a soul
7 Communing with the glorious universe.
8 Full often wished he that the winds might rage
9 When they were silent: far more fondly now
10 Than in his earliest season did he love
11 Tempestuous nights - the conflict and the sounds
12 That live in darkness. From his intellect
13 And from the stillness of abstracted thought
14 He asked repose; and, failing oft to win
15 The peace required, he scanned the laws of light
16 Amid the roar of torrents where they send
17 From hollow clefts up to the clearer air
18 A cloud of mist that, smitten by the sun,
19 Varies its rainbow hues. But vainly thus,
20 And vainly by all other means, he strove
21 To mitigate the fever of his heart.

●━━━ A5

1 And thus before his eighteenth year was told,
2 Accumulated feelings pressed his heart
3 With still increasing weight; he was o'er-powered
4 By Nature; by the turbulence subdued
5 Of his own mind; by mystery and hope,
6 And the first virgin passion of a soul
7 Communing with the glorious universe.
8 Full often wished he that the winds might rage
9 When they were silent: far more fondly now
10 Than in his earliest season did he love
11 Tempestuous nights - the conflict and the sounds
12 That live in darkness. From his intellect
13 And from the stillness of abstracted thought
14 He asked repose; and, failing oft to win
15 The peace required, he scanned the laws of light
16 Amid the roar of torrents where they send
17 From hollow clefts up to the clearer air
18 A cloud of mist that, smitten by the sun,
19 Varies its rainbow hues. But vainly thus
20 And vainly by all other means, he strove
21 To mitigate the fever of his heart.

●━━━ A6

   And thus before his eighteenth year was told,
2 Accumulated feelings pressed his heart
3 With still increasing weight; he was o'er-powered
4 By Nature; by the turbulence subdued
5 Of his own mind; by mystery and hope,
6 And the first virgin passion of a soul
7 Communing with the glorious universe.
8 Full often wished he that the winds might rage
9 When they were silent: far more fondly now
10 Than in his earliest season did he love
11 Tempestuous nights - the conflict and the sounds
12 That live in darkness. From his intellect
13 And from the stillness of abstracted thought
14 He asked repose; and, failing oft to win
15 The peace required, he scanned the laws of light
16 Amid the roar of torrents where they send
17 From hollow clefts up to the clearer air
18 A cloud of mist that, smitten by the sun,
19 Varies its rainbow hues. But vainly thus,
20 And vainly by all other means, he strove
21 To mitigate the fever of his heart.

Figure 5.4. Graphs showing the order of direct quotations used in each participant response to poetry extract one

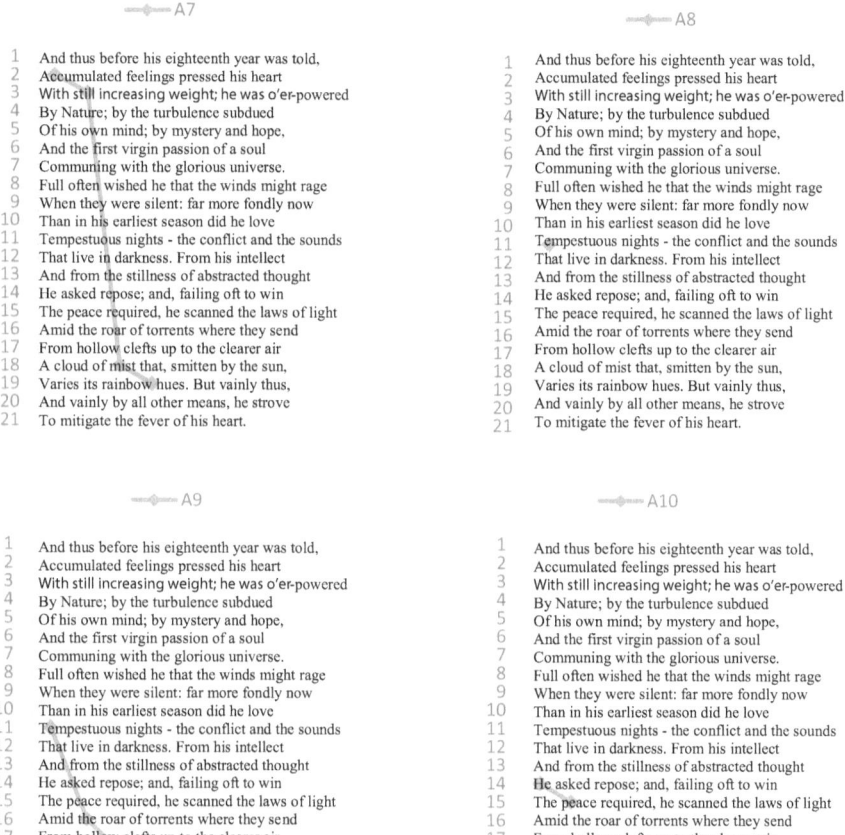

Figure 5.4. (*Cont.*)

There are parts in there with 'turbulence' and 'tempestuous' and 'darkness' and then it mentions 'peace' and 'sun' and 'rainbows' and the light is breaking through … He is talking about 'tempestuous' and 'turbulence' and 'the winds might rage', so it conjures up a scene of darker clouds, walking through more of a bleak landscape, but visually I see a darker landscape. Walking through the wind with your head down, battling against it to get through it, and then the sky becomes lighter and then, I don't know, life becomes brighter. (A5)

The changing pronouns used here, '*He* is talking about', '*I* see' and '*your* head down', suggest that a live relationship exists between the reader and the poem.

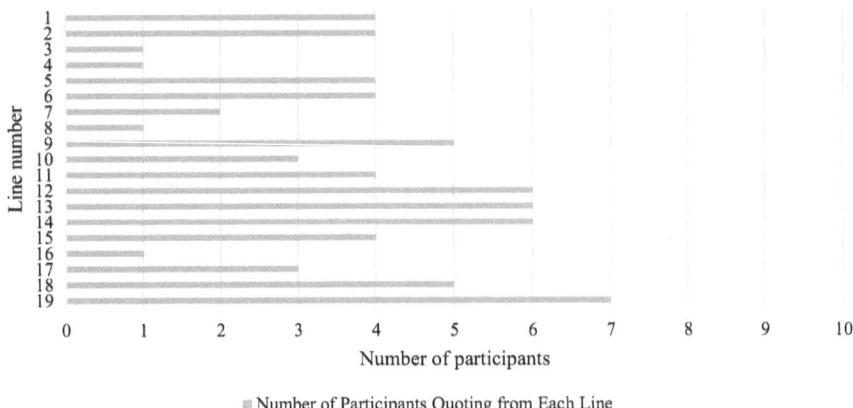

Figure 5.5. Graph showing the most frequently quoted lines of poetry extract two

The shift to the third-person singular 'your' indicates an indistinct but shared experience. The capacity to shift between pronouns has been related to a range of positive health outcomes in extensive research by James Pennebaker, therefore making these small grammatical shifts particularly noteworthy and perhaps indicative of more substantive mental shifts.[14] In the final sentence of this example – just as in the poem – the external physical landscape and the internal mental landscape are blended together and 'walking through *the wind*' becomes 'battling against *it* to get through *it*'. The shift from noun to pronoun indicates that this is not simply a battle against the weather, but rather some more indefinite 'it'. The move from '*the sky* gets brighter' to '*life* gets brighter' again provides evidence of the blending of external and internal, the physical and the emotional.

This process of analysis was repeated for the second extract of poetry. Figure 5.5 shows the number of participants who quoted from each line of the passage.

There was a particular focus – across much of the group – on lines 12, 13, 14 and 19, which were quoted in their entirety by the majority of participants. These findings are illustrated by the following graphic which indicates that rather than quoting single words or small fragments of the passage, as they had tended to do in their responses to the first extract of poetry, participants were now generally quoting much longer chunks of the text (Figure 5.6).

Each individual reading pattern was again plotted on a graph (Figure 5.7).

- Participant A1 demonstrates the same linear reading pattern as he did in response to the first extract of poetry.

> It would have grieved
> Your very soul to see her
>   my heart
>   my spirit clings
>   poor woman
>   her manner, and her look,
>   presence
>   goodness
> **A momentary trance**
>   I seem to muse
> By sorrow laid asleep
> **A human being destined to awake**
> **To human life, or something very near**
> **To human life, when he shall come again**
> For whom she suffered
>   evermore
> Her eyelids drooped, her eyes downwards were cast
> And, when she at her table gave me food,
> **She did not look at me.**

Figure 5.6. The most frequently quoted sections of poetry extract two

- The graphs for participants A2, A3 and A4 do jump vertically up and down the lines. Participant A3 appears to implicitly recognise the relationship between 'to see her' in line 2 and 'she did not look at me' in line 19. However, reading patterns for the second extract are generally more linear.
- Participant A5 used no direct quotations from the second extract of poetry, despite being among the most 'active' readers of the first passage of poetry. This was perhaps due to her sense of unease with the content of the second passage and desire quickly to skip past it, 'This makes me feel, I don't know, slightly depressed if I read too much more of it' (A5).
- Participants A7, A8, A9 and A10 again quoted less frequently – if at all – from the text. Despite the minimal use of quotations in the responses of participants A9 and A10, they still seemed to be tuning into the places within the poem which held particular significance for the group as a whole.

Distraction versus Emotional Focus

Participants appeared to become distracted quickly when responding to the news article and after making brief summary statements they tended to either

114 RETHINKING THERAPEUTIC READING

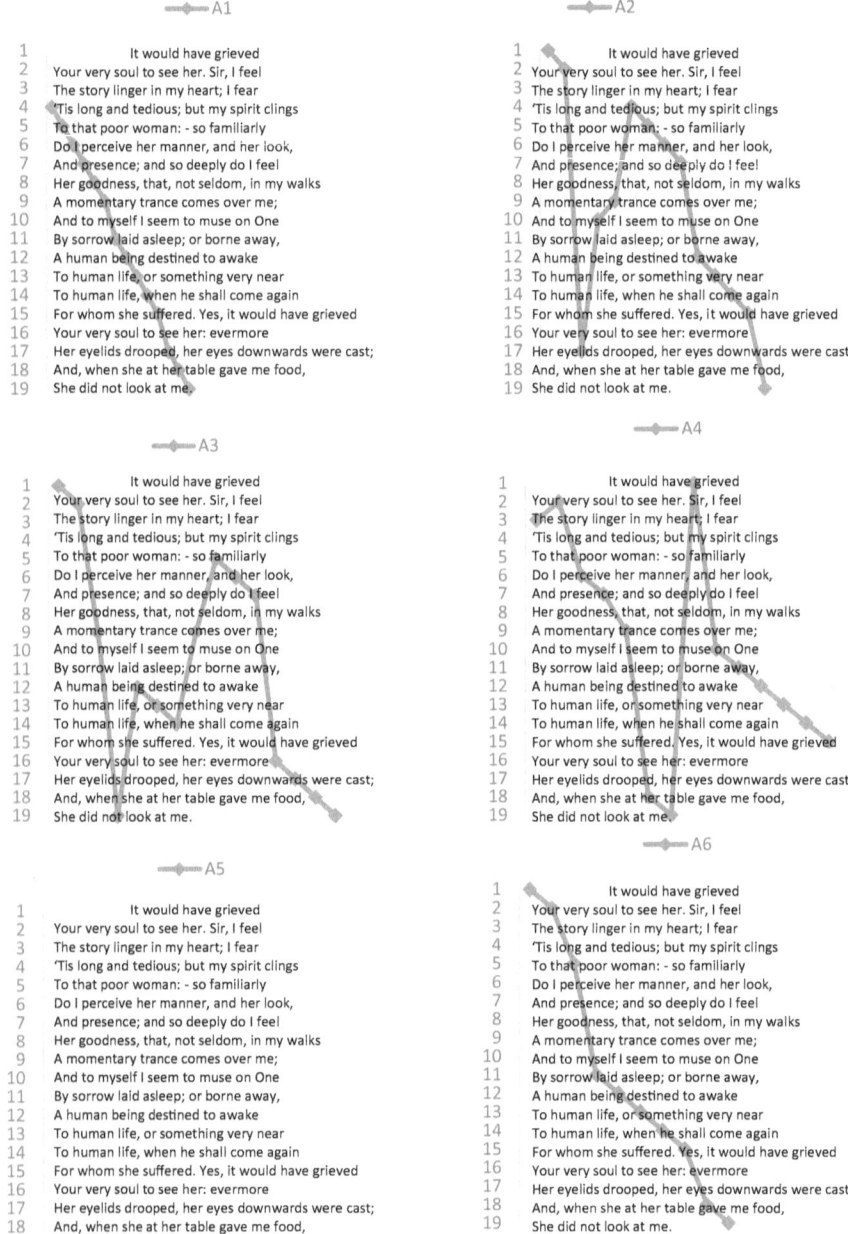

Figure 5.7. Graphs showing the order of direct quotations used in each participant response to poetry extract two

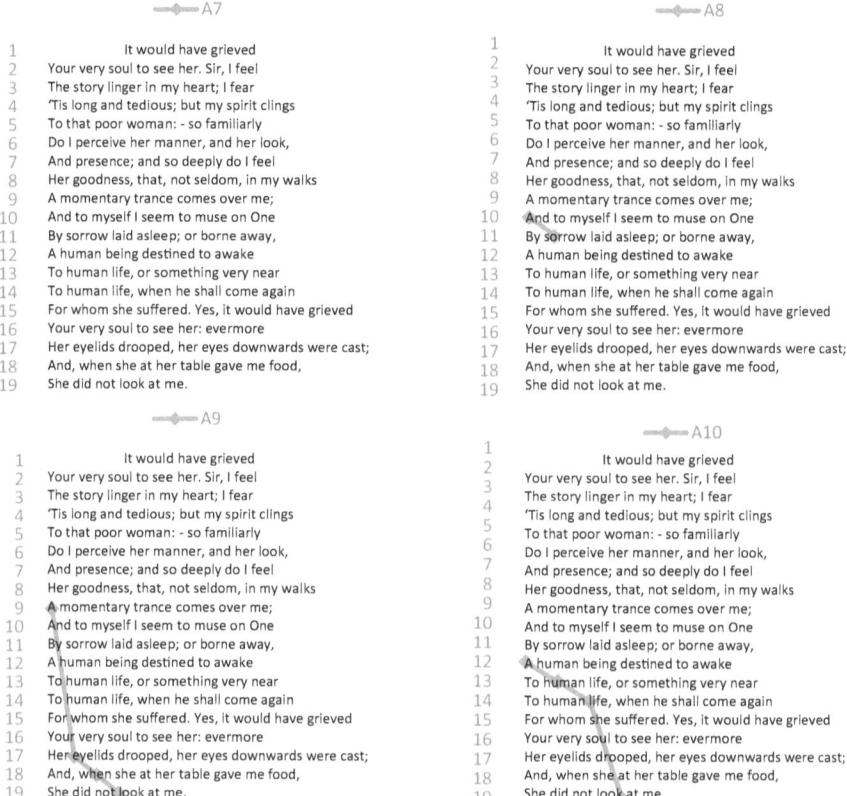

Figure 5.7. (*Cont.*)

abruptly stop talking or veer away from speaking about the text. In contrast, participants appeared to be able to maintain greater focus in their responses to the poetry, not only because of their increased use of direct quotations from the text, as previously discussed, but also because they often seemed to be able to establish a personal connection with the content of the poetry.

After reading the news article, participant A3 commented:

> It's hard to find it powerful and moving because it's very dry, very factual […] I don't know, I'm going to move on to the next bit. (A3)

While participant A5 stated:

> She was a ninety-two year old woman so obviously she had had a lifetime of um … well a lifetime of, well a long time of umm of upset, with

> losing a first husband and it doesn't say whether she got over that or whether … well it sounds like she's gone onto marry again umm but at ninety-two she's had quite a long, happy life, well I say happy life … she's had a long life. Obviously she has wanted to sell poppies all that time, umm and maybe it was just an age thing that saw her off or she'd given up, as people tend to do once they're around that age. (A5)

Participant A5 repeatedly pauses as she struggles to give even the most basic assessment of Olive Cooke's life. The initial 'obviously' is followed by a series of pauses and self-corrections as she drifts away from the actual emotional content of the article. Ignoring or perhaps having already forgotten the fact that Mrs Cooke committed suicide, she instead suggests that 'it was just an age thing that saw her off'. Participant A2's fragmented response to the news article also ignored much of its emotional, human content.

> As for the day of death or the date of the pronouncement of death, the 6th of May, because I'm interested in politics that's usually election time, we will have elections this year on the 5th of May, so that date stuck out for me. (A2)

He flits between different topics that have only a tenuous link to the text itself and becomes preoccupied with inconsequential details. His focus on the date of the pronouncement of Mrs Cooke's death is one good example of a participant missing the point of the article.

In contrast, A1's repetition of 'for me' in his response to the first extract of poetry appears to draw the focus towards the reader's own emotional experiences. In cases like this, 'me' is needed when 'I' does not go far enough in creating a personal connection.

> He says that up to the point of his eighteenth year there have been 'accumulated feelings', 'accumulated feelings' that only increase in weight. I would agree, although *for me* it was probably not at eighteen years, *for me* it was twenty or twenty-one. But the idea is still the same, the feelings are still the same. There is a point of transition when the teenager moves into adulthood. I agree that there will be a point when there will be a difference, the person will feel a difference. (A1)

Participant A1 was able to relate on a personal level, not only to the overall themes of the poetry extracts, but even to individual words within each passage:

> 'Trance' is a very strong word for me … It points to a very deep connection. I can definitely relate to this. (A1)

This ability to forge an emotional connection with the text appeared to help this participant to produce highly nuanced, focused and sensitive responses to the poetry:

> He is saying that the woman – the one 'by sorrow laid asleep' – either died from her sorrows or she died with her sorrows. Probably suffering if not on the outside, then on the inside. (A1)

In this example, participant A1 both imagines and differentiates between Margaret dying '*from* her sorrows' and '*with* her sorrows'. This is a thought which is borne out of Wordsworth's own literary language, in which subtle emotional changes are often held within the smallest of words. It is also a product of the close, emotional relationship that this reader has forged with the text and an example of what Terence Cave describes as poetry's capacity to create 'possibilities for imaginative leaps into the blue or into the minds of others'.[15]

In a final example taken from participant A10, pronouns are particularly good indicators of the emotional connection that I am suggesting is being built between the reader and poetry:

> It sounds like, and I know I'm a long way from my teenage years, but you're full of all those conflicting thoughts and emotions and growing pains and life choices and this is this person confused and overwhelmed by love and by all the thoughts going around in his head, trying to still everything, to slow it down and find out where he sits in all that, becoming a man. He asks for repose, looking for rest, looking for peace of mind, but there is so much going on when you're young, so much going around in our head that it seems to allude him. I think it's very powerful because it does demonstrate how difficult life can be. I particularly like, 'he asked repose' and 'failing oft to win the peace required' because that seems to be what we are all looking for, some peace and some time to reflect and be calm, and it's just not there. (A10)

In her mental mobility, this reader shifts between 'I', 'you' and 'he' as she describes her own experiences of the feelings contained within the poetry. The third-person singular 'you' acts here as a bridge between the reader as they are now, their past teenage self and the pedlar. 'You' offers a more impersonal way of speaking about the self than 'I', but halfway through this example there are further shifts from 'you' to 'our' and then 'him': 'There is so much going on when *you're* young, so much going around in *our* head that it seems to elude *him.*' The unusual use of 'our head' in the middle of this sentence seems to be a real point of psychological and emotional blending between the reader and the poem. It is followed by a shift to the first-person plural, 'what *we are all* looking for', further evidence of the emotional concordance between the reader and poetry.

Certainty versus Imaginative Uncertainty

Responses to the news article tended to mirror the matter-of-fact tone of the article itself. In several cases, a premature sense of certainty appeared to close down thinking. Participant A10 provides evidence of the over-certain approach that was typical of the news article responses:

> Obviously she was a dedicated woman who had dedicated herself to a cause and to helping others and as I said before had been moved to take action to be part of a charity generating income and interest in the British Legion. (A10)

By beginning with a word like 'obviously', the possibility for new thinking is immediately eliminated and A10's response becomes repetitive and stuck in summary mode.

In contrast, responses to the poetry passages appeared to be characterised by a greater sense of uncertainty. While a number of participants approached the poetry tentatively, unsure that they would be able to understand it by themselves or have anything to say about it, in most cases, this initial caution gave way to what I have termed 'imaginative uncertainty'. The poetry responses which adopted a tone of imaginative uncertainty contained more expansive, flexible thinking. Research has shown that a person's tolerance of uncertainty can influence their well-being, for 'when individuals are able to tolerate ambiguity and thus manage uncertainty, they may more effectively respond to negative life events'.[16] It was therefore important to begin to establish whether the poetry was encouraging participants to embrace uncertainty in ways that the news article was not, and furthermore, whether uncertainty was being put to use to fuel more imaginative and complex responses.

One example of a reader using their own uncertainty to fuel a more imaginative and complex response to the text can be found in participant A3's transcript:

> Well he repeats the word 'heart' at the beginning and at the end so I think that's quite important … The heart is interesting because it's something very bodily and very functional and yet, humans sort of consider it as an emotional centre of the human body as well, it's kind of like a soul or something like that. It says 'by the turbulence subdued of

his own mind' he seems to be subdued by turbulence … maybe because it's very powerful? Because his own mind is so powerful, he feels sort of vanquished? Vanquished by it? Something like that. (A3)

The pauses here lead onwards into second thoughts while the cluster of question marks indicate that this participant is actively working through a problem or place of uncertainty. The words 'sort of', 'kind of', 'something', 'yet' and 'seemed' all help to create openings for the tentative development of new ideas, while also mirroring the language of the poetry itself and Wordsworth's own sense of 'imaginative uncertainty'.

Three further examples, which all relate to the final line of the second extract of poetry, 'She did not look at me', provide evidence of how uncertainty within the poetry responses signal the places where participants are making breakthroughs in their understanding of the text:

> 'When she at her table gave me food, / She did not look at me.' So there is *some kind of* … she is inviting him in for food but she doesn't look up at him. There is *some kind of* distance there which *she can't, she can't* get past. (A3)

> In the final part of the poem he writes 'her eyelids drooped, her eyes downwards were cast; / And when she at her table gave me food, / She did not look at me.' Interpreting this, this woman is in a very bad way, *but if I understand correctly*, she has invited him in to eat and by not looking at him she is, *I don't know, perhaps* ashamed. (A9)

> 'She did not look at me.' That's just very sad. It's her own self-esteem, *as if* she's not worthy of being a person in her own right. (A10)

There is a particular bareness to the line 'she did not look at me' – already identified as the most frequently quoted part of the second extract of poetry – which calls to be met by greater imaginative engagement from the reader. There is nothing difficult in these words, yet they convey a small, silent, almost imperceptible, but also utterly recognisable moment between two people. For big things so often pass between people in small moments. It is often only later, in retrospect, that we can pinpoint the touch, the look, the words or perhaps – as here – the very absence of all those things that mark some larger internal shift. That this is something that *did not* happen means that it requires a greater degree of imagination to activate the line. In many of the responses it is as if participants are trying to flesh out some of this bareness and ambiguity as they tentatively speak. In contrast, there are no gaps to fill or ambiguities to struggle with in the news article. Less is demanded from readers and as such, less is produced by readers in their responses.

In only one case, the vocabulary of 'imaginative uncertainty' was used in relation to the news article. This was the only time that a participant was able to avoid summary mode and respond to the news article in a more contemplative manner:

> I think that what is particularly powerful is the um well I'm trying to think of the word … What I found really moving was that a ninety-two year old lady would take her own life. It seems that if it was suicide, it seems that a lady of this age would not be one for suicide really. From a larger perspective, what I find quite sad really is the bigger picture of how older people are quite disconnected from our society, because if she was suffering from depression then of course that could be partly due to the fact that we don't really take notice, or listen to or make use of the elderly very much and if we did she would possibly be alive today. (A9)

The words 'or', 'if', 'partly', 'seems', 'may' and 'possibly' create openings for deeper and more expansive thoughts. 'I'm trying to think of the word' is an indicator of a live, pre-articulate thinking process, where the sense that something 'particularly powerful' is contained within the article precedes the reader's ability to express it in words. This response moves out towards the 'larger perspective' or 'bigger picture' of what this specific story can tell us about our wider society. The long final sentence is not a conclusive summary, rather it is an attempt to get a bigger thought out of the small individual tragedy of this one woman's life. The participant is reading in a literary manner, making literature out of the news.

One way of beginning to quantify levels of imaginative engagement with the text was to isolate and compare the range of verbs used across the two sets of transcripts. Lexical richness, and in particular, verbal diversity has been recognised as an indicator of creativity, fluency and flexibility.[17] Research has also found a positive correlation between verbal fluency and well-being.[18] Because 'I' is used with almost equal frequency in the news article and poetry responses, in this analysis the range of verbs used in the first person were specifically selected for comparison. The following figures show the difference in the variety of verbs used within the two sets of transcripts. Positive and negative forms of each verb, in the present and past tenses are combined in the analysis here, for example, Do = Do / Do not / Don't / Did / Did not / Didn't (see Figures 5.8 and 5.9):

- Only 12 verbs were used in the first person across the entirety of the news article responses. In contrast, 39 verbs were used in the first person in the poetry responses.

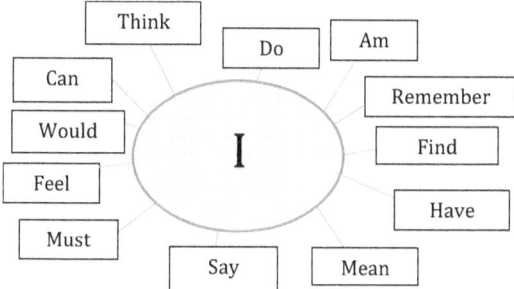

Figure 5.8. Verbs used in the first person in response to the news article

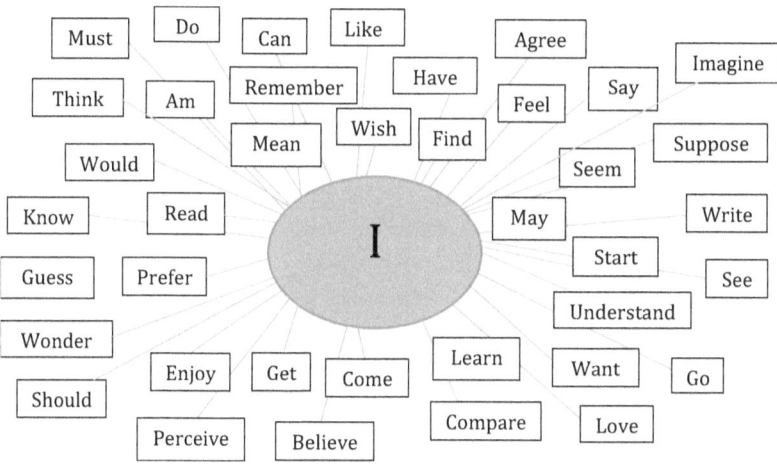

Figure 5.9. Verbs used in the first person in response to the poetry extracts

- The verb 'think' dominates both sets of transcripts. In 27 per cent of cases where 'I' is used in the news article responses it is followed by the verb 'think', while in the poetry responses the figure is 30 per cent. However, in 75 per cent of the instances where 'I' is used in the news article responses it is followed by one of four verbs ('think', 'do', 'am', 'remember') while in the poetry responses the top four most frequently used verbs ('think', 'do', 'am', 'like') make up 57 per cent of the cases where 'I' is used. Participants are using a smaller number of verbs more often in response to the news article and a larger range of verbs in response to the poetry.
- All 12 of the verbs that are used in the first person in the news article responses can also be found within the poetry responses, yet in the poetry

responses an additional 27 verbs are used that are not found within the news article responses.
- The verb 'imagine' does not occur in any form in response to the news article and nor do the verbs 'like', 'love', 'agree', 'enjoy', 'prefer', 'suppose', 'perceive', 'wonder', 'compare', 'guess', 'wish', 'start', 'learn', 'read' or 'write'. These are all verbs which would be useful for emotional or imaginative thinking and their absence from the news article responses and presence within the poetry responses supports the view that the poetry is encouraging more imaginative thinking from participants

Participant A6 provides what is perhaps the best example of 'imaginative uncertainty' in her response to the final lines of the second extract of poetry, using a range of verbs and constructions that are not found in responses to the news article:

> Her eyes are down, she doesn't look up, so again I've got the image of a downcast, lonely old woman. Ohh it's really sad. But she sounds really generous, 'when she at her table gave me food, / She did not look at me'. So she doesn't even make eye contact with people, she is that alone in her grief, but obviously she's giving people food, there is some interaction there. She is generous, she sounds like a good person. That line makes me think that oh she is feeding this guy who has come to her cottage, she gives food and she is generous but she does not even want to look up, she is so deep in her grief I think. Her grief has isolated her so much that she can't even look at anybody else, she's just, I don't know, functioning but asleep. I've got a picture of her, she is in her mid-sixties, she is wearing grey, living in this isolated cottage, her eyes are down. I imagine her being very very thin and dour looking. Other than her eyes looking down, there is no physical description of her, that is just my interpretation of her and of what grief has done to her or what this abandonment has done to her. It has left her half-alive, half-awake. (A6)

This reader has shifted the past tense of the poem into the present tense so that 'her eyes downwards were cast' has become 'her eyes are down' and 'she did not look at me' has become 'she doesn't look up'. These grammatical readjustments suggest that the reader is imaginatively re-living the lines in the present. Constructions like 'I've got the image', 'I've got a picture of her', 'my interpretation of her' and 'I imagine her' all provide evidence to support the argument that the literary texts are triggering this reader's capacity for producing mental imagery. These are all constructions that do not occur in responses to the news article. This suggests that the ability to visualise the subject of a text may be a particular feature of literary reading and it is this triggering of mental imagery which may lead readers towards more imaginative, exploratory and personal reflection.

Looking on the Bright Side versus Looking Back and Thinking Again

Readers often seemed to be attempting to extract a positive message from the news article. They appeared to be keen to move on from the tragic reality of Olive Cooke's life and displayed an insistent need to re-interpret her story and grasp at any form of consolation that they could find within it. Participant A2 reacted to the news article by saying:

> My overall thought on reading the article was one of sadness at the circumstances of the elderly woman, but also reflecting on her long years of service, seventy-six years to the Royal British Legion which was inspiring. (A2)

Participant A8 commented:

> It's a very sad case, erm, a ninety-two year old, I mean she probably didn't have an awful lot longer to live but it is very sad and if it has promoted or provoked some work being done by charities about how they actually raise their money, then perhaps some good has actually come out of it. That's kind of the main point of it for me, but she's certainly had a good life and she's made a big contribution and I think that her life should be celebrated. (A8)

Participant A5 displayed a particularly distinctive tendency to 'look on the bright side' when reading the news article:

> But yeah I think it's a moving story and a sad story, but then it's a nice story that she actually collected for the Poppy Appeal for all those years, for 76 years, and that's most of her life and she did that every year. So obviously the charities have, well the Poppy Appeal has benefited from her helping that. (A5)

In these examples 'but', 'perhaps' and 'if' appear to be being used to shift towards positivity and transform the traumatic content of the article into something more palatable.

After reading the two extracts of poetry, three participants (A4, A6 and A7) chose to look back and think again about the news article. In doing so, they were able to revise their initial overly certain, reductive or falsely optimistic responses to the text. In the cases where this happened, it was as if the poetry – and specifically the second extract of poetry relating to Margaret – was demanding that they turn back and reconsider the life and death of Olive Cooke. The contrast between participant A6's initial reaction to the news article, and her reassessment of it after having read the poetry is particularly striking evidence of this argument. After her first reading of the news article, participant A6 said:

> Yeah, it's a sad story isn't it? But you think, well she's ninety-two, so that's a long long life. (A6)

Having read the two extracts of poetry, she began to speak again about the news article:

> I think reading the two Wordsworth pieces and then thinking back to the original article about Mrs Cooke – Olive Cooke – you see I'm noticing the name now, after the last piece and Margaret I'm taking notice of the name now. Looking again, Mrs Cooke was identified by her grandson so she obviously had a family, so even though before I said that she was lonely after her husband died in the war. Maybe she remarried, but it doesn't say anything about that. She was depressed at being old. She strikes me as a lonely figure ... But I see some similarities in some of the themes between the news article and the second Wordsworth piece. (A6)

Having read the poetry she begins to reimagine the emotional reality of Olive Cooke's story from out of the impersonal flatness of the news format. While in the news article responses Mrs Olive Cooke is named only once by a single participant, in the places where, after having read the poetry, participants begin to reconsider the news article, she is named 13 times. As participant A6 herself notes, it seems to be the poetry which is causing participants to name and notice Mrs Cooke in a way that they had not previously done.

Participant A4 provides perhaps the best example of a reader reassessing their previously over-simplistic response to Olive Cooke's life by thinking about her again in parallel to Margaret. By blending together the lives of Olive Cooke and Margaret he is able to use the poetry as a trigger for more imaginative thinking about the news article:

> What person would somebody like Olive Cooke not have looked at? Whether it must have felt extremely awkward to see somebody who

was of the same age as her husband, or somebody for whatever reason, resembled her first husband. I would in those situations, be somebody who would cast my eye downwards for there would be some kind of emotional swing hitting me ... The idea of being asleep clearly and musing, 'To human life when he shall come again / For whom she suffered. Yes, it would have grieved / Your very soul to see her', um anyway, if you link that to Olive Cook, maybe again there is this link to the life lost, again her husband. It's not said, it would not really find a place in a newspaper article, but we do not know whether her father had been injured in the Great War, whether he died soon after, whether he was still alive when her own husband was killed in action, we do not know that. But either of these people, coming back, are haunting her in her sleep, so it could be possible, its mere speculation. But if you put these two texts side by side, nothing but that can be done. (A4)

The poetry holds within it a reminder of what the news article does not have a place for, namely the layered experiences of loss that have made up Mrs Cooke's life. Despite everything that 'we do not know' about Olive Cooke's life, this participant comes to know her imaginatively by blending her into the poetry. The suggestion here is that it is the poetry which causes this participant to think more deeply about Olive Cooke's psychological state in a way that the news article itself did not. Participants were not instructed to think back to the newspaper article after reading the poetry, it was an instinctive backwards move made by three of the ten participants. In the places where this 'thinking back' happens, participants appear to show some recognition of the limits of what can be contained within a news article and – it can be argued – it is the poetry which then serves to stretch those limits.

Conclusion

The results of this study give some indication that reading poetry can trigger greater levels of emotional focus, attentiveness and imagination than reading a news article and suggest that further research is required on how literary texts can be used to stimulate particular human capacities and qualities of thought.

Participants tended to speak for longer and in more detail about the poetry than the news article. They quoted extensively from the poetry itself within their responses yet very rarely made specific reference to words within the news article. When speaking about the poetry, participants continued to puzzle through some of the difficulties or ambiguities within the texts and in these cases appeared to use quotations from the poetry to make the lines live again for a second time as they actively thought a way through them. The familiarity of the news article format and the surface simplicity of its language and content meant that participants often appeared to be confident that they could understand the text without having to read it attentively. In contrast, the poetry extracts were unfamiliar to the participants, the language initially appeared more difficult and the lines that they were given to read only contained fragments of a much larger narrative. Consequently, it can be argued that the poetry demanded attentive, considered reading.

Participants tended to become distracted when speaking about the news article. They drifted away from the core content of the article, became preoccupied with inconsequential details within the text or cut their responses short as they ran out of interest in the article. In contrast, participants appeared to express feelings of emotional connection or recognition as they spoke about the poetry and as such demonstrated a greater degree of focus in their responses to the extracts from 'The Ruined Cottage'. Despite the emotive content of the news article, participant responses were generally unemotional. Participants did not make links between their own personal experiences and the news article in the way that they did in response to the poetry. This is evidenced by the frequent use of the verb 'feel', the noun 'feeling' and the pronouns 'me' and 'myself' in the poetry responses in comparison to their scarcity in the news article responses.

Participants seemed to have no difficulty understanding the content of the news article and their responses were therefore confident and often opinionated. In contrast, participants were less practised in reading poetry and were initially doubtful about their ability to understand the texts that they had been given. The levels of certainty displayed in the news article responses had a tendency to limit or cut short participant responses. The 'certainty' that participants displayed when speaking about the news article was largely replaced in the poetry responses with 'imaginative uncertainty'. It was this 'imaginative uncertainty' that appeared to become a tool for getting closer to the less explicit meaning held within the poetry. Participants seemed inquisitive and contemplative in their responses to the poetry in ways that they had not been when speaking about the news article. Participants frequently made connections as they were reading the poetry, often prior to quite knowing the meaning of the texts. Not knowing seemed to trigger more imaginative thinking than too easily knowing did.

Certain participants appeared to display a tendency to 'look on the bright side' in their responses to the news article. They attempted to extract some 'positive' message from Olive Cooke's life so as to distract from the tragedy of her suicide. Three participants reassessed the news article after reading the extracts of poetry. By speaking about the life of Olive Cooke in relation to the life of Margaret in 'The Ruined Cottage' these participants appeared to begin to think about the emotional content of the news article in a way that they had not previously been able to. Within these second thoughts about the news article the characteristics of 'imaginative uncertainty' and 'emotional focus' that had been triggered by the poetry can be identified and are being used to reflect back on the non-fiction account of Olive Cooke's life.

The four main characteristics identified in participant responses to the poetry extracts often overlap and interact with one another. For example, greater emotional focus can lead to an increase in active reading. Active reading can in turn lead to heightened emotional focus and encourages more exploratory, imaginative uncertainty. It is important to note that participants were not simply demonstrating these particular modes of thinking in isolation. When reading the poetry, participants started to demonstrate several, if not all, of the characteristics in combination. It is poetry's capacity to trigger this complex *blend* of responses which may have particularly important implications for its potential therapeutic usage.

Notes

1 Iain McGilchrist, *Against Criticism* (London: Faber & Faber, 1982), p. 35.
2 Felski, p. 191.
3 Terence Cave, *Thinking with Literature* (Oxford: Oxford University Press, 2016), p. 157, hereafter cited as 'Cave'.
4 David West, 'Practical Criticism: An Early Experiment in Reader Response', *Language and Literature* 26(2) (2017), pp. 88–98 (p. 88).
5 I. A. Richards, *Practical Criticism* (London: Kegan Paul, 1930), p. 309.
6 Ibid., p. 5.
7 Michael Paffard, *Inglorious Wordsworths* (London: Hodder & Stoughton, 1973), p. 251.
8 Ibid.
9 Ibid., p. 228.
10 David S. Miall, 'Empirical Approaches to Studying Literary Readers: The State of the Discipline', *Book History* 9 (2006), pp. 291–311.
    David S. Miall and Don Kuiken, 'The Form of Reading: Empirical Studies of Literariness', *Poetics* 25 (1998), pp. 327–41.
11 All 10 participants reported that they regularly read for pleasure – as would be expected from individuals responding to an advertisement about a study on reading. Half of the participants stated that they specifically read poetry for pleasure. Three participants had studied English Literature at degree level and had studied Wordsworth's poetry, although none had previously read the specific poetry being used in this task. Any future experiments could target recruitment at non-readers and advertise within the wider community. The approach chosen for this study was used to speed up the recruitment process, and every effort was taken to ensure that advertisements reached students and staff from across a wide variety of academic and non-academic departments within the university.

12 Participants were given two extracts of poetry to read so as to allow them to become more comfortable with this unfamiliar and difficult format and to counteract their inevitable familiarity with the news format. The news article was 268 words long and the combined length of the two poetry passages was 300 words. This minimal difference reduced any bias created by the fact that participants were given only one news article and two passages of poetry to read.
13 Virginia Braun and Victoria Clarke, 'Using Thematic Analysis in Psychology', *Qualitative Research in Psychology* 3(2) (2006), pp. 77–101 (p. 78).
14 Sherlock R. Campbell and James W. Pennebaker, 'The Secret Life of Pronouns: Flexibility in Writing style and Physical Health', *Psychological Science* 14(1) (2003), pp. 60–65.
15 Cave, p. 27.
16 Mark H. Freeston, 'Why Do People Worry?', *Personality and Individual Differences* 17(6) (1994), pp. 791–802 (pp. 791–92).
17 Paul J. Silvia, Roger E. Beaty and Emily C. Nusbaum, 'Verbal Fluency and Creativity: General and Specific Contributions of Broad Retrieval Ability (Gr) Factors to Divergent Thinking', *Intelligence* 41(5) (2013), pp. 328–40.
18 Nicola Gates et al., 'Psychological Well-being in Individuals with Mild Cognitive Impairment', *Clinical Interventions in Aging*,9 (2014), pp. 779–92 (p. 783).

Chapter 6

EXPERIMENT TWO: SLOWING DOWN AND TUNING IN

The aims of this second reading experiment were:

1. To continue and extend the work begun in Chapter 5 by exploring the impact that sustained private engagement with Wordsworth's poetry can have on readers.
2. To investigate the value of diary-assisted reading as a means of encouraging and capturing serious engagement with literature.
3. To develop a clearer understanding of the potentially therapeutic role that poetry can play in modern society.

Private reading is an elusive and complex process and in *The Limits of Critique*, Rita Felski sets out some of the incongruities and challenges that this study had to contend with:

> Readers are not autonomous, self-contained centres of meaning, but they are also not mere flotsam and jetsam tossed on the tides of social or linguistic forces that they are helpless to affect or comprehend. When they encounter texts, they do in all their commonality and quirkiness, they mediate and are in turn mediated, in both predictable and perplexing ways.[1]

It was important that this study was able to capture the reading process in action, rather than relying too heavily on retrospective analysis, in order to record some of the reciprocal shifts described by Felski and to avoid unhelpful overgeneralisations. It was equally vital that the design of this study created enough space to accommodate the specificity of individual responses, allowing 'both predictable and perplexing' ways of thinking to exist.

Study Design

A group of 18 adults were recruited via advertisements displayed across the University of Liverpool campus and in public libraries in Liverpool and

London. All participants were required to be at least 18 years of age and fluent in English. Participants were aged between 19 and 71 and consisted of 11 females and 7 males.

Recruits were invited to complete a short questionnaire about themselves and their reading habits and were then divided into three groups. Age, gender, profession, education and reading habits were taken into account during the allocation process and every effort was made to create balanced groups so as to reduce the effects of individual differences on the results of the study (see Table 6.1).

The eight participants allocated to group one were given a blank notebook and asked to spend 30 minutes per day for 14 consecutive days writing about anything that they felt to be important or interesting to them. This group were not asked to read any poetry.

A further eight participants in group two were given a 'poetry diary' containing a copy of Wordsworth's poem 'The Ruined Cottage'. The 1,009-line poem had been split into 14 sections of approximately seventy lines each. Participants were asked to spend 30 minutes per day, for 14 consecutive days, reading a section of the poem and writing down anything that seemed important or interesting to them about the text.

The remaining two participants were asked to complete both tasks. They were given the poetry exercise to complete first because it was judged to demand greater levels of concentration and motivation due to the unfamiliar reading material. One month later they were given the second diary task to carry out.

Two weeks after the completion of their diaries, participants were invited to attend individual semi-structured interviews which typically lasted between one and two hours. During interviews, extracts of the diaries that participants had written, and/or passages of the poetry that they had studied, were read back to them, triggering further discussion.[2]

It is important to remember that it is a specifically Wordsworthian conception of 'therapy' that is being considered here; an oblique process that acts almost by stealth to meet needs that may not even be known consciously to exist. Wordsworth described this process in Book 4 of *The Prelude*, in his autobiographical account of returning home for the summer holidays after a difficult first year at Cambridge:

> While I walked, a comfort seemed to touch
> A heart that had not been disconsolate:
> Strength came where weakness was not known to be,
> At least not felt; and restoration came
> Like an intruder knocking at the door
> Of unacknowledged weariness.[3]

Table 6.1. Experiment two: Sample information

Participant Number/Case Study Pseudonym	M/F	Age	Profession	Do You Read for Pleasure?	Do You Read Poetry?	Have You Studied English Literature?	Have You Read Wordsworth's Poetry?
Group 1: Control Task							
B1 'Nathaniel'	M	46	ESOL Teacher	Yes	Yes	Masters	Yes
B2 'Rachel'	F	31	Charity Worker	Yes	Yes	Masters	Yes
B3	F	19	Undergraduate Student	Yes	Rarely	A-Level	No
B4	F	45	Marketing Manager	Yes	Rarely	A-Level	Small Amount
B5 'Juliet'	F	53	University Administrator	Yes	Rarely	O-Level	Yes
B6	M	27	Personal Trainer	Yes	No	GCSE	No
B7 'Lucas'	M	31	PhD Student	Yes	No	GCSE	No
B8	F	21	Undergraduate Student	Yes	Rarely	GCSE	No
Group 2: Poetry Task							
B9	M	71	Retired Adult Education Teacher	Yes	Yes	O-Level	No
B10	F	43	Housewife	Yes	Occasionally	A-Level	No
B11 'Samantha'	F	43	Secondary School Head Teacher	Yes	Rarely	Masters	Yes
B12	F	41	Charity Manager	Yes	Yes	A-Level	No
B13	M	25	PhD Student	Yes	Occasionally	GCSE	No
B14 'Michael'	M	26	Waiter	Yes	Very Rarely	GCSE	No
B15	F	27	Waitress	Yes	Yes	Masters	Yes
B16	F	23	Unemployed	Yes	Yes	Masters	Yes
Group 3: Both Tasks							
B17 'Peter'	M	65	Artist	Yes	Yes	O-Level	A Small Amount
B18 'Mary'	F	61	Primary School Teacher	Yes	Occasionally	O-Level	A Small Amount

With this idea of implicit therapy in mind, the design of this study largely avoided quantitative measures. It did not screen participants on the basis of their well-being or mental health and it did not use an established therapeutic programme or task – such as a series of Cognitive Behavioural Therapy (CBT) self-help exercises – as a comparator to the reading intervention. These were conscious choices intended to create space for the particularities of each individual participant's response to develop without any sense of explicit therapy being introduced.

The tasks that participants were asked to complete were intentionally challenging. Individuals were required to spend a substantial amount of time each day for a period of two weeks on their diaries. This strict framework was designed to help participants to establish a routine and to force them to slow down and engage in a period of daily focused reflection. In the case of those completing the poetry diary, the intention was for readers to slow their pace and thus align themselves with the slow pace of the poetry itself. It was important that the tasks did not resemble academic exercises, in order that all participants, regardless of their previous educational experience, would find themselves in a position of testing uncertainty, and thus be more likely to avoid habitual modes of thinking and instead engage in personal reflection.

Diary-writing is not an explicitly therapeutic activity, although diary-assisted counselling is an established therapeutic practice and in a number of studies, daily, reflective writing has been shown to improve mood and well-being. James Pennebaker, for example, has carried out a considerable amount of research which has shown that 'writing about emotional upheavals can affect people's psychological and physical health'. In one study in particular, a group of students were asked to spend 15–30 minutes per day for between three and five days writing about either emotional or superficial topics. Pennebaker found that those who wrote about emotional subjects subsequently reported a reduction in physician visits, improved medical markers of health and higher grades.[4]

It was hoped that the diaries completed during this study would help to illuminate the live processes of reading and demonstrate how engagement with a literary text over time may trigger shifts in thinking. The aim was to capture reading in action and thus avoid – as far as possible – reductive summary mode. During participant interviews the diaries were used to bring the reading process back to life in the minds of participants, to encourage greater specificity of thought and to avoid generalisation. This diary-assisted interview process was informed by the successful use of video-assisted interviews by researchers at the Centre for Research into Reading, Literature and Society (CRILS). By video recording shared reading sessions and then replaying clips of salient moments to those involved during interviews, researchers at CRILS have been able to re-establish the power of the shared reading experience in the interview room and enable participants to revisit and re-evaluate their own first responses.[5]

The analytical method used in this study is rooted in techniques of literary analysis. All diaries, transcripts and questionnaire responses were treated – as far as possible – as literary texts and subjected to the kind of close reading that has been demonstrated throughout Part I of this book. The analytical method was also informed by the interdisciplinary work of CRILS which has used a combination of literary, linguistic and psychological analysis to assess the impact of shared reading interventions.[6]

It was important to be able to identify themes within the data without losing a sense of each participant's individuality. Initially, all data was read and coded to allow connections within as well as between individual diaries to begin to be identified. Categories and themes were then formed, which were reviewed and refined by the research team at CRILS. In order to cross-check themes and help to mitigate against researcher bias the full texts of six randomly selected participant diaries were given to four postgraduates from the University of Liverpool's Institute of Psychology, Health and Society trained in qualitative analysis. This group were asked to read through and code the data that they had been given. Their annotations of each diary were tabulated and categorised into themes which were then verified by each cross-checker during a follow-up meeting. Throughout this chapter precedence has been given to themes which were identified and corroborated not only by colleagues and expert academics, but also by the participants themselves during their individual interviews or in their post-task questionnaires.

A series of case studies from each of the three groups are presented here in order to demonstrate some of the range, variety and nuance of individual responses to the reading and writing tasks while also illustrating some of the broader themes which connect individual participants together. These case studies indicate the value of the diary-assisted reading methodology as a means of generating data for the study of the complex subtleties of private reading. While these brief case studies offer only a snapshot of the rich data compiled over the course of this study, they begin to show some of the implicit therapeutic properties of literature and illustrate some of the ways in which literary texts can offer readers a space outside of the everyday and enable them to cast off default patterns of thought and to get quickly into the thick of their inner, emotional lives.

Case studies are used here as a means of illuminating the specific, local detail of each individual participant's response. If, as Terence Cave argues, 'literature always operates via the particular',[7] this approach – focusing on the particularities of each individual – is an attempt to respect the literary material that the study centres around as well as the literary modes of thought that it sought to encourage. The case studies presented here belong to participants of different genders, ages, professions and educational backgrounds. For example, 'Samantha' is a 43-year-old head teacher of a large secondary school. She is an experienced English teacher and holds a master's degree in English literature. Twenty-six-year-old 'Michael' left school at 16 after completing his GCSE's and is currently working as a waiter. These two case studies work to ally the misconception that a literary-based therapeutic task might only be suitable for those with some type of literary background or training. As will be explored in Samantha's case study, her extensive literary education had to be cast off in some respects in order for her to engage with the task on a more personal, reflective level. All names and identifying details have been changed in the case studies that follow.

Control Task

Case Study One: Daily Routine

Nathaniel teaches English at a further education college in Merseyside. He is 43 years old and is currently completing a master's degree in English language. He is married with two children and his diary entries focused primarily on details of his daily life at work and with his family. The tone of Nathaniel's diary was casual and chatty, as these selected examples demonstrate:

> Well today was a normal Tuesday spent with my daughter [...] we went strawberry picking which was fun. It's nice to go when nobody's there. Then home and dinner. (Day One)
>
> End of the first week in the job. I've been thinking about it and think it was a bit of a lukewarm start and I don't know why. I felt a bit disconnected for the first few days. (Day Nine)
>
> Summer has arrived! Had a great trip to the common. We first climbed the little summit there with a view you can never tire of. Then we found a swing on a tree and had a real 'Famous Five' moment of pure summer innocence. (Day Twelve)
>
> Last Tuesday was so hot I took off after work to go for a swim in the lake. It was wonderful and not too cold at all! It proved to me that I can just go for an evening and still get back in time for bed at a reasonable hour. I'd wanted to camp but the tent was broken so I headed home. Can't wait until I can get back there again. (Day Thirteen)

Nathaniel's approach to the task was characteristic of participants in the control group, the majority of whom wrote in each entry about what had been happening to them that day. This set of diaries could be perceived to lack breadth or depth. After analysing a random selection of three diaries from the control group, the independent cross-checkers commented that they were typically 'not as emotionally deep, less reflective and contain a less diverse set of topics'. The control diaries were categorised as being 'event-driven' and one cross-checker remarked that 'Participants struggle to think so much about what is important to them' and that 'Participants wrote about things that were happening in their life currently, they did not delve into past memories.'

While Nathaniel's diary did focus entirely on the present, during his interview he began to discuss a particularly important period from his past. When asked whether he had ever kept a diary before, he began to speak about a six-month period, twenty-five years previously, that he had spent travelling through Alaska. He described in detail a geographical research trip that he had been involved in as a young student and discussed the meticulous diaries he had kept during his travels. The trip culminated in Nathaniel staying with an American family in a tiny village in the middle of the Alaskan wilderness. Being in Alaska had been a transformative experience for him, and during the interview he talked at length about what he had experienced there, becoming more and more expressive:

> That Alaskan experience was a massive life-changing thing. It was a massive smack in the face really. I'd done walking in the UK, in the Lake District and Wales, but when I went to Alaska, it was so extreme, it was so big and so wild and so dangerous. It was a massive learning curve. When I came back and went to the Alps a year later, I remember thinking it was so small. I'm very aware that there was a massive spiritual element to the experience as well. The nature contact was so so strong as if it was pushing onto you. It was almost as if – for me anyway – it was imposing, it was a threat, nature was so strong and all the senses were just impacting on you all the time. It was just so dramatic and so beautiful and so wild and so empty. It was such a life-changing experience, it was the big moment of my life, so I don't always want to talk about it. I think about it quite a lot though because it was such a big thing really. (Interview)

It was during the interview stage, in conversation with a stranger, that Nathaniel began to open up about this 'big moment of my life' and to discuss the broader implications of his past experiences in a way that he had not done at all within his diary. In writing Nathaniel had focused entirely on details of his daily life; however, during the interview he started to reveal and to revel in stories from his past that were particularly important to him. The interview appeared to create the space for him to consider the wider span of his life in a way that the diary had not. After the interview, when looking back at the content of Nathaniel's diary, it was possible to recognise how the outlook nurtured during his youth in the wilderness of Alaska has been translated into his daily life and family routines, and to notice more clearly all the places in his diary that Nathaniel had demonstrates both his appreciation of nature and his desire to be 'in' nature.

Case Study Two: Non-Disclosure

Rachel is 31 years old and currently works for a charitable organisation in Merseyside. She completed her diary over a period of two weeks, yet was not willing to submit it for analysis. Instead, she agreed to be interviewed about her experience of doing the task. During her interview she explained why she had not wanted her diary to be read:

> I did stick to the instructions rigidly, and I did want to give it time – two weeks wasn't it? – to see if you know, anything shifted or became valuable. Oh, and that's right, I'd been asked to do a similar thing before, I think about eight or nine years ago, I went to a counsellor for a little while and she did sort of CBT stuff and I dunno, talking therapies, chatting, she had given me something similar to do. It was first thing in the morning, before you do anything else, you give yourself half an hour and you just write whatever's in your head, and then you just tear it up and throw it away, you don't keep it or look back at it. It's just kind of like a flushing out exercise. I remember thinking about that a little bit as I was doing this. So, I did stick with it, but to be honest I found it terribly unhelpful and I can't really pinpoint why. There was this awareness in me of having to write about something important, which I did give a lot of thought to. I felt like I was going backwards, almost through a mental filing cabinet to find stuff and to be honest it felt like I was making it up. It felt like I was telling a story and through the writing it felt like it was out of date and untruthful. I remember writing actually, I have kept it, even though I've said you can't have it. It's not just me being terribly private, it didn't feel truthful and it didn't feel like I was doing anything worthwhile ... I did try to write about stuff that I enjoy, because that's important – where I find joy and pleasure – but it just felt a bit silly, maybe a bit forced ... wrong is I guess the best word I can come up with, and almost like it felt forcibly revealing, not of any fact that I'm ashamed of, just that I wouldn't want to show myself doing something that didn't

feel truthful and didn't really give me anything. I wouldn't want to give that to someone. Invasive isn't the right word, but I think I would feel exposed in some way. (Interview)

Rachel had felt pressurised by the requirement to write about something 'important' and was concerned that what she had chosen to write about seemed forced or untruthful. Unlike her previous experience of 'therapeutic writing' as part of a programme of CBT, where writing was used to 'flush out' mental clutter and nothing she wrote was ever reread or kept, this diary felt worryingly permanent. She did not withhold her diary because it was too revealing but because she felt that it revealed an untruthful version of herself.

Case Study Three: Avoiding the Past

Juliet is a 53-year-old university administrator. She lives with her husband and has a large extended family, being one of six siblings. Her diary appeared to be the most reflective of the control group. Although she too tended to focus in her writing on her daily routines and work habits, she also wrote extensively about her family:

> My mum was widowed young and my brother's wife died of cancer at thirty-nine. I wonder how I would cope – someone just not being there anymore. I've been married for more than half my lifetime and I just couldn't think what life would be like on my own. The loss of security / doing things together / doing things apart but there at the end of the day at home. I'd like to think that I could be strong – but you just don't know. My brother had some sort of crisis and is now an alcoholic, life can be very hard and the repercussions tough. (Day Four)

At several points in her diary and during her interview Juliet expressed a dislike for her own tendency to want to look back and think about the past:

> As I get older I seem to look back more and think about choices made as a young person. I mustn't allow myself to wallow in the past – cannot change the past/turn the clock back. (Day Eleven)

In her writing she seems to be both drawn to the past and fearful of the dangers of regret. At interview, she described how she had refrained from rereading any of her diary entries for the same reason that she had tried to stop herself from looking back over her own past:

> There could be two consecutive days where I've written exactly the same thing because I didn't ever go back, because I don't really like going back on things, so I just left it alone. I try not to go back but sometimes it does happen. Yes, I try not to go back. You've made a decision or something's gone wrong years ago. You just have to get on. You can't unpick something that has happened years ago … like to my brother five years ago, you can't say … you have to just move on. (Interview)

Her conscious mind attempts to stop herself from looking back and trying to amend the past in some way, and this part of her is perhaps most dominant during the interview stage. In the pause after 'you can't say' she abruptly stops herself from articulating what it is exactly that it is now too late to say to a brother who fell into alcoholism after the death of his wife. But within the diary itself, where her unconscious mind seems to surface, she finds that she cannot stop herself from looking back into the past, she cannot simply, 'leave it alone', 'get on' or 'move on'.

On day twelve there is no linear progression from the past to the present to the future; instead, fragments of each are mixed together, creating a more accurate representation of what thinking and feeling across time is really like:

> I rang my niece earlier to wish her luck for her new start in London on Sunday. I saw her when she was just twenty-four hours old – the first niece / nephew in my family – she is sensible and I hope she settles in soon and makes friends. She means a lot to me. I found some old pictures of her and emailed these around the family. I shall be thinking of her a lot over the next few weeks as the new intake starts at the University. I used to find this a difficult time of year, thinking back to when I started and how it could have been different, but I don't feel like this now. It has happened and I have to make the most of the situation I'm in now. (Day Twelve)

There are a whole series of shifts in this passage: she begins by looking to the future, then flips backwards in the second sentence to the birth of her niece, before switching to the present and then moving into her own past experiences and difficult memories of starting university. Here the past does not belong to a separate mind compartment that can be cut off from the present or the future. Instead, Juliet appears to be able to look backwards here without regret and without needing to amend the past.

The interview stage of this task proved to be particularly important for several participants in the control group, including Juliet. In conversation she was able to demonstrate greater levels of self-awareness and to clarify and build upon what it was that she had gained from the writing exercise:

> I hadn't realised how much I think about and worry about my family. Because we have had some problems. I'm one of six and my youngest brother has had some problems, and it's been going on for years and he seems to be … it's … well sometimes it's a bit of a pain to just have to think about them all, but actually you have to support them and you expect that from them if you needed it. So yeah, I didn't realise because I don't really think that I am that close to the members of my family, but maybe I am more so than I thought. You know I expect more from them and I want them to expect that back from me because it's family. It did hit home a bit more than I had realised. I think it crystallised my ideas about my family and how important they are. (Interview)

Juliet's deeply held concern for her family keeps surfacing as she writes, revealing something about her own core feelings that she had not previously – or consciously – known to be true. Writing a diary helped her to see herself with greater clarity:

> It was good for me to do because it brought some things into focus. It was good at the end of the day to think about some things that had happened and to get some separation from life. Actually I've missed it. I've sort of missed having to sit down and separate myself from what's going on. (Interview)

When asked whether the interview stage had added anything to her experience of writing the diary, Juliet responded: 'It helped me to explain it, to say it out loud. It is one thing to write, but another to actually say it.' It was by speaking that she was able to cash in on the discoveries she had made while writing.

Case Study Four: Confession

Lucas is a 31-year-old PhD student who wrote a highly confessional diary in which he described at great length his struggles with depression. He had volunteered to participate in the study with the explicit hope that writing a diary would be therapeutic for him in some way. He writes about putting his PhD studies on hold and taking a job at a postal sorting office and this punishing workplace provides the backdrop for much of the diary:

> The sorting job is exactly the kind I was looking for. It is menial, low-skilled, at nights, with absurdly long commuting. This serves as a punishment for my errors. I was however expecting it to be harder, more exhausting, stressful, fast-paced, challenging. (Day Two)

Lucas is almost compulsively confessional in his diary, as if lacking any instinct for self-preservation. On day thirteen he shows his eagerness to communicate to somebody just what he was going through and to find some companionship through confession:

> Yesterday a man at work admitted to having had clinical depression a few years ago, so I looked for an opportunity to admit my problems to him. However, the guy cringed and appeared uninterested when I told him. (Day Thirteen)

At first, Lucas seems to be using the diary to collect together evidence to support his own negative beliefs about himself and as he is writing there is nothing to stop him from doing this. When asked what he had learned from writing the diary, he responded simply, 'That I am a really uninteresting person.' Yet, during his interview, he spoke about how the diary had helped him:

> I think writing can definitely help to avoid overthinking. You have to turn what could have been murky as a thought, into a phrase. You have to structure the problem. It limits digressions and deflections, and even when they appear, it's easier to look back at the text and return to the main line of thought. This actually reminds me of the method of psychodynamic psychotherapy that I took in the past. At first I got annoyed when I was saying a lot about my problems but finding the therapist was silent, not commenting at all or maybe only saying a few words after minutes of silence. Later I realised that just expressing my problem made me think about it in a different way, I was trying to guess what the other person might be thinking. As a result, I often find new ideas about my problems after a period of silence. Even if I'm writing for myself, I am thinking what a reader might think, so I am thinking in a different way. (Interview)

The writing process appears to have helped Lucas to limit his tendency for rumination. Writing helped to clarify his thoughts, turning 'murky' ideas into distinct phrases, shaping and structuring his thinking. The pace of writing forced his mind to slow down and focus on one single 'main line of narrative', simplifying his overcomplicated thought-processes and cutting back on 'digressions and deflections'. He connects the act of writing on the blank pages of the diary with speaking into the silence of the therapy room. In both cases there is somebody listening to and observing him from behind the silence, either the therapist or a real or imagined reader. It is the silence – or in the case of the diary, the blank page – which allows Lucas to get outside of his own mind.

The interview stage was particularly significant for Lucas because rather than simply imagining 'what a reader might think', he was faced with his actual reader and had to listen to them reading his own words back to him (In all subsequent examples the interviewer is indicated by italics):

Ok, I'm going to read the bit you mentioned earlier where you were at work and were trying to stop yourself from crying in front of everybody.

Oh that was really a hard moment. Oh this was actually quite a dramatic thing. This was well, the tip of the iceberg of my feelings.

'She opened the truck bay gate and went for her break without setting the platform. I was busy talking with a mate and my trolley fell into the gap. She was called back and reluctantly finished the setting while I dragged my trolley and hid far from her, blushing with shame. I carried on working with eyes full of tears, I struggled not to actually start crying. I decided I could not hide in the toilet, I had to do the work. I kept making errors and I was mortified that apparently I am too stupid to even push a trolley. For the rest of the shift I was on the verge of crying. A mate asked if I was ok and later even the girl asked if I am managing. I started to tell her that it had not been a good day, but then we were separated. What is the actual difference between managing and not? I said that I am managing, but it is just that I could not say that I am not managing.'

Oh yes, this was actually quite an emotionally packed moment ... Yeah, it was ... I was helpless.

How did it feel hearing me read your diary?

It felt better actually ... Yes, actually I am quite surprised about how much we have really processed it. I'm really glad, I'm really happy that this has happened. I didn't expect it to look like this. It has helped me to look at the inside, a bit at least, from the outside, so yes definitely it was useful. It did enhance my view of myself. So yes, I think it was really helpful. (Interview)

Lucas is beginning to see how he might separate the version of his self that is inside the diary from the self that is on the outside reading the diary, and to find some room to manoeuvre in the space between these two selves. His case study demonstrates how writing can perhaps lead to the development of more objective and less punishing attitudes by creating a way for somebody to look in at themselves from an external perspective, particularly when combined with a secondary process of being read.

The combination of diary and interview here resembles certain 'two-chair' therapeutic interventions, in which patients physically move between two chairs and as they do so take on different mental positions. Sitting in one position they have the chance to speak to a person or a part of their own self that they imagine to be sitting in the chair opposite; then by moving to sit in that opposite chair they can embody the person or part of themselves that they have been addressing and begin to view themselves from that alternative perspective.[8]

Poetry Task

Case Study Five: Triggering Memories

Peter is a 65-year-old artist currently living in London. From the first day of the task, the poem reminded Peter of his own childhood growing up in a rural landscape not dissimilar to the Lake District setting of the poem. In his diary Peter wrote about the broader span of his life, but also within that span, he focused with great specificity on particular experiences, usually from his childhood. For example, on day six, in response to a section of the poem which begins: 'Sometime his religion seemed to me / Self-taught, as of a dreamer in the woods' (ll. 409–10) he wrote:

> This first bit brings back memories of my Baptist chapel upbringing and one Sunday evening when I was sitting on a big rock overlooking the common, when an older couple from the church saw me and said, why hadn't I gone to church and I said from the top of my rock, 'This is my Church.' (Day Six)

The poem appeared to trigger a broad range of memories in many of the participants in this group. This was corroborated by the independent cross-checking team who noted that 'The poem acts as a trigger for memories', 'The poetry stimulated memories', 'Diaries contain very detailed and emotive memories' and 'Participants reflect on the poetry in relation to their own lives, especially with a focus on memory.' This is in direct contrast to the diaries written by the control group, which concentrated overwhelmingly on the daily routines and habitual preoccupations of each participant.

Peter felt a strong sense of correspondence between the character of the pedlar and his own former best friend. On day one he wrote:

> I remembered John, my great school friend who popped into my mind half way through the reading. It really was my 'best delight to be his chosen comrade'. His friendship fed my soul and was as cool as refreshing water. I had never experienced that feeling with a man before, or since, and in a way, I'm pleased about that as it makes it even more special. It ended badly of course, but the early times were wonderful. (Day One)

In the post-task questionnaire Peter described his own surprise at how vividly memories of this formative relationship had been recalled by the poem: 'I had a real surprise when I found myself writing about John.'

Peter immediately felt that Wordsworth was addressing him directly and articulating feelings that he himself had not always been able to articulate. Yet he was also concerned that he was somehow manipulating or 'using' the text by making his responses all about him:

> This seems to be talking directly to me, the poet seems to have been there when I grew up, hiding behind a rock, observing my every movement and thought. He has given voice to my confused suspicions and vague imaginings, but I also feel guilty and self-centred for feeling like this. The poet makes me feel like he is my ally, someone like John. (Day Two)

> The words constantly make me think of myself and my past. They ring so true, it's like I've been there. The poet seems to be talking about himself and his childhood and what made him a poet which beautifully illustrates to me the feelings that I have no words for. This poem makes me feel less alone. I feel this poem is like a true friend. (Day Three)

The poem appeared to act as a companion in thinking for Peter, guiding him back into his past and leading him through his own parallel memories into spaces of shared experience. Like a friend or ally, the poem is a supportive presence, it seems to already know him and to share his own viewpoint. But also, like a friend, the poem provides Peter with something that he would be incapable of providing for himself, in this case, a rich and complex language for articulating feelings that he has 'no words for'.

On day eleven, Peter read a section of the poem in which the pedlar recounts his final meeting with Margaret:

>   And when,
> In bleak December, I retraced this way,

> She told me that her little babe was dead,
> And she was left alone. She now, released
> From her maternal cares, had taken up
> The employment common through these wilds, and gained,
> By spinning hemp, a pittance for herself;
> And for this end had hired a neighbour's boy
> To give her needful help. That very time
> Most willingly she put her work aside,
> And walked with me along the miry road,
> Heedless how far; and, in such piteous sort
> That any heart had ached to hear her, begged
> That, wheresoe'er I went, I still would ask
> For him whom she had lost. We parted then –
> Our final parting; for from that time forth
> Did many seasons pass ere I returned
> Into this tract again. (ll. 893–910)

There was a distinct shift in the tone of Peter's diary in the entry that followed. This is the only occasion where he wrote about his current, pressing concerns, rather than memories of the past:

> I missed yesterday, my wife was ill and I couldn't concentrate, for a few short hours I felt some pangs of sadness and worry that my imagination magnified into a monster which was too close to the poem, she was suffering and I was helpless. There followed a night of fitful sleep and worry about my son and my inadequacies as a father, followed by a morning of relief and business as usual, and back to the poem. It was like my life was giving me a little snippet of insight into the poem, a warning of what could happen to anyone at any time. The Wanderer comes in, is sad, and then goes again, then he comes back, sympathises, and then goes again. Each time he comes, it gets worse, he agonises and he goes again, back to his life of roaming. He cannot get drawn too deeply in. He feels helpless and he has to get away. My life is intruding into this poem, my son's birthday, my feelings about him, my wife's worries about him, the Wanderer, Margaret and her absent husband, the dead baby all seem part of the same poem – poetry and reality mixed up. (Day Eleven)

Peter's present appears to infiltrate his reading of the text and as it does so he begins to speak about the poem in the present tense: 'He cannot get drawn too deeply in. He feels helpless and he has to get away.' In these places it becomes less clear whether he is speaking about the pedlar or about himself or both.

The poem no longer appears to be distinctly separate from the reader. In the final sentence of this diary entry the syntax breaks down into a 'mixed-up' list of people and feelings that belong partly to the external life of the reader and partly to the internal world of the poem, and which are then drawn back together with 'all seem part of the same poem', so that they then coexist in a third, shared space between the text and self. This kind of blended thinking is the product of slow, immersive and regular reading over an extended period of time and provides evidence of Peter's growing attunement to the text.

Case Study Six: Wise Passiveness

Mary is a 61-year-old primary school teacher who lives in London. In common with a majority of the participants in the poetry group, she wrote extensively about her own past in her diary. Certain words within the poem appeared to trigger specific memories for Mary. This initially helped her to develop a personal understanding of this complex and unfamiliar piece of poetry. However, as the task progressed and she seemed to become more deeply engaged with the poem, memories became places of live, shared feeling and indicated a growing sense of convergence between reader and text.

On day two of the task, Mary read a passage of the poem in which the pedlar recounts his childhood growing up in the Lake District. The passage includes the following lines:

> He, many an evening, to his distant home
> In solitude returning, saw the hills
> Grow larger in the darkness; all alone
> Beheld the stars come out above his head,
> And travelled through the wood, with no one near
> To whom he might confess the things he saw.
> So the foundations of his mind were laid.
> In such communion, not from terror free, (ll. 126–33)

The words 'terror' and 'in solitude returning' appear to lead Mary to write about her own specific childhood memories of returning home alone:

> When I was young – probably from the age of seven, I often returned home from evening activities alone. The most memorable was from Brownies / Guides. The way home was often in the dark and the streets were very quiet. There was one particular part which filled me with 'terror' every time. It was only a low wall around the back of the chapel, but I always imagined someone / something lurking behind the wall

who would jump out on me. My heart would be in my mouth as I passed every time. I never told anyone about it when I was young. When I see the word 'terror' this is the feeling I remember. (Day Two)

As Maryanne Wolf writes in *Reader, Come Home*, 'Words contain and momentarily activate whole repositories of associated meanings, memories, and feelings, even when the exact meaning in a given context is specified [...] each word can elicit an entire history of myriad connections, associations, and long-stored emotions.'[9] Mary's own memory of childhood 'terror' sits adjacent to the content of the poem here, but it is these first strands of recognition – often triggered by only single words – which help her to form an initial attachment to the text.

By day nine it appears that Mary is beginning to align herself with the text to a greater extent. The day's passage of poetry included lines which themselves describe a moment of emotional alignment between Margaret and the pedlar:

> This tale did Margaret tell with many tears:
> And, when she ended, I had little power
> To give her comfort, and was glad to take
> Such words of hope from her own mouth as served
> to cheer us both. But long we had not talked
> Ere we built up a pile of better thoughts,
> And with a brighter eye she looked around
> As if she had been shedding tears of joy. (ll. 721–28)

In her response, Mary wrote:

> I've been in this situation. I remember one time in particular – when I told a friend news about my family, I remember telling her 'with many tears' – but by the end after I had told her everything, although she was upset, we then started talking about things in a more cheerful way – just as they do in the poem. It's as if unloading the story onto someone else gives the storyteller a period of relief and you almost immediately feel more cheerful. You make someone very sad with your story – but then you have the resources to try and cheer them up. It's strange. (Day Nine)

Mary shifts here from writing in the first person about her own life experiences to using the second-person plural 'you'. This move from singular to plural, individual to more communal, suggests a growing recognition that Mary's own particular experiences belong to something bigger than her individual self. This is not detached autobiography. Mary integrates the quotation 'with many tears' into her own story and as she refers back to the poem she is keen to reinforce the link between herself and the text, writing that she and her friend had reacted 'just as they do in the poem'.

While Mary appeared to experience moments of emotional alignment with the poem throughout the course of the task, there were also places within the text which caused her much confusion and annoyance. She found it particularly difficult to grapple with the character of the pedlar because he did not appear to fit any of the pre-existing templates that she held within her mind of a good or virtuous person. The fifth day of the task, where she learnt more about the pedlar's past, was especially troubling for Mary:

> From his native hills
> He wandered far; much did he see of men,
> Their manners, their enjoyments, and pursuits,
> Their passions and their feelings; (ll. 340–43)

It was specifically the words 'much did he see of men' which triggered her frustration:

> Does the word 'see' mean he didn't get involved – just stayed outside – observing? Because I believe that life is all about making mistakes and learning from them, and that sometimes involves trusting or getting involved too closely with people, and that can mean upsets, unhappiness, problems. He seems to have achieved wisdom in a different way. Maybe quite a selfishly indulgent way. Yet he seems to have approval from all around him. I read it through and wonder what kind of man I am expected to imagine. (Day Five)

The pedlar does not match up to any of Mary's ideas of what a friend is, what a wise person or good person is, yet the poem is telling her that he is all of these things. She cannot imagine him, she cannot understand him and she cannot understand other people's reactions to him.

During her interview, Mary spoke again about her initial reaction to the pedlar and how being faced with such an unrecognisable character had triggered a shift both in her way of thinking and her way of approaching certain problems in her own life:

> *How did you initially feel about the character of the pedlar?*
> I think it was really difficult because it was as if he was being revered as this really wise person. He is made welcome everywhere, everyone is

happy to see him, but I just felt as if he was acting in an almost very superficial way as far as my standards go. Yeah, I just found that almost impossible to understand how those two things could go together, being wise and not getting involved when you come across people, just observing them. But yes, it has given me a new pathway for thinking really, it's very hard, it's a very hard path to follow, but it's also a very good path to follow, definitely for me anyway [...] To feel empathy, but not to feel too much, to be realistic as well, to be far more realistic. To look after myself as well as worrying about a situation. I've felt I've built up a picture of myself which is wrong and I've had to change it dramatically over the last five years. And it was like, that I'm a really good helper, I love helping people, I'll go out of my way to help people and people like me to help them. And ... I got into a situation where that was making me ill. I had to stop and think and I've had to partially ... I've partially undone that a little bit and this poem has made me realise that I need to go further, I've got to go even further, I've got to get rid of the idea that I need to go around helping people all the time. I've got to completely undo it, it's really unnecessary and it's really not good for you.

When you said that you need to change your idea of yourself as 'the helper' do you think you have to replace that with something else?

No, no I don't think so. Because by being a helper, you are also a controller. It is a way of controlling people and I really want to get away from that, from that part of me. I want to get rid of that part of me now. So no, I don't want to replace it with anything.

The poem appears to have challenged Mary's understanding of what 'help' can look like and has led her towards a more Wordsworthian stance of 'wise passiveness'. Having originally harshly judged the pedlar for not giving Margaret any practical support, she comes to see him as somebody from whom she can learn. After spending a lifetime building up a 'picture' of herself that has proven to be damaging, she begins here to strip away constraining ideas of herself, casting off the role of 'helper' which is synonymous for her with the role of 'controller'. The final assertion, 'I don't want to replace it with anything', suggests that she has realised the need to try now to exist in her own bare vulnerability.

This case study offers some evidence of how poetry might challenge a reader to shift out of habitual patterns of thought or behaviour and explore new, unexpected ways of thinking about themselves. There is no suggestion here that any other reader faced with 'The Ruined Cottage' should or would reach the same conclusions as Mary or steer themselves – as she did – towards a philosophy of 'wise passiveness'. This is however a specific, localised example of how literature can – often unexpectedly – meet the particular needs of an individual reader, by offering up new perspectives and a new language for thinking with.

Case Study Seven: From Academic to Emotional

Samantha is the head teacher of a secondary school in the South of England. She teaches English and has studied English literature to postgraduate level. She is familiar with the poetry of Wordsworth, and in her initial diary entries she frequently referred to what she had formerly learnt about Wordsworth at university. A member of the cross-checking group noticed Samantha's repeated references to her 'uni days' and commented that 'this is a key part of the person's narrative that they draw on'. This commentator also identified the clear shift in tone that occurs towards the middle of Samantha's diary entries: 'The writing has changed from earlier entries, it sounds almost poetic. The poem seems to be influencing the reader in a reflective way, which is influencing how they see the world, maybe this is coming through in their writing.' Over the course of the task Samantha appeared to move away from her default 'academic' mode and shifted to a more personal way of reading and writing.

The poem opens on a hot summer's day with the character of the poet meeting an old acquaintance – the pedlar – beneath the shade of some elm trees:

> 'Twas summer, and the sun had mounted high:
> Southward the landscape indistinctly glared
> Through a pale stream; but all the northern downs,
> In clearest air ascending, showed far off
> A surface dappled o'er with shadows flung
> From brooding clouds; shadows that lay in spots
> Determined and unmoved, with steady beams
> Of bright and pleasant sunshine interposed; (ll. 1–8)

In response to the first passage of the poem, Samantha attempted to draw on her literary training to analyse the text:

> I think that the description of the sun alongside the 'brooding clouds' description, with the impact of both together on the land, creates a metaphor for the world that I remember from my uni days that this poet inhabited – beauty of nature but something 'brooding' around the

corner. I can't remember the detail now of the whole perspective he had, but I have a sense that the man lying so relaxed may face disruption like that the world faced then and certainly faces now. (Day One)

In contrast, on day seven of the task, Samantha is involuntarily jolted into a more vulnerable, emotional position by the description in the poem of Margaret's overgrown garden. She is no longer writing as a teacher or a student, she instead begins simply to respond to the poem as a daughter coming to terms with her mother's recent cancer diagnosis:

> It was a plot
> Of garden ground run wild, its matted weeds
> Mark'd with the steps of those, whom, as they passed,
> The gooseberry trees that shot in long lank slips,
> Or currants, hanging from their leafless stems,
> In scanty strings, had tempted to o'erleap
> The broken wall.
> […]
> "I see around me here
> Things which you cannot see: we die, my Friend,
> Nor we alone, but that which each man loved
> And prized in his peculiar nook of earth
> Dies with him, or is changed; and very soon
> Even of the good is no memorial left." (ll. 452–74)

I had quite a shock then, reading a description of the overgrown garden, with words like 'matted', 'leafless', 'long lank', 'scanty strings' leading then into the man saying what he says about death, and all that we 'prize' changing and going with us as we die. I wasn't wanting to think about that, as mum prepares for her op. I'm thinking about gentle pauses, her lovely garden staying just fine at home for her while dad waits for her to recover and all proceeding forward as it should. I am also a little repelled by the idea that there's no 'memorial left' even of good. (Day Seven)

She finds the passage uncomfortable to read, but it is the shock of being faced by this image of decay that forces her to drop her previous detached, academic default mode. The poem leads her to consider what – in the aftermath of her mother's cancer diagnosis – her mind had been working hard to avoid. In this case, her requoting of words from the text is a good thing to come out of her student/teacher experience as it creates a more focused, live reading of the poem. Two weeks later at her interview, I read aloud this same passage of poetry about Margaret's overgrown garden and Samantha spoke again about the fear that it had initially triggered in her:

> Not wanting anything to alter or adjust at all and how like the processes of nature happen anyway no matter what you do and that is quite scary. I've found that, I like that, I really love that passage and I really connected with that passage but at the same time it showed a really powerful advancing of time and nature that is a little bit scary, especially if you are faced with illness at a particular point. The garden itself reminded me of where we lived as kids, they or we had a big garden and I imagine it like now, I imagine it like that, even though they don't live there now. I imagine that if they did, that if mum, I mean mum's getting better, but if she wasn't, there would be that sense of that happening there, and how sad that is. I think that that is a really overwhelmingly sad passage, really powerfully, really powerfully. And how when you go and revisit places, I don't like going and revisiting places particularly because I often find that the experience that you had is altered and not always in a good way. I think that is why that spoke to me as well really strongly in terms of mum's illness, because I don't like going back to where we lived as children in case it's all gone wrong. You know that sort of idyllic quality is gone. (Interview)

Reading can perhaps be one way of imaginatively restoring a place that cannot be returned to in reality. Here in the interview, after a second reading of the text, Samantha is reading and relating to the text in a very different way to how she had in the first half of her diary. Reading appears to have become an intensely personal and imaginative process. Rereading this passage of the poem during the interview seemed to help Samantha to quickly get back into the thick of the feelings that the text had initially triggered in her. As soon as I had finished reading the passage, she began to speak – not in fully formed sentences – but urgently mid-sentence, keen to articulate, however roughly, the mixture of emotions and memories that the poetry had activated.

During her interview, Samantha was asked about the changes that had taken place for her over the course of the task. She had noticed, as she was writing, that she was beginning to think about and respond to the poem in a different way and had felt the benefit of this change:

> For a start, well, I'm an English teacher for a start, so before you know you start going into the tried and tested ways of reading and analysing that you have learnt to do for a really long time and that you have asked young people to do for years and I liked it for that because I found that

I was able to stop doing that as I went through. Initially I was doing that, I was very much trying to find the answer to what stuff meant and in that, do you know what I mean? In that kind of English student kind of way, I was definitely, that's where I defaulted to because if I see a poem that's what I do, like a dog running for a bone, the same process. Whereas as it went through, you probably can tell in the writing, I was much more personally connected to the poem and finding, as you say, space to think. It's a combination not just of the task but of the subject matter as well. It's the poem that takes you there actually, because some poems I might never have done that, I might have carried on trying to analyse.

I think the points that were most interesting for me to read were when your knowledge and understanding of Wordsworth or literature falls away.

Yeah, absolutely.

They were the most interesting points and as you've said already, a more direct, personal connection comes through at those points.

Yeah and I liked the fact that I couldn't remember very much what I used to know. I kind of knew some headlines, but I couldn't really remember any detail. But actually that was really good because to start with I thought I'd be putting it through a filter from my undergraduate days, which as you said, initially I started to do a bit. But actually I couldn't do that, I couldn't remember anything and it was better that I couldn't. I stopped trying to remember and it was even better. (Interview)

This case study is particularly important as it demonstrates that the study design was successful – at least for Samantha – in creating a non-academic space to engage carefully and attentively, but on a more personal level, with literature. Samantha felt the benefit of putting aside her theoretical knowledge of how to approach a text. As she began to stop processing the task in her habitual, learnt manner, she started to leave herself open to surprises and thus formed a new understanding of how to relate – as a human rather than as a student or a teacher – to the poem.

Case Study Eight: Less Is More

Michael is a 26-year-old from London. He left school at age 16 after completing his GCSE's and is currently working as a waiter. He has a keen interest in art and design and enjoys reading for pleasure; however, he has little experience of reading poetry and described his initial reticence about the task in his post-task questionnaire and during his interview. In his first two diary entries Michael wrote long, descriptive summaries of the poetry. For example, on day one:

> He meets his friend and you're given the sense of relief that his journey has come to an end and that his eagerly anticipated meeting has arrived. There is a real sense of affection growing and intrigue as to who this man is and the nature of their relationship. Even in the previous passage 'be welcomed with livelier joy' indicates his excitement. (Day One)

However, on day three Michael abruptly changed his method. After reading the day's passage, he highlighted the following lines:

> he had felt the power
> Of Nature, and already was prepared,
> By his intense conceptions, to receive
> Deeply the lesson deep of love which he,
> Whom Nature, by whatever means, has taught
> To feel intensely, cannot but receive. (ll. 191–96)

He then stopped paraphrasing the poetry and instead began to write much briefer notes about how the task was making him feel and what he was learning from it:

- Stop thinking/being so analytical – feelings/instincts are real and important.
- I feel I must take this on board? (Day Three)

As Michael himself explained in his post-task questionnaire: 'My approach to the task changed dramatically. At first I couldn't help but describe the poem rather than describe how it made me feel. As soon as I began to try and describe my feelings I found it harder to write but was more absorbed by the poem.' After changing his stance on the third day, Michael went on to write about deeply personal topics. In particular, he wrote about the different experiences of grief that he and his mother had gone through after his father had died, ten years earlier.

During his interview – which took place two weeks after the completion of the reading diary – Michael spoke about his conscious decision on the third day to shift away from his default tactic of superficial description and towards a more emotional approach:

> *I wanted to ask you about that shift that you have just mentioned from the first few days where you were very descriptive to when you later became much more emotional*

and personal. You said at the end that it became harder when you started doing that, but also much more rewarding.

Yes, definitely. Well at first I wanted you to be impressed by me. I was writing in my best handwriting, in straight lines, I was worried in a very naïve young way about making it look like I'd really put in the effort. Then I then just thought, you know what actually I can't not ... I'm just describing the poem rather than doing anything of any difference. I'm basically rewriting it in a really stupid way. And then I was like, this is stupid, I'm going to try and get the best from it. And I did. I think that from the look of it, the more I absorbed the less actually I wrote down.

So it was a conscious decision to do that then? You thought, stop describing and start talking about how this is making me feel?

I can remember on like the third day, I read back, there wasn't long into it, I thought this is ridiculous, I read back the first one and I thought, this is just a complete waste of time. I was like, she doesn't want this. I did think she doesn't want this. I'm gonna have to start bullet-pointing it. I was slightly worried that you might think I had been too lazy to do it. But I thought I'm getting as much down doing bullet points as I am sentences you know, in terms of emotional delivery. I think I put more down after that point because I wasn't going sentence by sentence. (Interview)

Michael quickly realised that his default mode was inadequate. As his responses became increasingly personal, the diary entries became significantly shorter and more fragmented. All the unnecessary paraphrase was stripped away and instead he appeared to focus on the task of getting closer to the emotional core of the poem.

On day twelve Michael read a passage of the poem which recounts Margaret's spiralling decline into despair and her subsequent neglect of her young child, following her abandonment by her husband. The passage includes the lines:

Her infant babe
Had from his Mother caught the trick of grief,
And sighed among its playthings. (ll. 868–70)

In response to this passage, Michael wrote:

Grief is Contagious.

– It seems strange to me that she would seem so affected by her husband's grief yet so unaffected by the death of her child. Or I suppose her husband's death had so affected her that the remainder of him (her child) was a burden.

– Makes me jealous of that kind of love.

You want to scream at her "pull yourself together" which makes me feel as though I'm unsympathetic and dead inside myself. (Day Twelve)

Here Michael is writing simultaneously about both Margaret and his own mother, about Margaret's husband and his own father and about Margaret's child and his own self (as 'remainder' rather than 'reminder' of the father). The poem is allowing him to get close to his own parallel experiences and to think and say what would be difficult – if not impossible – for him to say to his mother, 'Pull yourself together' or 'I'm jealous of that kind of love.'

In his post-task questionnaire, Michael wrote that 'This poem made me think about myself as someone who may have been affected by grief unknowingly.' During his interview Michael spoke in more detail about how reading the poem had led him to think about his own grief in a way that he might otherwise have avoided:

You wrote about being 'unknowingly' affected by grief, what did you mean by that?

Yes. Because I only have become a little more tolerant of talking about my own father in the last I would say year or so. Because I never really liked talking about it or anything else and I can't say I was consciously affected by it at the time. It was not, because in the poem I know it talks about this old woman, and I very much saw my own mum in it. Because she is not the same woman ... even now. She is nowhere near what she was. And that was what kind of ... I can see how I'm probably a bit more severe in my own nature because she was so miserable. Because I was quite happy go lucky really before that ... you know ... because I don't like saying it was ... you know because I can't say I ever got on with him, I can't say I ever really liked him, I can't say it was a big loss personally. It was just that thing of how it affected my mother and subsequently how that affected me. Because that was in the poem, I think I just couldn't not write what I wrote. (Interview)

The poem has caused Michael to begin to think about the ways in which grief was transferred between his mother and his own teenage self after the death of his father. This new sense of previously unrealised feeling is articulated here in the pauses between words as well as in the words themselves. All of the things that Michael feels that he 'can't say' build up to create a negative space around which the form of all that is left unspoken is in some way solidified. This is a small example of a kind of creative inarticulacy that can prove to be therapeutic. It was moments of personal breakthrough such as this – triggered by immersive, contemplative reading – that this experiment sought to explore, document and analyse. For they demonstrate how poetry can guide readers into areas of serious emotional depth and provide them with a language for thinking that helps previously unformed thoughts to surface. For while Michael has for many years avoided the subject of his father's death, the poem meant that 'I just couldn't not write what I wrote.' That double negative form is itself borne out of the literary language that this reader has absorbed, a language which can help us to take hold of those things that we so often do not have the words for, or cannot bear to say.

A Comparison of the Two Tasks

Mary and Peter, the two participants allocated to group three of the study, were asked to complete both the poetry diary and the control task. These two participants therefore followed a 10-week programme:

Week 1–2	Poetry Task
Week 3	Break
Week 4	Poetry Task Interview
Week 5–6	Break
Week 7–8	Control Task
Week 9	Break
Week 10	Control Task Interview

The assessments made by both during each of their interviews were particularly valuable. Their personal analysis of the two tasks greatly contributed to the process of identifying and verifying themes across the whole data set.

As previously discussed in Case Study Five, Peter had strongly identified with the text of 'The Ruined Cottages' and in his poetry diary he had written primarily about memories of his childhood. In contrast, during the control task he wrote exclusively about the present, focusing on family life, his work and daily routine, just as the majority of participants in this group had also done:

> Saturday is always a bleary-eyed day for me. A day of rest after the week's exertions. Lots of newspaper reading and drifting around supermarkets like a wandering ghost. I love this domesticity, with my wife leading me, doing ordinary, everyday things, just like everybody else and I love being with my wife. (Day Twelve)

In his post-task questionnaire Peter described the positive effect that keeping a regular diary had had on him: 'It felt good to put some things down on paper rather than just thinking about it. It's good to put some things down.' Yet he also outlined some of the shortcomings of the task: 'I couldn't express myself fully [...] I could only be superficial, I could only write about things that I know about.'

In Peter's second interview he gave a detailed analysis of the two tasks and explained the differing demands that they had placed upon him as a thinker:

> With the poem I was dealing with other people's thoughts and words, I had to decipher those words, I had to make sense of them, whereas when I was doing the diary, they were my own thoughts, I knew exactly what I was thinking, it was just a matter of writing them down [...] with the poem I was dealing with other people's words and the words were conjuring up memories, I wasn't dealing with my own words and my own words could only conjure up what I could see in front of me in the present. Whereas when I was reading Wordsworth's words that set my memory going. The poem made me think about the past. The poem made you think about your whole life, not just what happened today and once you start thinking about your whole life, you start to go much deeper don't you. You start to think about the things that are really stuck in your mind from fifty years ago or more. Whereas the diary I think is much more superficial. There was much more scope for deep thinking with the poem. You can't help getting into a deeper level you know. (Interview)

Peter had struggled to get beyond the surface detail of his immediate surroundings and daily experiences as he was writing his control diary. In contrast, during the poetry task, the poem itself appeared to have taken him out of the present and into deeper and often unexpected areas. The poem seemed to expand the scope of Peter's thoughts and guided him into areas of perhaps only partially known but deeply held memory and feeling.

During the poetry task Mary had initially found the character of the pedlar difficult to understand or accept. However, over the course of the two weeks that she spent reading 'The Ruined Cottage', her attitude shifted and she began to take on board the more Wordsworthian approach of 'wise passiveness' that the pedlar advocates. One month after completing the poetry task Mary began the diary task. She managed to write six entries over a period of 14 days with an eight-day pause between the fourth and fifth entries. She felt unable to continue the task beyond this point and submitted her six diary entries before being interviewed two weeks later. The six diary entries are full of anxiety and raw emotion:

> On Thursday I started off feeling quite anxious. I started worrying about going down to look after my mother. I booked the bus so it made the event more real. Then in the afternoon I spoke to my mother. She wanted to talk for ages. The way my mother was talking to me made me feel quite repulsed, it's like I'm suddenly her favourite child, after only a few weeks ago I wasn't good enough. So when I lay down to have a sleep, my thoughts were very dark. (Day Five)

In her post-task questionnaire Mary explained why she had needed to stop writing the diary:

> By writing about things as they are actually happening it has felt like I'm talking about them too early – even if I've written about them one or two days later. So I have to stop. I hope you understand. I found it difficult to share when the emotions I was experiencing were so raw. It made me feel vulnerable and wasn't the way I would normally resolve my problems. (Post-task Questionnaire)

The interview stage of the task did however provide Mary with a second chance to readdress the perceived permanency of what she had written in her diary: 'It was good to talk in person about the struggle I'd had in writing the diary and to think about it again with some hindsight.' The interview stage appeared to create the opportunity for Mary to say in a different way what it was that she had not been able to write. During the interview she was able to redeem something 'good' from the task. After the rash, raw, primary emotion of her diary, the interview seemed to create the chance for secondary, contemplative and more objective thinking.

In Mary's final interview, she gave her own analysis of the two tasks:

> Well the poetry task was very structured. It focused you on what was being said in the poem, so it focused your mind on things that were not necessarily happening at the time, it focused … well, it brought up a lot of memories, and it kind of kept you thinking outside yourself in a way, you were trying to understand the poem, you were studying the poem and trying to get out of the poem as much as you could. I liked doing it and it was a real challenge. Writing the diary wasn't a challenge, it didn't have that feel at all. (Interview)

The poem appeared to have a widening effect, not only on Mary, but on a number of participants' way of thinking. In contrast, those in the control group could only really think about what was immediately around them or what they already knew or thought. They appeared less likely to have new thoughts or new ideas when writing, they were less challenged and less likely to change their ways of thinking over the course of the task.

Conclusion

The interview stage often seemed to elicit more from participants in the control group than the diary-writing process had. During the interviews, participants spoke about much more than just their daily routines. They often began to talk in detail about the past and about the wider span of their whole lives. They gave an overview of their lives during the interviews, while in the diaries they had mainly written from within their own small, daily concerns. Perhaps this is due to the fact that during the interviews, thoughts which had become their text had to be translated back into speech and shared or exchanged in some way with another person. The interviewer, when reading the diaries aloud, enabled participants to consider what they looked like from the outside and to embody that external perspective. This suggests that participants were no longer thinking and writing in isolation, and that they could therefore begin to see themselves through the eyes of their reader and also – in certain cases – to become their own readers.

Both tasks seem to work best where there are exchanges taking place, or where more than one mind is at work. For the control group, there was much greater opportunity for this to happen during the interviews than at the initial writing stage. For many of the participants in the poetry group, there appeared to be an almost constant process of exchange and conversation taking place between the poem and the reader as they read the poem and wrote their responses to it each day.

The interview therefore seemed to be more significant to participants in the control group than to those in the poetry group.

In an interview in which the psychoanalyst and essayist Adam Phillips discusses the relationship between literature and psychoanalysis, he describes the importance of two minds working together:

> In conversation things can be metabolized and digested through somebody else – I say something to you and you can give it back to me in different forms – whereas you'll notice that your own mind is very often extremely repetitive. It is very difficult to surprise oneself in one's own

mind. The vocabulary of one's self-criticism is so impoverished and clichéd. We are at our most stupid in our self-hatred.[10]

The literary form that Adam Phillips identifies as closest to psychoanalysis is the essay, and for him the most important quality that writing an essay calls for in a person is 'to be reflexively self-revising.'[11]. Participants in all groups were allowed to write about almost anything that they wanted to, yet for some participants the act of writing felt too permanent to allow self-revision to happen. Instead, it was with the help of either the poetry – which appeared to take readers out of their own daily, habitual thinking patterns – or the interviewer, that these moments of 'reflexive self-revision' more commonly took place.

Over the course of this study, participants in the poetry group appeared to adjust the ways in which they were reading, writing about and relating to 'The Ruined Cottage', in order to meet the challenges that the poem was placing upon them. The poem did not simply consolidate what participants already knew or felt, although in certain cases the first step towards a deeper understanding of the text came from readers recognising their own selves within it and matching their own memories onto the poem. The length, complexity and unfamiliarity of the poem, as well as the study's specific demand to read it slowly over fourteen 30-minute sessions, made this a difficult and, in some ways, disruptive exercise for many, if not all participants. It was not a task that could be easily absorbed into the routine of a person's life. The structure of both the task and the poem challenged default habits of thinking, and in certain cases the content of the poem also tested participants' established beliefs about themselves and those around them.

The poetry triggered particular capacities and qualities of thought that are not necessarily available elsewhere in everyday life and which did not seem to be triggered by mere information processing. The text appeared to take participants quickly into the thick of their inner, emotional lives and led them instinctively to explore areas of emotional depth and complexity, to shift between different mental positions and thus move away from automatic or default mode and towards potentially healthier patterns of thought. The poetry appeared to help participants to think about the wider span of their whole lives. The poetry triggered memories and therefore seemed to transport participants into more unconscious or unexpected areas of thinking as they wrote. They appeared to be guided by the poem to reflect upon parts of their lives that those who were writing diaries without any literary stimulus did not think about, in particular, specific moments from their childhoods. In accordance with Wordsworth's commitment to the avoidance of emotional wastage, several participants who read 'The Ruined Cottage' seemed to transform their own fixed ideas or unprocessed traumas, not getting rid of emotional matter as Stoic therapy would demand, but instead putting it to some use within their own minds.

Notes

1 Felski, p. 171.
2 The independent measures study design eased recruitment by reducing the amount of time and work required of each participant and helped to increase the quantity of data collected. In a cross-over or repeated measures design, participants would have had to commit themselves to spend twice as much time on the study in order to complete both tasks, potentially resulting in participants dropping out, losing motivation or failing to comply with the requirements of the study. The third group, consisting of two participants who did both of the tasks, was however included in the study to mitigate against the limitations of an independent measures design – namely the problem of participant variables – and allowed for some initial direct comparisons to be made between the two different tasks.
3 *Prelude*, Book 4, ll. 143–48.
4 James W. Pennebaker, Matthias R. Mehl and Kate G. Niederhoffer, 'Psychological Aspects of Natural Language Use: Our Words, Our Selves', in *Annual Review of Psychology* 54 (2003), pp. 547–77 (p. 567).
5 Eleanor Longden et al., 'Shared Reading: Assessing the Intrinsic Value of a Literature-Based Health Intervention', *Medical Humanities* 41(2) (2015), pp. 113–20, hereafter cited as *Shared Reading*.
6 Ibid.
7 Cave, p. 152.
8 S. H. Kellogg, 'Transformational Chair-Work: Five Ways of Using Therapeutic Dialogues', *NYSPA Notebook* 19(4) (2007), pp. 8–9.
9 Maryanne Wolf, *Reader, Come Home* (New York: Harper Collins, 2018), p. 33, hereafter cited as *Reader, Come Home*.
10 Adam Philips, 'The Art of Nonfiction No. 7', interview by Paul Holdengraber, *Paris Review*, 208 (2014), https://www.theparisreview.org/interviews/6286/adam-phillips-the-art-of-nonfiction-no-7-adam-phillips, accessed 15 April 2016.
11 Ibid.

Chapter 7

EXPERIMENT THREE: WRITING BACK

This final chapter sets out the findings of a third reading study, designed to further explore the kinds of thinking within individuals that can be triggered by serious reading. In this study, rather than poetry, the focus was on prose. A group of four participants were asked to read four selected chapters from George Eliot's *Silas Marner*, and in response to their reading, write a series of imaginative letters between themselves, the characters within the novel and the author.

By serious reading I do not mean formal or academic study, instead the objective here was to trigger attentive, thoughtful and personal engagement with a difficult literary text. For as George Eliot herself wrote, as she was working on *The Mill on the Floss*, 'My books are deeply serious things to me, and come out of all the painful discipline, all the most hardly-learnt lessons of my past life.'[1] These 'deeply serious things', forged out of all the accumulated, complicated material of George Eliot's life demand to be taken seriously and they – in turn – and unlike so much of the material that we consume nowadays – are books that take us – as readers – seriously.

George Eliot places quite unique demands on her readers, but these demands are also what form the foundations of all that is potentially therapeutic within her novels. The aim of this study was, in part, to explore how modern readers might respond to those demands.

Further objectives were:

1. To examine whether readers were able to enter into and engage with the complex circuitry of the novel.
2. To explore whether George Eliot's prose could expand a reader's capacity to hold onto and shift between multiple different perspectives.
3. To allow some part of the interchange that takes place during reading between reader, character and author to be captured.
4. To examine whether readers can in some way replicate or participate in the process of projection and feedback that takes place between George Eliot and her characters.
5. To discover how George Eliot's mobility and breadth of thought impacts upon her readers.

Reading and Empathy

Theory of Mind is the ability to attribute mental states to other people and is a skill that is typically developed during early childhood: 'It is mind reading, empathy, creative imagination of other's perspective; in short, it is simultaneously a highly sophisticated ability and a very basic necessity for human communication.'[2] A positive correlation has been found to exist between reading literary fiction and 'Theory of Mind'[3]. This has spawned a growth in interest, among psychologists and others, in the psychological effects of reading. In *Why We Read Fiction: Theory of Mind and the Novel*, Lisa Zunshine argues that reading fiction allows us to test, hone and also to relish the flourishing of our Theory of Mind skills:[4]

> Our enjoyment of fiction is predicated – at least in part – upon our awareness of our 'trying on' mental states potentially available to us but at a given moment differing from our own.[5]

Maryanne Wolf echoes this sentiment in her own study of the science behind the phenomenon of reading:

> Reading enables us to try on, identify with, and ultimately enter for a brief time the wholly different perspective of another person's consciousness [...] Through this exposure we learn both the commonality and the uniqueness of our own thoughts.[6]

But the relationship between literature and what we today call empathy has long been understood by generations of writers and readers. In Michael Paffard's second book – *The Unattended Moment* – he explores the close ties between literature, imagination and empathy:

> John Stuart Mill called imagination this 'power by which one human being enters into the mind and circumstances of another,' and Wordsworth thought it 'the mightiest lever known to the moral world.' [...] We can call this power of entering into the mind and circumstances of another person's imagination empathy or sympathy or morality indifferently, for the impossible union, like all unattended moments goes beyond the reach of ordinary words.[7]

George Eliot is a novelist who is deeply concerned with sympathy and in her writing she not only enters into the minds of her characters to look out through their eyes, she also leads us – the reader – into the rich density of multiple

Table 7.1. Experiment three: Sample information

Participant Pseudonym	Gender	Age	Profession	Do You Read for Pleasure?	Have You Previously Studied English Literature?
Marsha	F	27	Waitress	Yes	Masters
Mary	F	61	Teacher	Yes	O-Level
Rachel	F	31	Charity Worker	Yes	Masters
Peter	M	65	Artist	Yes	O-Level

perspectives that make up each of her novels. Her sympathy extends beyond the internal world of her novels, out into the world of her readers. It is these complicated interactions that perhaps go beyond what can be held within the terms 'empathy' or 'Theory of Mind' that this final study sought to explore.

Study Design

Four people from the pool of 28 who had previously taken part in either experiment one or experiment two were recruited to take part. Table 7.1 provides some basic information collected from each participant through their pre-task questionnaires.

The criteria for inclusion in the study was that participants had to be over 18, fluent in English, and have previously read *Silas Marner* in its entirety, at some point in their lives. Because although this experiment focuses on four specific chapters of *Silas Marner*, it was important that participants had a sense of the whole text. In initial trials, those who had not previously read the entire novel and were given only short extracts to read found it too difficult to develop any depth of feeling or understanding of the characters.

Each participant was asked to read chapters 3 and 9 of *Silas Marner* and then to write two letters, each with a minimum length of 150 words. The first letter was to be written from themselves to any one character that they had encountered in chapters 3 and 9. The second letter was to be written from the perspective of that chosen character, either back to the reader, or to George Eliot herself. Participants were then asked to read chapters 13 and 18 of the novel, and repeat the letter-writing process.

Letter writing was used in this study to encourage risk and creativity while also reducing participants' sense of self-exposure. It was important that the exercise did not feel like an academic task, but rather a more authentic private exchange between readers, characters and the novelist. As Maryanne

Wolf writes in *Reader, Come Home*: 'Letters invite a kind of cerebral pause in which we can think with each other and, if very fortunate, experience a special kind of encounter.'[8] The task was designed to encourage focused, careful reading and extended reflection. Letter-writing is commonly used to supplement established forms of therapeutic practice. In Narrative Therapy for example, letters written by both patient and therapist are used to help externalise a patient's problems, increase their sense of agency and turn the therapeutic process into a more collaborative effort.[9] It was essential, however, that the letter-writing task in this study did not have an explicitly therapeutic function, for, as in experiments one and two, it was important to create space for the particularities of each individual reader's response to the text to develop without any sense that they were participating in a form of therapy.

There is a shift in methodology here, away from the *intrapersonal* method of experiments one and two, where participants were writing and speaking largely from within their own perspective, and towards an *interpersonal* approach, as participants wrote letters from the perspective of different characters within the novel. This shift not only reflects a move from poetry to the novel but also corresponds with George Eliot's own concern for a wider community of lives which encompasses both the characters within her novels and the readers on the outside of her novels.

Leading on from the initial findings of experiment two, one of the objectives of this study was to explore whether reading and writing about literature could serve as a way for one person to internalise some of the psychological work of dialogue that is otherwise carried out between two people during conventional therapeutic interventions. The dual reading and writing task asks participants to project an aspect of themselves out into a character of the novel and then to imaginatively listen to that character speaking back to them. This study was intended to bridge the gap between theory and practice and potentially to lay the foundations for the development of literary-based therapeutic interventions.

Silas Marner tells the story of a lonely weaver who, having left his home after being betrayed by those closest to him, is now living alone in a cottage in the village of Raveloe. He exists in an almost comatose state of semi-existence, his only joy comes from counting the fortune of gold coins that he has accumulated throughout his life. But one night, after he suffers from an epileptic fit, his money is stolen. It is only with the arrival of a mysterious, abandoned baby, that Silas is brought back to life again. The novel follows closely in the tradition of Wordsworth and its epigraph is taken from Wordsworth's poem 'Michael': 'A child, more than all other gifts / That earth can offer to declining man, / Brings hope with it, and forward-looking thoughts.'[10]

The chapters that were selected for participants to read – 3, 9, 13 and 18 – were chosen because, alongside Silas himself, they focus heavily on the life of Godfrey Cass. These four chapters contain the majority of Godfrey's story arc. Godfrey is important to this study because he is a man who is stuck in the thick of a post-religious world of psychology, struggling with guilt and confession – problems which previously would have belonged to the realm of religion.

Godfrey begins chapter 3 in a seemingly impossible situation. He is being blackmailed by his brother Dunstan and is torn between confessing to his father that he has secretly and regretfully married a woman called Molly Farren, or remaining silent, in hope of somehow in future marrying his new, respectable love Nancy Lammeter.

In chapter 9 Godfrey makes a partial confession to his father, revealing that he has lost £100 of the squire's money, that Dunstan has gone missing and that one of their horses has been killed. But he fails to confess anything about his secret marriage.

In chapter 13, Silas Marner finds a small child in his cottage and then discovers its mother Molly Farren in the snow outside. He carries the child to the squire's house to get help. Godfrey recognises the baby as his own child but does not claim it and instead travels back to Silas's cottage to make sure that Molly is in fact dead and that his secret can remain intact.

Chapter 18 takes place 16 years later and it is here – after Dunstan's dead body is found and he is exposed as the thief that stole Silas Marner's fortune – that Godfrey reveals his whole secret to his second wife Nancy.

Analysis

The small sample size of this study is an obvious limitation, but it did also mean that the process of analysis could be a little more thorough. The 16 letters that my four participants wrote were on average 500 words long, nearly four times longer than the minimum length that I had stipulated in the task instructions.

The analytical method used in this study was rooted in techniques of literary analysis and informed by the interdisciplinary work of the Centre for Research into Reading, Literature and Society (CRILS) which has used a combination of literary, linguistic and psychological analysis to assess the impact of shared reading interventions.[11] Initially, each letter was carefully read. Categories and themes were then formed, which were reviewed and refined by the research team at CRILS. In order to cross-check themes and help to mitigate against researcher bias, all letters were additionally read by four postgraduates from the University of Liverpool's Institute of Psychology,

Health and Society, trained in qualitative analysis. This group were asked to read through and code the data that they had been given. Their annotations of each letter were tabulated and categorised into themes which were then verified by each cross-checker during a follow-up meeting. After completing their sets of letters, each participant was asked to comment on any elements of the reading and writing process that had seemed significant to them. These commentaries provided a further level of verification during the analysis of the letters.

The results of this study are presented in two sections. The first section focuses on who the participant chose to address their letters to, and will discuss:

1. Cases where participant's choice of character was motivated by a felt sense of kinship.
2. Letters written to George Eliot.

In the second section, a series of three case studies will demonstrate the varying degrees to which different participants were able to change perspective as they wrote their set of four letters. Case studies are used here to illustrate the range and nuance of individual responses to George Eliot's novel.

Addressing the Letters

A Sense of Kinship

The first decision that participants had to make was to which characters they were to write their letters. Then they had to determine whether that character should respond back to themselves or to George Eliot the novelist. Figure 7.1 sets out to whom and from whom each letter was written.

Of the 16 letters that were written in total by the four participants, 10 were either addressed to or written from Godfrey. This was an expected outcome because Godfrey is – arguably – the dominant character in all four of the chapters that participants had been given to read during the study. However, more striking was the consistent reason that participants gave for choosing Godfrey as the focus of their letters. Readers did not say that they simply knew more about Godfrey; instead, they described their choice as motivated by a sense of kinship with Godfrey and tended to describe a feeling of affinity with his internal conflict, sense of guilt and struggle with confession.

Marsha wrote directly to Godfrey, telling him in her third letter: 'I feel a connection to you and those inner struggles you have faced.' While in Mary's commentary on the task, she wrote: 'I felt a strong connection with Godfrey as a mother of a son who has gone astray.' In Rachel's first letter, also written

EXPERIMENT THREE: WRITING BACK 169

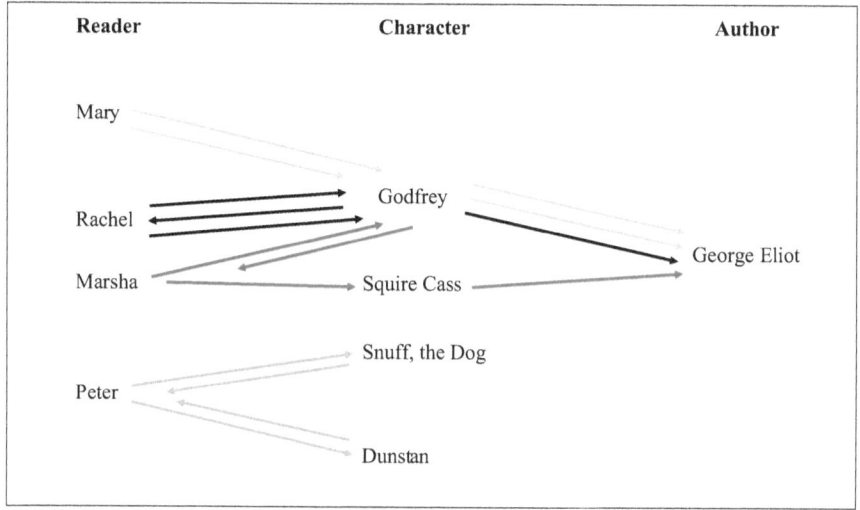

Figure 7.1. The letters written by each participant in experiment three

directly to Godfrey, she described her sense of familiarity with Godfrey's predicament:

> It's painful to read because it feels familiar. I feel that George Eliot is showing us both that we are part of something beyond what feels so painfully ours alone [...] Maybe company will lessen the sense of being alone in our foolishness – make it more forgivable and part of a greater pattern.

Her choice of language immediately places her not only alongside Godfrey, but also, in relation to George Eliot, alongside the novelist who is 'showing us both' – reader and character alike – 'that we are part of something beyond what feels so painfully ours alone'. The repeated word 'alone' is used here to mean both solely and solitarily and acts as a counterpoint to the pronouns 'us', 'we' and 'ours'. Here Rachel has found herself occupying a shared space where the lives of the character, reader and novelist intersect and impact upon one another.

During the cross-checking process, independent researchers identified this sense of kinship, noting that, 'The readers have clearly connected with the character', 'The readers connect with Godfrey's experiences and his emotions resound deeply in them' and with specific relation to Mary, who saw not herself, but her own son in the character of Godfrey, one of the cross-checkers commented that, 'She wishes to do more than just read the story, she wants to have a deeper understanding or insight or connection. The reader wishes to nurture Godfrey.'

Peter was the only reader who did not write any of his letters to or from Godfrey; instead, after reading chapters 3 and 9 he chose to write to and from the perspective of Godfrey's dog, and after reading chapters 13 and 19 he wrote letters to and from Godfrey's dead brother Dunstan. In his commentary Peter explained these unusual choices, noting that he had also considered writing a letter to Godfrey's unclaimed baby:

> The dog, the baby and the dead man, what's the connection for me? I suppose they are all unable to speak, all inscrutable in their own way […] The dog, the baby, Dunstan, I could identify and feel sympathetic towards. I wanted to try and give them an opportunity to say something about themselves […] I thought about Dunstan lying there dead in the stone pit while all these things were happening, the elephant in the room. The idea of writing to and from a dead, unlamented man was irresistible.

Peter saw the task as an opportunity to give extra voice to these silenced characters and to get into unusual perspectives in an imaginative and almost playful manner.

'Dear George Eliot'

Four of the letters produced by the group were addressed to George Eliot. In each of these letters the novelist is considered to have a god-like perspective and understanding of the characters' internal lives, like a sort of super-counsellor. This was corroborated by one cross-checker who commented that in Rachel's letter, addressed to George Eliot and written from the perspective of Godfrey, 'The first paragraph feels like a conversation with a higher being (God).' In several of the letters to George Eliot a certain resentment is imagined to exist within characters towards the all-seeing novelist. Marsha – in a letter written from Godfrey's father – admonishes George Eliot:

> What am I to make of it all? This is why I am writing to you: I am deeply disturbed, as I have said, and crave guidance from you. You must tell me what to do. You have the power to fix this. What could possibly be stopping you? And as for Dunstan, he will never listen to me and you know it. Do something for him.

Squire Cass angrily demands help from the author, but this fantasy is something that the realist novel cannot itself fulfil. There are no simple solutions here, and there cannot be an easy way out.

In Rachel's second letter, written from Godfrey to George Eliot, she imagines the anger and shame that her character must have felt, not only within the world of the novel, but also in the external space that reader, character and author are now all occupying, as he is forced to read the story of his life and address his author:

> I am angry at you for being able to see my mistakes, it only makes me feel all the more stupid. Why didn't I see this coming? Where was that clarity, that overview, when I was so desperate? By being forced to look at myself I seem to suffer more than if I were just left to the business of living.

Godfrey is ashamed that George Eliot is able to see all that he most really and truly is. It is as if in reading the novel for himself, through this imaginative letter-writing process, Godfrey has seen too late – through George Eliot's eyes – what he wishes he could have already been able to see for himself. There is no clear or formal distinction between reality and fiction; and the author in the midst is seen as someone who can help not only the character within the internal reality of the novel, but also the reader in the outside world.

Mary addressed two of her four letters to George Eliot. Both letters are written from the perspective of Godfrey Cass, the first when he was a young man struggling to hide his secret marriage from his father, and the second, 16 years later, written after Godfrey has finally revealed his secret to his second wife Nancy Lammeter.

In Mary's first letter to George Eliot, Godfrey pleads with the novelist to help him: 'Why have you given me such a huge problem with no one to turn to for advice? [...] Please send me a solution.' However, in the second letter, the older Godfrey is no longer a helpless supplicant; instead, he has become a conscious actor in his own life:

> I wrote to you sixteen years ago when I was a bitter and angry young man. I railed against you for dealing me such a bad hand of cards and I asked you to send me a solution. I realise now that there have been times in my life when I have been given choices by you to do the right thing [...] I am grateful to you for not imposing your solution on me.

Mary appears to demonstrate not only the capacity to imagine the mental state of a person other than herself at one particular point in time, but also imaginatively to shift with that other person over time into a new perspective. After reading Mary's letters, one cross-checker noted:

> It is interesting that the reader can flip perspectives and understand the complexity of his situation. They've understood the problem from different perspectives really well. This is interesting. Not a lot of people can do this in everyday life. The fourth letter is very different to the previous one written in this way. There is a much greater sense of maturity. There is an understanding of the growth and complexity of the character. They must have quite a deep connection with the character for them to understand it in this way.

The capacity to 'flip perspectives' was a key feature of the letters produced by all four readers in response to their reading of *Silas Marner*, and will be considered more closely in the three case studies that follow.

A Different Perspective

Marsha

In her third letter, Marsha described to Godfrey an act of betrayal from her own past that she had struggled to come to terms with. In her commentary, Marsha explained why she had chosen to write in this manner to Godfrey: 'I found out what it was that connected me with this character and I simply went straight to that.' Her confession is an attempt to align herself with the character that she is writing to:

> Many years ago – almost ten years it must be – I did something which seemed, and still does seem so opposite to the character I believe I am, and would have others believe in, that I quite simply could not accept or own it. I was unfaithful to a partner. I felt terrible for having done it, but even more so for the prospect of telling my partner about it and in the end I couldn't. I went half-way to a confession, told a half-truth which eased some of the pressure and guilt and, so I told myself, saved my partner from the pain of the full truth. It saved me, in that moment from the pain of the full truth – and from the consequences of it.

This letter illustrates some of the secret dangers of giving yourself too narrow a remit to exist within, or of conceiving of yourself and your life in terms of a conventional narrative. The point at which a person might suddenly have to face the reality that who they are and what they are capable of does not fit neatly into the story that they might have told themselves about themselves, becomes a real crisis point. It is this kind of psychic narrowness that George Eliot is fighting against within her novels. Free indirect discourse in the novels is the language of this suppressed consciousness, either seeking to break the bounds or hide within them.

In chapter 13 of *Silas Marner* Godfrey had tried to persuade himself – just as Marsha did 10 years previously – that by not confessing he would be protecting not only himself but also the person that he had secretly betrayed. The four small words that Marsha inserts into her letter to Godfrey, 'so I told myself', signal that she has now realised the flaw of self-deception in that secret logic. It is a realisation that Godfrey too will reach, 16 years later in chapter 18 of the novel.

In her fourth and final letter, Marsha writes from the perspective of Godfrey, back to herself. She commented after the task that, 'It felt right then to write back to myself and I realised that although I was writing as someone else, at points in the letter, I was also writing as myself, speaking to myself.'

One such point is where – writing as Godfrey – she appears to be speaking to herself in a way nonetheless different from the self-deceptive 'told myself' of the past:

> I think you can and must forgive yourself for that incident you speak about. Perhaps you already have forgiven yourself, but did not like to say and thought you should still blame yourself. Do not.

The final two words of this passage is a direct order given to Marsha – via Godfrey – from herself. It is here that the turn from '*writing as* myself' to '*speaking to* myself' can be felt. She is not simply saying something to herself as she did in her time of real-life guilt: with greater shifts of level and positon, she is now writing as Godfrey (or her version of him, from her perspective as a sort of would-be George Eliot figure of counsel) speaking to herself.

Nonetheless, while Marsha may have felt as if she was thus occupying two positions, her own perspective still tends to dominate all of her letters. She does not quite manage to get out of herself and into Godfrey's mind, for Godfrey is all too prone to forgive himself anyway and hardly needs this encouragement. The letters therefore become arguably too self-confirming and too self-forgiving as she is simply repeating back to herself things that she already knows and believes. While self-forgiveness and self-acceptance would be encouraged by modern psychological therapies, these letters demonstrate how a kind of self-acceptance that is too easily won might shut down the possibility of genuinely therapeutic and more difficult thinking, and instead allow us still to hold onto narrow or neat conceptions of ourselves even in repentance.

Peter

For his third letter Peter made the unusual choice of writing to Godfrey's dead brother Dunstan. He imagines addressing the corpse of the disgraced thief, whose body lay undiscovered for 16 years after he drowned in the quarry pit beside Silas Marner's cottage:

> Dear Dunstan,
>
> Unsung hero,
> The catalyst for things to happen,
> Lost faith in your family early,
> Saw through their hypocrisy,
> Became a rebel, lost your faith,
> You were forgotten and not missed.
>
> These were the words I wrote while thinking about you on the bus going to work today. I wanted to write to you because I feel you had an unhappy life and now you are dead and seemingly mourned by no-one. You fell in the stone pit and for sixteen years you laid there, wedged between two great stones, an unloved brother. What a terrible disgrace you brought to your family. What was it like to lie there for sixteen years, unloved?

In response to this letter Dunstan wrote back:

> Where do I begin? I'm in a timeless land without boundaries. I have no memories, only vague feelings that something happened. Only doubt exists here and yet I am here. You must realise that you are not writing to me but to yourself who is pretending to be me, you and I are the same person. We do this when we pray maybe, and who knows the power that has. Not I.

While Marsha had felt in her letters as though she was simultaneously 'writing as someone else' and 'as myself' in her letters, her own perspective still tended to dominate throughout. Here, in Peter's fourth letter, the opposite seems to be happening. Peter is writing as Dunstan, warning himself that 'you are not writing to me but to yourself who is pretending to be me'. It is as if he is trying to remind himself that there is only one mind at work here but doing that through Dunstan in a complex and self-checking way, creating a double perspective in the very act of querying its veracity.

It is Peter who makes, arguably, the biggest imaginative leap in his letters, getting – as he does here – into the head of a dead man. In this letter, Peter demonstrates a level of empathy for Dunstan that the character never receives within the world of the novel, either while he is alive or after his death.

Rachel

Rachel had previously taken part in experiment two, where she had written a diary but refused to submit it for analysis at the end of the task. Here she had no such problem submitting her letters. This task was less explicitly about the participants themselves. The primary focus was on the literature and therefore, in this case in particular, participants felt less exposed by what they had written, even when they began writing about more personal details. The task appears to have become a kind of therapy by stealth. In experiment two Rachel had felt the act of writing a diary to be dauntingly permanent, as if she was setting down a version of herself in stone that could not possibly be a truthful representation. During the letter-writing task a dialogue built up between herself and the people to whom she was writing. This is a form of writing that more closely resembles speech than inscription and as such seemed to be a less worrying challenge for her.

In her third letter Rachel wrote about her own personal connection to Godfrey:

> I want to judge you, but something happens in me when I go to that feeling. I am so sad about it all. I feel sad for all of us. I am saddened for you – for me – next to Silas who seems to love before anything else. I myself have told half-stories, even in the moment of confession or at the point of being found out.

Her own struggles with confession led her to take a more compassionate stance towards Godfrey which in turn implicitly leads her to judge herself less harshly. The shifting progress of Rachel's empathy can be traced in three steps: (1)'I am so sad *about it all*', (2)'I feel sad *for us all*', (3) *for you – for me* – next to Silas'. The addition of 'for me' is a small moment of sudden self-directed compassion and evidence that Rachel is writing in some way back to herself at the same time that she is writing to one of the characters within the novel. Rachel demonstrates a mobility of perspective here in the swift, informal shift between pronouns, from 'I' to 'you' to 'us', then unpacked into 'you' and 'me'. The 'us' in particular suggests that a more complicated dialectical relationship is being built between the reader and the novel that goes beyond simple one-way empathy. Rachel was the only reader who brought Silas Marner into comparison with Godfrey within her letters, as she does here with the insertion of 'next to Silas'. By placing alongside one another the stories of these two men who are both fathers to baby Eppie, one biological and the other adoptive, George Eliot was tacitly demanding that such a comparison be made.

In Rachel's final letter, addressed to herself and written from the perspective of Godfrey, she produced what is arguably the richest and most complicated of all 16 letters submitted in this study. One independent cross-checker commented that this letter 'shows the complexity of humans and recognises that we have many different levels to us in many different situations':

> Writing this – and reading my story with you – I am being taken back to conversations with my father. Particularly the desire for discipline that though vague I do remember. All this feels connected to that. I love only Nancy, but my love for her seemed at some point to need things hidden, though now I see that – in a way I can't quite put into words – it is the discipline I have always needed, but not allowed myself to want. After all, was it not her that prompted me to tell all in the end? Was it not the thought of myself seen through her eyes – her look – that made me need to be true? It is as if I am only the man who I want to be when I imagine who I am through Nancy. She seems to have a better sense of things, she has never behaved in a way that she would wish or need to conceal. It feels sometimes as though I borrow myself from Nancy. I think perhaps, reading your letter to me, that you feel more like me than you do Nancy. You seem to want to distance yourself from me, but cannot quite. I can understand that and am oddly reminded of how, even now, I wish to distance myself from Molly. It is strange how, by being pushed to do what I always wanted least, I feel larger than I did. I could not have imagined quite how things would play out, how different Nancy was to how I predicted.

Rachel is not writing as herself here but as Godfrey, sitting in parallel to herself. Rather than taking over his world with her own perspective, Godfrey instead draws her into the periphery of his world, he is 'reading my story with you'. Rachel shifts out of herself and into the mind of Godfrey in this letter. But also, as she writes from his perspective, she is able to make a second and then third imaginative leap from his mind out into Nancy's and then back again: 'Was it not the thought of myself seen through her eyes – her look – that made me need to be true? [...] It is as if I am only the man who I want to be when I imagine who I am through Nancy [...] It feels sometimes as though I borrow myself from Nancy.' Rachel goes one step further in this letter than any other participant in the study and begins to produce the kind of rich content and density of thought that was not fully realised in other participants' letters. By getting outside of herself and becoming involved in the dense overlapping layers and multiple viewpoints of the realist novel itself, Rachel widens and deepens the possibilities for herself and is able to activate new thoughts. The now blended consciousness of participant and character has effected some kind of realisation of kindred singularity and shared psychology. For in the construction, 'You seem to want to distance yourself from me, but cannot quite. I can understand that and am oddly reminded of how, even now, I wish to distance myself from Molly,' there is a recognition of something that is crucial to George Eliot: namely, that 'I' – and all the complexity of my individual psychology – am one of many, and that 'you' have an individual psychology of your own that is just as complicated as my own.

While it could be argued that Rachel has simply demonstrated an ordinary, adult capacity for Theory of Mind, the notable feature of her final letter is her shift beyond one-directional empathy. Rather than simply demonstrating an ability to understand and embody the mental state of a fictional character outside of herself, she uses that new-found perspective to look back – with a degree of understanding and compassion – at her own self: 'I think perhaps, reading your letter to me, that you feel more like me than you do Nancy. You seem to want to distance yourself from me, but cannot quite. I can understand that.' This is multi-directional thinking. For Rachel, an area of emotionally resonant engagement is created, which enables self-reflective and even self-critical thinking within a form of non-psychological therapy. In this final letter Rachel draws back into herself the density of thought of the realist novel and illustrates the richness of thought that can potentially come out of the widening mental shifts that are triggered during reading. She is for that moment a practical psychological novelist.

Conclusion

The epistolary form of this study appeared to be successful in minimising participants' self-consciousness or hesitancy. The task felt less like a formal, academic exercise and letters averaged at 511 words each, much longer than the 150-word minimum requirement per letter set out in the instructions given to participants at the beginning of the task.

Throughout the task participants appeared to demonstrate – to different degrees of success – an ability to get outside of themselves and into somebody else's mind through the action of reading and writing. Readers were then able to look back at themselves through the eyes of the external character, while also still writing partly as themselves. It is these complex and important mental shifts that can potentially trigger wider, deeper and denser thinking.

In therapeutic letter-writing programmes, patients write to themselves in order to externalise problems that are often lodged deeply within themselves.

Here – without any prompting, other than from the text itself – participants appeared to have found themselves either writing to themselves or writing to elements of their own selves that they saw lodged within certain characters within the novel. In doing so, they provide evidence to support the position that reading can create the beginnings of self-directed therapeutic dialogue.

The letter-writing task set up a whole series of potential relationships between reader, character(s) and novelist, and as such created the conditions for a more complex circuitry of thinking to develop. This helps to illustrate the psychological processes that are demanded of the reader by the realist novel and which exceed simple one-way empathy. By changing perspective, through the imaginative act of reading and writing, participants potentially, can access a whole repertoire of thoughts that they didn't previously have so available within them. The outside can be drawn back inside so as to get something inside that was not consciously there initially. As Feuerbach writes in *The Essence of Christianity*, 'Thought originally demands two. It is not until man has reached an advanced stage of culture that he can double himself, so as to play the part of another within himself.'[12]

In certain cases and to differing degrees within this study, most particularly in the example of Rachel, the literary stimulus did seem to be expanding readers' capacities to hold and to shift between multiple different perspectives. Through a combination of attentive reading and imaginative writing, readers were able to enter into and become a part of the rich web of connections contained within the realist novel.

Narrative therapies and modes of analysis have become increasingly popular within the discipline of psychology. However, the problem with many of these trends is that they often mistakenly understand a narrative to mean an episodic, linear structure that has a definite beginning and end. There is a mistaken belief that a person must be able to tell the story of their life in order to live it and even more so that the story that they tell should be episodic and linear and somehow conclusive. However, the fundamental oversimplification of what a narrative is means that through these stories we can only ever come to understand a simplified, single, flattened out version of ourselves. Galen Strawson has argued persuasively in his essay 'Against Narrativity' that the prevailing belief that the ability to construct an episodic narrative about yourself is a possible marker of health is a restrictive and damaging trend in psychology.[13] George Eliot offers an alternative to this false understanding of what a narrative can be and what it can do. The most important implication of this experiment is that, in its most successful places, it demonstrates how literature could form the basis of therapeutic interventions or aids which did not stick rigidly to limiting narrative theories.[14]

Notes

1. GEL 3, p. 187.
2. Paula Leverage et al. ed. *Theory of Mind and Literature* (West Lafayette: Purdue University Press, 2011), p. 1.
3. David Comer Kidd and Emanuele Castano, 'Reading Literary Fiction Improves Theory of Mind', *Science* 342 (2013), pp. 377–80.
4. Lisa Zunshine, *Why We Read Fiction: Theory of Mind and the Novel* (Columbus, Ohio State University Press, 2006), p. 19.
5. Ibid., p. 17.
6. Maryanne Wolf, *Proust and the Squid: The Story and Science of Reading* (New York: Harper Collins, 2007), pp. 7–8.
7. Michael Paffard, *The Unattended Moment* (London: SCM Press, 1976), p. 44.
8. *Reader, Come Home*, pp. 9–10.
9. Mary Ann Majchrzak Rombach, 'An Invitation to Therapeutic Letter Writing', *Journal of Systematic Therapies* 22(1) (2003), pp. 15–32.
10. 'Michael', *Wordsworth's Poetical Works*, ii, l. 146–48, p. 85.
11. *Shared Reading*, pp. 13–20.
12. Ludwig Feuerbach, *The Essence of Christianity*, trans. George Eliot (New York: Prometheus, [1814] 1989), p. 83.
13. Galen Strawson, 'Against Narrativity', *Ratio* 17(4) (2004), pp. 428–52.
14. Josie Billington, 'Telling a New Story: Literary Narrative and Narrative Medicine', in *Is Literature Healthy?*, The Literary Agenda (Oxford: Oxford University Press, 2016), pp. 47–85.

CONCLUSION

This book has been an attempt to examine the ways in which literature can serves as:

- A repository for containing and exploring complicated emotional human matter
- A therapeutic and contemplative aid
- A place for and trigger of particular kinds of 'literary thinking' that, being of value to human survival and flourishing, can be hard to come by and difficult to preserve elsewhere in the modern world.

It has tried to show how non-contemporary languages and the ways of thinking implicit within them have been vitally preserved, transferred and adapted by humans, across time, through the evolving needs and strategies of human thinking within the processes of reading and writing.

This conclusion seeks to consolidate a new approach towards thinking about what a literary-based form of unformalised therapy is and can be by focusing on four particularly important aspects of what I have called 'literary thinking' involved throughout the chapters of this book. It is these four crucial elements that I want to bring together and emphasise here:

1. Blending
2. Widening
3. Re-positioning
4. Reappraising

If these are prime constituents of therapeutic progress, then by therapy, I mean here any tool or process that aids us to make psychological progress, and by progress, I do not mean, over-literalistically, merely forward movement in a straight line, but rather the development of complex and flexible shapes in which to do thinking in the midst of dilemmas. In their role within this development, these four interrelated functions have been shown in action not only within individual chapters, but also in the interrelations across chapters between different writers, and in the practical examples of the modern-day readers who took part in the three reading experiments.

Blending

The concept of elemental blending sits at the heart of the Stoic cosmology, and Seneca's writing – when considered as a whole body of work – demonstrates the danger as well as the potential held within a fluidly interconnected universe where no-thing and no-body stands in singular isolation. The capacity to hold a blend of more than one thought within our minds is central to developing healthier modes of being, even and perhaps especially in relation to material that feels far from safe.[1] I have argued that literature's particular therapeutic contribution is in its ability to model and to trigger different versions of blended thinking within readers' minds, especially in the blended interrelation to-and-fro between text and reader, and including areas in between simple good or bad, safe or dangerous. Through a literary language, that blended area that exists for a reader between life and text is a trial model for thinking about real life without full and helpless exposure but without unemotional withdrawal. Serious reading of serious literature gives readers access to a blend of more thoughts than one single mind can either produce or hold within it, particularly during times of trauma.

I have shown how different writers have absorbed and adapted the work of those who came before them, to create a blend of stored human thought. This further development of blending through reading and writing is shown in action in Montaigne's personalised use of Seneca and then again in the experimental work of the final three chapters in which modern readers, engaging with the writing of Wordsworth and George Eliot, instinctively began to create and inhabit blended mental spaces. This was a process from which, for the most part, they seemed to benefit greatly, in following the creative mental leads implicitly left by the selected modellers of this book – Montaigne, Wordsworth and George Eliot. For reading gives people the opportunity to think with the power and scope of more than one mind, enlarging our own capacity for thought beyond the limits of the single selves that we have partly constructed for ourselves, or the seemingly fixed circumstances that we inhabit.

If we are to have any chance of making sense of the reality of our lives, we need ways of thinking that can match the continually shifting blends and compounds of feelings and experiences that we face. While modern psychology has attempted to develop replicable solutions to human suffering, therapies that overgeneralise or oversimplify their restrictively named subjects risk diminishing the complexity and multiplicity of individual lives and individual blends or compounds. Literature is by its very nature a richly linguistic product of that complexity and multiplicity and as such it can aid us in places that formal psychology – in its current form – cannot always reach.

Widening

I have argued that literature offers readers a means through which they can widen their own mental capacity, stretching the space within which they are able to think. I began in Chapter 1 by looking at Stoic philosophy and its version of therapy which advocates the elimination of damaging emotional material from our lives. But literature exists not by exclusion or subtraction but by creating through its forms an inclusive holding ground for the freer exploration of powerful emotional material. While in normal, everyday life it is difficult to escape narrow, linear, black-and-white frameworks and their repetition, literary forms contain within them a set of distinctly different blueprints. For example:

- The vast scope of a Senecan tragedy creates a wide external space within which emotional forces that exist internally, within our minds, can be seen playing *out* in full.
- Montaigne's essay form offers a model of wide-ranging mental flexibility, related to his own reading and thinking, in which there are no preset routes and where self-revision is always possible.
- Wordsworth's use of lineation creates a circuitry on the page which demands to be matched within the extended mind of the reader, opening up unrealised internal spaces.
- George Eliot's syntax exists to accommodate all the rich density of reality and to create beyond ego a certain extended mental width for her characters, and for readers made imaginatively sympathetic to them, often when the characters are least able to create it for themselves.

In the reading experiments, literature's specific capacity for triggering an excited degree of mental widening is demonstrated in the places where participants shift out of their default modes, rethink their lives and past experiences, and managing to get outside of their own minds, see themselves from different perspectives.

Re-Positioning

The ways in which literature can help readers mentally to re-position themselves have emerged as an important finding within this book. Re-positioning yourself and/or the emotionally charged material under which you might be suffering is not to seek a cure or an explicit solution, instead it is an attempt to minimise the wastage of trauma and to reconfigure it (as art itself can) into something that can be of act or service.

When Seneca wrote to his mother to comfort her while he was in exile, he was struggling to reconcile his dual positions as both the cause of her troubles and the possible source of relief. He was also struggling to reconcile the general precepts of Stoicism with the particulars of his individual reality. The difficulty and also the necessity of inhabiting multiple psychological perspectives recur throughout the book. George Eliot's capacity to shift between different mental positions – between the general and the particular as well as between different character centres – offers perhaps the clearest demonstration of how literature can create greater imaginative mobility within the width discussed above. Across each of the chapters, syntax and a strong language are shown again to be a tool for the reconfiguration of thoughts and the re-positioning of the self.

In the experimental chapters, certain participants demonstrated how reading and/or writing provided them with a route out of their own singular, fixed positions, allowing them – in certain places – to look back in at themselves from the outside.

Reappraising: Revising and Going Back Over

The revisionary modifications to Stoic thought made by Montaigne, Wordsworth and (for George Eliot) Spinoza have led towards an implicit model of therapy which no longer seeks merely to withdraw from or diminish emotional trauma. Instead, acts of returning, and rethinking, within places of deep emotional richness have been shown to be crucial processes.

As a holding ground for emotionally charged human material, literature serves to prevent wastage, and while there can perhaps be no cure or solution to a trauma, the very capacity to hold onto something of it until it can be better placed, used or accepted is important. Without these holding grounds for reappraisal, it is difficult to avoid becoming caught up in damaging cycles of rumination.

The literary models of Chapters 1 to 4 provide an alternative version of going back over, or looping back into, that is not rumination. They also demonstrate a version of progress that is not merely forward motion. The capacity to go backwards must be acknowledged as a part of progression, and not simply seen as a feature of failure through regression or stuckness. Going back with added levels of understanding may be far more significant than simply trying to 'move on'. In the reading experiments, certain participants again instinctively demonstrated a capacity for self-revision, rethinking and backwards-reflection, which was being triggered by the literature that they were reading.

These four elements of blending, widening, re-positioning and reappraising have a crucial relation to the capacities found within a literary language. I have argued that literature offers readers a language which can serve as an alternative or challenging addition to formal psychological therapies or theories. It is a language which is distinctly difficult – and necessarily so – in order to counter the overfamiliar superficiality of much ordinary discourse. This (in particular in Wordsworth as poet and George Eliot as novelist) is an extraordinary language for ordinary people and ordinary lives. While a difficult language poses the risk of alienating readers or leading quickly to dismissal or distraction, in the reading experiments it is often the difficulty of the literature given to participants within what are nonetheless powerful emotional areas that appears to have been a crucial trigger of:

- Spontaneity
- Attentiveness
- Speculative thinking
- Greater depth and range of thinking

Easier reading material or tasks that merely required information processing tended to allow participants to remain within their practised default modes and to be over-certain, opinionated or distracted in their thinking.

We need a language within which we can recognise ourselves and which – through the mirroring processes of reading and writing – can recognise us. For it is difficult, if not impossible, to know what or who you are and how you feel (at least consciously) until you see it written – in some form – outside of yourself. It is then that it becomes possible to place that conscious knowledge back into yourself. This is what it means to find a language with which to think. That language – if it is to be effective – must have the requisite complexity, density and richness to bear witness to and record the difficult complexity of real life.

In a book in which individual specifics counter overgeneralised theories or ruminations, I end with one final example. In *A Fortunate Man*, John Berger gives an account of the work of a country doctor, which provides a useful example of how literary language and literary thinking can be applied within the practical world of the doctor. It is an account that has proved foundational in its influence on a generation of GPs interested in a more holistic medicine.

Berger describes the role of the doctor – in particular when treating a depressed patient – as first of all to recognise the sick man, but also to be a person in whom the sick man can recognise himself:

> If the man can begin to feel recognised – and such recognition may well include aspects of his character which he has not yet recognised himself – the hopeless nature of his unhappiness will have been changed: he may even have the chance of being happy [...] How does a doctor begin to make an unhappy man feel recognised? [...] The recognition has to be oblique [...] This can be achieved by the doctor presenting himself to the patient as a comparable man. It demands from the doctor a true imaginative effort and precise self-knowledge. The patient must be given a chance to recognise, despite his aggravated self-consciousness, aspects of himself in the doctor.[2]

I would argue that literature can and does play an analogous and therefore therapeutic role of oblique recognition, standing before the reader in a way that is related in its own medium to how an imaginative doctor stands before a needy patient.

Notes

1. Gilles Fauconnier and Mark Turner set out the argument that 'conceptual blending [...] is responsible for the origins of language, art, religion, science, and other similar human feats, and that it is indispensable for basic everyday thought as it is for artistic and scientific abilities' in *The Way We Think: Conceptual Blending and the Mind's Hidden Complexities* (New York: Perseus Books, 2002), p. vi.
2. John Berger and Jean Mohr, *A Fortunate Man* (Harmondsworth: Penguin, 1967), pp. 75–76.

BIBLIOGRAPHY

Primary Works

Eliot, George, *Adam Bede* [1859], ed. Carol A. Martin. Oxford: Oxford World's Classics, 2008.
———, *Daniel Deronda* [1876], ed. Graham Handley. Oxford: Oxford World's Classics, 1988.
———, *The George Eliot Letters*, ed. Gordon S. Haight, 9 vols. New Haven, CT: Yale University Press, 1954–78.
———, *Middlemarch* [1872], ed. David Carroll. Oxford: Oxford World's Classics, 2008.
———, *The Mill on the Floss* [1860], ed. A. S. Byatt. London: Penguin Popular Classics, 1994.
———, *Scenes of Clerical Life* [1857], ed. Graham Handley. London: Everyman, 1994.
———, *Selected Essays, Poems and Other Writing*, ed. A. S. Byatt and Nicholas Warren. London: Penguin Classics, 1990.
———, *Silas Marner* [1861], ed. Terence Cave. Oxford: Oxford World's Classics, 1996.
Montaigne, Michel de, *The Complete Essays*, trans. M. A. Screech. London: Penguin Classics, 1991.
———, *Les essais de Michel de Montaigne*, ed. V. L. Saulnier. Paris: Presses Universitaires de France, 1965.
———, *The Essays of Michael, Seigneur de Montaigne*, trans. Charles Cotton. London: Ward, Lock, and Tyler, 1693.
———, *The Essayes of Michael Lord of Montaigne*, trans. John Florio, ed. Henry Morley. London: George Routledge, 1885.
Seneca, Lucilius Annaeus, 'Consolation to Helvia', in *On the Shortness of Life*, trans. C. D. N. Costa. London: Penguin, 2004, pp. 34–67.
———, *Eight Tragedies*, with an English trans. John G. Fitch, The Loeb Classical Library, 2 vols. Cambridge: Harvard University Press, 2002.
———, *Epistulae Morales*, with an English translation by Richard M. Gunmere, The Loeb Classical Library, 3 vols. Cambridge: Harvard University Press, 2006.
———, *Four Tragedies and Octavia*, trans. E. F. Watling. Harmondsworth: Penguin, 1966.
———, *Moral Essays*, with an English translation by John W. Basore, The Loeb Classical Library, 3 vols. Cambridge: Harvard University Press, 1932.
———, *Naturales Quaestiones*, with an English translation by Thomas H. Corcoran, The Loeb Classical Library, 2 vols. Cambridge: Harvard University Press, 1971.
Wordsworth, William, *The Borderers*, ed. Robert Osborn. Ithaca, NY: Cornell University Press, 1982.
———, *The Excursion*, ed. Sally Bushell, James A. Butler and Michael C. Jaye. Ithaca, NY: Cornell University Press, 2007.
———, *Lyrical Ballads and Other Poems 1797–1800*, ed. James Butler and Karen Green. Ithaca, NY: Cornell University Press, 1992.

———, *The Prelude: The Four Texts (1798, 1799, 1805, 1850)*, ed. Jonathan Wordsworth. London: Penguin, 1995.

———, *The Prose Works of William Wordsworth*, ed. W. J. B. Owen and Jane Worthington Smyser, 3 vols. Oxford: Clarendon Press, 1974.

———, *The Ruined Cottage and the Pedlar*, ed. James Butler. Ithaca, NY: Cornell University Press, 1979.

———, *Wordsworth's Poetical Works*, ed. Ernest de Selincourt and Helen Derbyshire, 5 vols. Oxford: Clarendon Press, 1940–49.

Wordsworth, William, and Dorothy Wordsworth, *The Letters of William and Dorothy Wordsworth: The Early Years 1787–1805*, ed. Ernest de Selincourt, 2nd edition, rev. Chester L. Shaver. Oxford: Clarendon Press, 1967.

———, *The Letters of William and Dorothy Wordsworth: The Middle Years: Part II, 1812–1820*, ed. Ernest de Selincourt, 2nd edition, rev. Mary Moorman and Alan G. Hill. Oxford: Clarendon Press, 1970.

Secondary Works

Andreas-Salomé, Lou, *The Freud Journals*, trans. Stanley A. Leavy. London: Hogarth Press, 1965.

Arnold, Matthew, 'The Function of Criticism at the Present Time', in *Essays in Criticism*. London: Macmillan, 1875.

———, *Selected Poems*, ed. Miriam Allott. Oxford: Oxford University Press, 1995.

Baker, Carl, 'Mental Health Statistics for England: Prevalence, Services and Funding', House of Commons Briefing Paper, 25 April 2018.

Beer, Gillian, *Darwin's Plots*. Cambridge: University of Cambridge Press, 2000.

Berger, John, and Jean Mohr, *A Fortunate Man*. Harmondsworth: Penguin, 1967.

Bernard, Barnett, *You Ought To! A Psychoanalytic Study of the Superego and Conscience*. London: Karnac, 2007.

Billington, Josie, *Is Literature Healthy?: The Literary Agenda*. Oxford: Oxford University Press, 2016.

Bollas, Christopher, *The Mystery of Things*. New York: Routledge, 1999.

Boutcher, Warren, *The School of Montaigne in Early Modern Europe*, 2 vols. Oxford: Oxford University Press, 2017.

Brad, Inwood, *Reading Seneca: Stoic Philosophy at Rome*. Oxford: Clarendon Press, 2005.

Braun, Virginia, and Victoria Clarke, 'Using Thematic Analysis in Psychology', *Qualitative Research in Psychology* 3(2) (2006), pp. 77–101.

Byatt, A. S., *Unruly Times: Wordsworth and Coleridge in Their Time*. London: Hogarth Press, 1970.

Byron, Lord Gordon George, *Life, Letters and Journals of Lord Byron*, ed. Thomas Moore. London: John Murray, 1892.

Campbell, Sherlock R., and James W. Pennebaker, 'The Secret Life of Pronouns: Flexibility in Writing Style and Physical Health', *Psychological Science* 14(1) (2003), pp. 60–65.

Cates, Joanna, 'Cognitive Behavioural Therapy Is Not Always the Answer for Anxiety and Depression', *Huffington Post*, 10 March 2015, https://www.huffingtonpost.co.uk/joanna-cates/cognitive-behavioural-not-always-the-answer_b_6814562.html, accessed 20 March 2015.

Cave, Terence, *Thinking with Literature*. Oxford: Oxford University Press, 2016.

Clouston, T. S., *Clinical Lectures on Mental Disease*. New York: Lea Brothers, 1897.

Coleridge, Samuel Taylor, *Collected Letters of Samuel Taylor Coleridge*, ed. Earl Leslie Griggs, 6 vols. Oxford: Clarendon Press, 2000.
———, *Specimens of Table Talk of the Late Samuel Taylor Coleridge*, ed. Henry Nelson Coleridge, 2 vols. London: John Murray, 1835.
Comer Kidd, David, and Emanuele Castano, 'Reading Literary Fiction Improves Theory of Mind', *Science*, 342 (2013), pp. 377–80.
Daniel, Samuel, *The Complete Works in Verse and Prose*, ed. Alexander B. Grosart. London: Hazell, Watson and Viney, 1885.
Daniels, Elizabeth, 'A Meredithian Glance at Gwendolen Harleth', in *George Eliot: A Centenary Tribute*, ed. Gordon S. Haight and Rosemary T. Van Arsdel. London: Macmillan, 1985, pp. 28–37.
Davie, Donald, *Articulate Energy*. London: Routledge, 1955.
———, 'Syntax and Music in *Paradise Lost*', in *The Living Milton*, ed. Frank Kermode. London: Routledge, 1960, pp. 70–84.
Davis, Philip, *Reading and the Reader*, The Literary Agenda. Oxford: Oxford University Press, 2013.
———, *The Transferred Life of George Eliot*. Oxford: Oxford University Press, 2017.
DeBrabander, Firmin, *Spinoza and the Stoics: Power, Politics and the Passions*. New York: Continuum, 2007.
Deleuze, Gilles, *Spinoza: Practical Philosophy*. San Francisco, CT: City Lights Books, 1988.
De Quincey, Thomas, *Recollections of the Lakes and the Lake Poets* [1839], ed. David Wright. Harmondsworth: Penguin, 1970.
Donald, Frame, *Montaigne's Essais – A Study*. Upper Saddle River, NJ: Prentice-Hall, 1969.
Eliot, T. S., 'Seneca in Elizabethan Translation', in *Essays on Elizabethan Drama*. New York: Harcourt, Brace, 1956.
Emily, Wilson, *The Greatest Empire*. Oxford: Oxford University Press, 2014, p. 181.
Emerson, Ralph Waldo, 'Montaigne or The Sceptic', in *Representative Men*. London: Routledge, 1850, pp. 109–38.
Empson, William, *The Structure of Complex Words*. London: Chatto & Windus, 1977.
Evans, Jules, *Philosophy for Life and Other Dangerous Situations*. London: Rider Books, 2012.
Fauconnier, Gilles, and Mark Turner, *The Way We Think: Conceptual Blending and the Mind's Hidden Complexities*. New York: Perseus Books, 2002.
Felski, Rita, *The Limits of Critique*. Chicago, IL: University of Chicago Press, 2015.
Festinger, Leon, *A Theory of Cognitive Dissonance*. Stanford, CA: Stanford University Press, 1962.
Feuerbach, Ludwig, *The Essence of Christianity* [1841], trans. George Eliot. New York: Prometheus, 1989.
Freeston, Mark H., 'Why Do People Worry?', *Personality and Individual Differences* 17(6) (1994), pp. 791–802.
Freud, Sigmund, 'Beyond the Pleasure Principle', in *The Standard Edition of the Complete Psychological Works of Sigmund Freud* [1814], vol. 18, ed. James Strachey, 24 vols. London: Hogarth Press, 1953–74, pp. 7–64.
———, 'Remembering, Repeating and Working Through', in *The Standard Edition of the Complete Psychological Works of Sigmund Freud* [1814], ed. James Strachey, 24 vols. London: Hogarth Press, 1953–74, pp. 145–56.
Gates, Nicola, et al., 'Psychological well-Being in Individuals with Mild Cognitive Impairment', *Clinical Interventions in Aging* 9 (2014), 779–92.
Gendlin, Eugene T., *Experiencing and the Creation of Meaning*. New York: Free Press of Glencoe, 1962.

Gill, Stephen, *Wordsworth and the Victorians*. Oxford: Clarendon Press, 1998.
———, *Wordsworth's Revisitings* (Oxford: Oxford University Press, 2011)..
———, *William Wordsworth: A Life* (Oxford: Oxford University Press, 1989).
Glaser, Barney G. and Anselm L. Strauss, *The Discovery of Grounded Theory: Strategies for Qualitative Research* (New Jersey: Aldine, 1967).
Graver, Bruce, 'Wordsworth and the Stoics', in *Romans and Romantics*, ed. Timothy Saunders et al. (Oxford: Oxford University Press, 2012).
Greenberger, Dennis, and Christine A. Padesky, *Mind Over Mood: Change How You Feel by Changing the Way You Think* (New York: The Guilford Press, 1995).
Hazlitt, William, 'On Mr Wordsworth's *The Excursion*', in *William Wordsworth: A Critical Anthology* [1814], ed. Graham McMaster. Harmondsworth: Penguin, 1972, pp. 114–20.
Hegel, G. W. F., 'Freedom of Self-Consciousness, Stoicism: Scepticism: The Unhappy Consciousness', in *The Phenomenology of Mind* [1807], trans. J. B. Baillie. London: George Allen & Unwin, 1971, pp. 112–30.
Homans, Margaret, *Bearing the Word: Language and Female Experience in Nineteenth- Century Women's Writing*. Chicago, IL: University of Chicago Press, 1986.
Huisman, Rosemary, *The Written Poem: Semiotic Conventions from Old to Modern English*. London: Cassell, 1999.
Jarvis, Simon, *Wordsworth's Philosophic Song*. Cambridge: Cambridge University Press, 2008.
Jeanneret, Michel, *Perpetual Motion: Transforming Shapes in the Renaissance from Di Vinci to Montaigne*, trans. Nidral Poller. Baltimore, MD: John Hopkins University Press, 2001.
Johnsen, Tom J., and Oddgeir Friberg, 'The Effects of Cognitive Behavioural Therapy as an Anti-Depressive Treatment Is Falling: A Meta-Analysis', *Psychological Bulletin* 141(4) (2015), pp. 747–68.
Kellogg, S. H., 'Transformational Chair-work: Five ways of Using Therapeutic Dialogues', *NYSPA Notebook* 19(4) (2007), pp. 8–9.
Kolk, Bessel van der, *The Body Keeps the Score: Mind, Brain and Body in the Transformation of Trauma*. London: Penguin, 2014.
Leary, David E., 'Instead of Erklaren and Verstehen: William James on Human Understanding', in *Historical Perspectives on Erklaren and Verstehan*, ed. Uljana Feest. Berlin: Max Planck Institute for the History of Science, 2007.
Leverage, Paula et al., ed., *Theory of Mind and Literature*. West Lafayette, IN: Purdue University Press, 2011.
Lewes, G. H., *Problems of Life and Mind*, 5 vols. London: Truber, 1874–75.
London, E. H., 'The Q&A: Adam Phillips. Poetry as Therapy', *The Economist*, 29 March 2012, https://www.economist.com/blogs/prospero/2012/03/qa-adam-phillips, accessed 15 April 2016.
Longden, Eleanor et al., 'Shared Reading: Assessing the Intrinsic Value of a Literature-Based Health Intervention', *Medical Humanities* 41(2) (2015), pp. 113–20.
MacIntyre, Alasdair, *After Virtue*. Notre Dame: University of Notre Dame, 1984.
McGilchrist, Iain, *Against Criticism*. London: Faber & Faber, 1982.
———, *The Master and His Emissary: The Divided Brain and the Making of the Western World*. New Haven, CT: Yale University Press, 2009.
Miall, David S., and Don Kuiken, 'Aspects of Literary Response: A New Questionnaire', *Research in the Teaching of English* 29 (1995), 37–58.
Mill, John Stewart, *Autobiography* [1873]. Oxford: Oxford University Press, 1971.
Milner, Marion, *A Life of One's Own* [1934]. Harmondsworth: Penguin, 1952.
———, *On Not Being Able to Paint* [1950], (London: Heinemann, 1984).

Mind, 'We Need to Talk: Getting the Right Therapy at the Right Time' (2010), https://www.mind.org.uk/media/280583/We-Need-to-Talk-getting-the-right-therapy-at-the-right-time.pdf, accessed 12 February 2015.
Moreton, Cole, 'Author Diana Souhami: 'Why I 'Rescued' a Character Left in the Lurch by George Eliot'', *Independent*, 13 September 2014, https://www.independent.co.uk/arts-entertainment/books/features/author-diana-souhami-why-i-rescued-a-character-left-in-the-lurch-by-george-eliot-9729873.html, accessed 11 November 2017.
Myers, F. W. H., *Human Personality and Its Survival of Bodily Death* [1903]. New York: Dover, 2005.
Neu, Jerome, *Emotion, Thought and Therapy*. London: Routledge and Kegan Paul, 1977.
Orbach, Susie, *In Therapy: The Unfolding Story*. London: Profile Books, 2018.
Ost, Lars-Goran, 'Efficacy of the Third Wave of Behavioural Therapies: A Systematic Review and Meta-Analysis', *Behaviour Research and Therapy*, 46 (2008), pp. 296–321.
Paffard, Michael, *Inglorious Wordsworths*. London: Hodder & Stoughton, 1973.
———, *The Unattended Moment*. London: SCM Press, 1976.
Paris, Bernard J., *Experiments in Life: George Eliot's Quest for Values*. Detroit, MI: Wayne State University Press, 1965.
———, *Rereading George Eliot: Changing Responses to Her Experiments in Life*. Albany: University of New York Press, 2003.
Pennebaker, James W., 'Telling Stories: The Health Benefits of Narrative', *Literature and Medicine* 19(1) (2000), 3–18.
Pennebaker, James W., Matthias R. Mehl and Kate G. Niederhoffer, 'Psychological Aspects of Natural Language Use: Our Words, Our Selves', *Annual Review of Psychology* 54 (2003), pp. 547–77.
Perry, Ralph Bardon, *The Thought and Character of William James*, 2 vols. London: Humphrey Milford, 1935.
Philips, Adam, *Promises, Promises: Essays on Literature and Psychoanalysis*. London: Faber & Faber, 2000.
———, *The Penguin Freud Reader*. London: Penguin, 2006).
———, *On Balance*. London: Hamish Hamilton, 2010.
———, *Missing Out: In Praise of the Unlived Life*. London: Hamish Hamilton, 2012.
———, 'The Art of Nonfiction No. 7', interview by Paul Holdengraber, *Paris Review*, 208 (2014), https://www.theparisreview.org/interviews/6286/adam-phillips-the-art-of-nonfiction-no-7-adam-phillips, accessed 15 April 2016.
Pinney, Thomas, 'George Eliot's Reading of Wordsworth', *Victorian Newsletter* 24 (1963), pp. 20–22.
Prawer, S. S., *A Cultural Citizen of the World: Sigmund Freud's Knowledge and Use of British and American Writings*. London: Legenda, 2009.
Raber, Karen, 'Closet Drama', in *The Oxford Encyclopaedia of British Literature*, ed. David Scott Kastan. Oxford: Oxford University Press, 2006.
Redinger, Ruby, *George Eliot: The Emergent Self*. London: Bodley Head, 1976.
Reimer, Margaret, 'The Spoiled Child: What Happened to Gwendolen Harleth?', *Cambridge Quarterly* 36 (2007), 33–50.
Richards, I. A., *Practical Criticism*. London: Kegan Paul, 1930.
Ricks, Christopher, 'Wordsworth: "A Pure Organic Pleasure from the Lines"', in *William Wordsworth: A Critical Anthology*, ed. Graham McMaster. Harmondsworth: Penguin, 1972.
———, *The Force of Poetry*. Oxford: Clarendon Press, 1984.
Rieff, Philip, *Freud: The Mind of the Moralist*. London: Methuen, 1965.
———, *The Triumph of the Therapeutic*. Chicago, IL: University of Chicago, 1966.

Rombach, Mary Ann Majchrzak, 'An Invitation to Therapeutic Letter Writing', *Journal of Systematic Therapies* 22(1) (2003), pp. 15–32.

Rosenmeyer, Thomas G., *Senecan Drama and Stoic Cosmology*. Berkeley: University of California Press, 1989.

Rotenberg, Carl T., 'George Eliot – Proto-Psychoanalyst', *American Journal of Psychoanalysis* 59(3) (1999), pp. 257–70.

Rylance, Rick, *Victorian Psychology and British Culture 1850–1880*. Oxford: Oxford University Press, 2000.

Saul, Frampton, *When I Am Playing with My Cat, How Do I Know She Is Not Playing with Me*. London: Faber & Faber, 2011.

Scheler, Max, *The Nature of Sympathy*. London: Routledge, 1970.

Shuttleworth, Sally, *George Eliot and Nineteenth-Century Science*. Cambridge: Cambridge University Press, 1984.

Silvia, Paul J., Roger E. Beaty and Emily C. Nusbaum, 'Verbal Fluency and Creativity: General and Specific Contributions of Broad Retrieval Ability (Gr) Factors to Divergent Thinking', *Intelligence* 41(5) (2013), 328–40.

Spinoza, Benedict de, *Ethics* [1677], trans. George Eliot, ed. Thomas Deegan. Salzburg: Universitat Salzburg, 1981.

Starobinski, Jean, *Montaigne in Motion*, trans. Arthur Goldhammer. Chicago, IL: University of Chicago Press, 2009.

Stephen, Leslie, 'Wordsworth's Ethics', in *Hours in a Library* [1829], 3 vols. London: Smith, Elder, 1892, pp. 270–307.

———, *George Eliot*. London: Macmillan, 1919.

Stokes, Adrian, *A Game That Must Be Lost*. Cheadle: Carcanet Press, 1973.

Strawson, Galen, 'Against Narrativity', *Ratio* 17(4) (2004), pp. 428–52.

Sully, James, 'George Eliot's Art', *Mind* 6(23) (1881), pp. 378–94.

Trilling, Lionel, 'Freud and Literature', in *Freud: A Collection of Critical Essays*, ed. Perry Meisel. New Jersey, CT: Prentice Hall, 1971, p. 95.

Waddell, Margot, 'On Ideas of "the Good" and of "the Ideal" in George Eliot's Novels and in Post-Kleinian Psychoanalytic Thought', *American Journal of Psychoanalysis* 59(3) (1999), pp. 271–86.

Welsh, Alexander, *The Humanist Comedy*. New Haven, CT: Yale University Press, 2014.

West, David, 'Practical Criticism: An Early Experiment in Reader Response', *Language and Literature* 26(2) (2017), pp. 88–98.

Williams, John, *Wordsworth Translated*. London: Continuum, 2009.

Wolf, Maryanne, *Reader, Come Home*. New York: Harper Collins, 2018.

———, *Proust and the Squid: The Story and Science of Reading*. New York: Harper Collins, 2007.

Wordsworth, Christopher, *Memoirs of William Wordsworth*, ed. Henry Reed, 2 vols. Boston, MA: Ticknor, Reed and Fields, 1851.

Worthington, Jane, *Wordsworth's Reading of Roman Prose*. Connecticut: Archon Books, 1970.

Zunshine, Lisa, *Why We Read Fiction: Theory of Mind and the Novel*. Columbus, The Ohio State University Press, 2006.

INDEX

Acceptance and Commitment Therapy 10
Andreas-Salomé, Lou 82
Arnold, Matthew 53, 82

Bain, Alexander 73
Beer, Gillian 91
Berger, John 185–86
Bollas, Christopher 84
Byron, Lord Gordon George 41

Cave, Terence 100, 117, 133
Centre for Research into Reading,
　　Literature and Society, The 2, 105,
　　132–33, 167
Closet drama 41
Clouston, T. S. 86
Cognitive Analytic Therapy 10
Cognitive Behavioural Therapy 1, 9–10,
　　20, 22, 29, 103, 137
Coleridge, Samuel Taylor 46, 48, 60
Cooke, Olive 103

Daniel, Samuel 41, 48
Davie, Donald 58
De Quincey, Thomas 59
DeBrabander, Fermin 81

Eliot, George 2, 182–84
　　Adam Bede 67–69, 75–78
　　Daniel Deronda 86–93
　　Middlemarch 82–85
　　Scenes of Clerical Life 67–68
　　Silas Marner 67, 163, 165–77
　　The Idea of a Future Life 92
　　The Mill on the Floss 67, 69–72, 74–75,
　　　80, 163

Ellis, Albert 9, 29
Empson, William 58
Evans, Jules 9–10

Felski, Rita 3–4, 99, 129
Feuerbach, Ludwig 78, 178
Frampton, Saul 34
Free indirect discourse 83–84
French Revolution, The 41–42, 46, 48
Freud, Sigmund 1, 4, 37, 61–62, 89–90

Gill, Stephen 67
Grounded Theory 3

Hamans, Margaret 67
Hazlitt, William 54

Inwood, Brad 11

James, William 53–54

Kuiken, Donald 102

La Boétie, Etienne de 29
Leary, David E. 53
Lewes, George Henry 73, 80

MacIntyre, Alasdair 11
McGilchrist, Iain 63, 99
Miall, David S. 102
Mill, John Stuart 53, 73, 164
Milner, Marion 36
Montaigne, Michel de 1, 182–83
　　'Apologie for Raymond Sebond' 31–32, 48
　　'On Friendship' 29, 34
　　'On the Inconstancy of the Self' 36–37

Montaigne, Michel de (*cont.*)
  'On Practice' 30–31
  'On Repentance' 34–35
  'On Solitude' 28, 45
  'The Taste of Good and Evil
    Things' 29–30
  'On Vanity' 33
Myers, F. W. H. 60

Narrative Therapy 165, 178
Neu, Jerome 82

Orbach, Susie 38

Paffard, Michael 101–2, 164
Paris, Bernard J. 86–87, 92
Pennebaker, James 111, 132
Phillips, Adam 1, 4, 38, 160
Psychoanalysis 2, 37–39, 82, 86, 160

Raber, Karen 41
Reader Organisation, The 2
Richards, I. A. 3, 100–1
Ricks, Christopher 58
Rieff, Philip 4, 37
Rotenberg, Carl 86–87
Ruskin, John 53
Rylance, Rick 73

Scepticism 31, 35
Self-help 35
Seneca, Lucius Annaeus 1, 9, 27–30,
  41, 46, 182, 184
  Consolations 21–23
  Epistles 12, 18–21, 46
  Hercules 16–18
  Naturales Quaestiones 32, 48
  Phaedra 15–16
  Thyestes 12–15
  Tragedies, The 11–18, 45, 183
Shuttleworth, Sally 73
Spencer, Herbert 73
Spinoza, Baruch 2, 80–83, 184
Stephen, Leslie 49
Stoicism 1, 9, 11, 19, 27, 29, 37, 41, 50,
  81, 183
  Cosmology 12–13, 15, 18, 23, 182
Strawson, Galen 178

Theory of Mind 164, 177

Vallon, Annette 41

Waddell, Margot 86–87
Wilson, John 54
Wolf, Maryanne 146, 164–65
Wordsworth, Dorothy 52
Wordsworth, William 1, 41, 67–71, 99,
  164, 182–83
  'Answer to Mathetes' 54–55
  The Borderers 41–45, 49
  'The Character of the Happy
    Warrior' 46–47
  'Essays Upon Epitaphs' 60
  The Excursion 48–63, 69
  'Intimations of Immortality' 69
  Lyrical Ballads 68
  'Michael' 166
  'Ode to Duty' 46
  The Prelude 58–59, 130
  The Recluse 48, 52
  'The Ruined Cottage' 46, 49, 62, 102–3,
    130, 142–60
Worthington, Jane 41, 46, 48

Zunshine, Lisa 164

www.ingramcontent.com/pod-product-compliance
Lightning Source LLC
Chambersburg PA
CBHW021828300426
44114CB00009BA/370